45 min
67m

CASSETTE FROM MY EX

Also by Jason Bitner

LaPorte, Indiana
FOUND Polaroids

CASSETTE FROM MY EX

STORIES AND SOUNDTRACKS OF LOST LOVES

EDITED BY
JASON BITNER

St. Martin's Griffin New York

Author's note: Some of the names have been changed.

Design by Lissi Erwin/SplendidCorp.
Miscellaneous photography and collages by Lissi Erwin.

Printed in China. For information, address St. Martin's Press, 175 Fifth Avenue, New York, N.Y. 10010.

www.stmartins.com

Library of Congress Cataloging-in-Publication Data
Cassette from my ex : stories and soundtracks of lost loves / [compiled by] Jason Bitner. — 1st ed.
p.cm
ISBN 978-0-312-56552-7
1. Popular Music—Social aspects—Anecdotes. 2. Audiocassettes—Social aspects—Anecdotes. I. Bitner, Jason, 1974-
ML3918.P67C37 2009
306.4'8424--dc22
2009008411
First Edition: October 2009
10 9 8 7 6 5 4 3 2 1

MADE IN USA
Normal Bias
120 μs EQ
SIDE
NOISE REDUCTION
U.S.A.
REALISTIC®
SUPERTAPE®
GOLD
60

KEYSTONE
Compact Cassette
MADE IN U.S.A.
C60

SIDE
INDEX
C-90
CONCERTAPE®
Compact Cassette

2
Haydn The Seasons
#4
1A9279
90 MIN.
45 MIN. PER SIDE
Magnavox
90 Min.

TABLE OF CONTENTS

45 min
67m

CASSETTE FROM MY EX

7559-79111-4
killing my lobster gets some action - september 98 sf/la
THE
BIG BA
KATE
SURPRISE
TDK
D90
FLIP YOUr

INTRODUCTION

BY JASON BITNER

One recent summer, when I headed down to my basement to purge some boxes of belongings, I came across an old suitcase filled with cassettes. Among the musical gems in the collection, I discovered a mixtape from my first girlfriend. In a bout of nostalgia and curiosity, I popped it into a dusty boombox and was instantly transported back to 1991. The tape struck me, not only for the musical gems on there, but for the memories that flooded back when I listened to its hissy, worbly tracks.

Considering how much stuff I've lost or tossed in the past couple decades, it's remarkable I hung onto this mix for so many years. I mean, it's just a cheap plastic shell covering a tiny ribbon tape—there's nothing inherently special about it. So what was it about this tape that compelled me to hold onto it for so long, years after the demise of the cassette in favor of CDs and iTunes playlists?

It's got to be the memories. Mixtapes are like personal time capsules. Not only do you get the physical tape and homemade artwork, but you've got memories attached to each of the handpicked songs. Forget flowers and jewelry—cassettes were the perfect vehicle for expressing love. When you made a tape for someone, your intentions were clear: I'm into you. Whether it was a crush tape or a compilation of a couple's favorite songs, a mix could win over a lover in one listen, or nix a relationship just as quickly. No matter how the relationship ended, the mixtape lasts as a physical reminder of what took place between those two people.

Figuring that I wasn't the only one hanging onto these tapes, I soon enlisted the help of six good friends—Danielle Smith, Michael Hearst, Larry Smith, Katie Krentz, Dexter Randazzo, and Damon Locks—to help gather the stories that follow, and thus began *Cassette from My Ex*.

A
Still Love You
TDK Normal Bias D90 EQ 120μs
B
The World's A Mess – It's In My Kiss
OUT
TDK Normal Bias D90 EQ 120μs

THE WORLD'S A MESS, IT'S IN MY KISS

BY JOE LEVY

I made many and received few. It's like that for most boys, a slight reversal from the almost inevitable getting more and giving less that sets in as the years pile up. But from this girl, two tapes survive.

We met at a Women's Center dance. I'd DJ'd the music to tape. It was 1985. There was so much good music then—rock guitars getting it on with drum machines, hip-hop just starting to crash the party—even I couldn't screw it up. I was dancing with her friends. She joined in. Every song, no matter where the beat was, she did the same '80s move where one knee buckles and the other leg shoots out straight. You can see Molly Ringwald do it on the library steps in *The Breakfast Club*. Molly Ringwald did it better.

We met again months later. I was still a depressed boy, still years away from reasonably solving problems like the ones in my head, by listening to Smiths' records. In other words, a moron. She came into her friend Pam's room off campus. I can't remember who had the copy of Jean Toomer's *Cane*, her or Pam. I just remember flipping through until I found my favorite bit and reading it out loud: "Face flowed into her eyes. Flowed in soft cream foam and plaintive ripples, in such a way that wherever your glance may momentarily have rested, it immediately thereafter wavered in the direction of her eyes." When I left the room, she asked Pam if I was for real. Sadly, I was.

It took weeks longer, until sometime around Thanksgiving. We ended up driving all night, going nowhere. When the sun came up, a cop pulled us over. I had a broken taillight. We rode around until a service station opened. As the taillight was getting fixed, we sat and talked about where we wanted to live when we each had children to raise. This is how I found out she was a Red Sox fan, which we never again discussed. We had not yet kissed.

Her parents lived in Paris. I visited at Christmas. I brought a tape with me. It took hours to get right, though I no longer remember any of it, except for a local band's cover of "Blue Christmas." But it was love-struck and awesome. A few weeks later, she gave me a tape back. There's a French song, "Embrasse Moi Idiot!" that I always loved, as well as a segue from Crosby, Stills & Nash's "Since I Met You" to Elvis Costello's "The Greatest Thing," that is better to read about than it is to hear, and five Bad Company songs on side B. There's also a note on the case: "You can tape over it if you want. It's OK . . . "

This tape is from later. From a breakup, the first of many. Whatever else she did or didn't get from me, she got a lot of music. I still remember walking into her apartment the summer after she graduated during a reconciliation and seeing lyrics from songs I taped for her—Chuck Berry, Big Star—typed out and taped to the wall. When I put this tape on, it's cued to midway through side A, King Floyd's "Groove Me": *No other man, no other girl, can enter into our world.* Gulp.

I had a rule against two songs by the same artist back to back. (If you had two songs by the same artist, one was on side A and the other on side B.) This tape breaks that rule over and over. Three Drifters songs in a row on side A, each one compounding the heartbreak. *There's room enough for two, up on the roof. . . . There goes my baby, moving on down the line. Wonder where. . . . Don't forget who's taking you home, and in whose arms you're gonna be.* Side A ends with a Rickie Lee Jones song I haven't heard in so long I don't even recognize it at first. Simple, sad—the sound of intimacy receding down an endless dark hallway. *I will miss your company.* Rickie Lee Jones was the first concert I ever saw, at fifteen. Jesus.

I am not at all sure I ever listened to the tape all the way through. I don't know how I ever could have gotten past the Shangri-Las at the start of side B: *What will happen to the life I gave to you?* This song has never sounded so serious. It sounds more serious than the X song at the end of side B where Exene is trying to talk to her dead sister through the bathroom wall.

I'm still a music nerd, so as I listen I think: This tape could be better. That Tom Waits song on side A from *Rain Dogs*? That should have been "Blind Love." (*I wonder where you are, and I whisper your name.*) And Joan Jett's "I Love Rock N' Roll"? Talk about shattering the mood. But also, this tape could be no better. It is every breakup ever. *I can't help myself. Too many teardrops. I'm coming apart at the seams. The world's a mess. It's in my kiss.*

I have a longstanding theory that all music is about time. Time slowed or sped up or suspended. Time future. Time past. Here's Pavement articulating that theory for me: *3:03. The seconds, they are sequins.* And here's Richard Hell: *Only time can write a song that's really, really real.*

Last I knew, she lived in the same city where we went to college. (New Haven. Yale.) I live in the place I dreamed of that morning waiting for the taillight to be fixed—New York City, around the corner and up the street from CBGB, which is not even there anymore. That's just one of the ways time has made the dream completely different. And better.

THE WORLD'S A MESS—IT'S IN MY KISS

A DATE
N.R. ○ YES ○ NO.

The Supremes: I Can't Help Myself
The Velvet Underground: I Found a Reason
Tom Waits: Jockey Full of Bourbon
The Blasters: Marie Marie
The Blasters: I'm Shakin'
King Floyd: Groove Me
Chuck Berry: No Particular Place to Go
The dB's: Amplifier
The dB's: Living a Lie
The dB's: We Were Happy There
The Blasters: Border Radio
The Drifters: Under the Boardwalk
The Drifters: There Goes My Baby
The Drifters: Save the Last Dance for Me
Joan Jett & The Blackhearts: I Love Rock 'N' Roll
Rickie Lee Jones: Company

B DATE
N.R. ○ YES ○ NO.

Cat Stevens: Sad Lisa
The Shangri-Las: Remember
The Shangri-Las: Give Him a Great Big Kiss
Nick Lowe: Too Many Teardrops
David Lee Roth: Coconut Grove
Talking Heads: Road to Nowhere
Stevie Wonder: Signed, Sealed, Delivered I'm Yours
Tom Verlaine: Always
Tom Verlaine: Coming Apart
Ben Vaughn: You're Gonna Hurt Yourself
X: The World's a Mess; It's in My Kiss
X: Dancing with Tears in My Eyes
X: Come Back to Me
Elvis Costello: My Funny Valentine

Novios by Sara Lamm

ENERGY EFFICIENT AND ANTI-RESONANCE
CASSETTE MECHANISM
XL II 90
POSITION·HIGH
maxell
A
Blanca Nieves

I was a five-foot-eleven-inch North Carolina girl who had spent twelve months in Spain. Francisco was a six-foot-three-inch Mexican guy, who had spent sixteen years in North Carolina. "You two would make a good couple," some friends told us. "You're tall and you speak Spanish." And so I went over to his house, we got really high, and made Muenster cheese quesadillas. When he tried to kiss me, I started crying, which should have scared him off, but didn't. Thus we became *novios.*

It was my junior year in college and his senior year. I was convinced that I was dying, so I kept going to the student health clinic for HIV tests. Francisco had bouts of rage and threw beer cans at his dog. Together we orchestrated an honor-code violation that I can't write more about because I am still afraid that if anyone discovers it the university will take away our diplomas.

Still, there were the good things. A trip to Old San Juan for spring break. The purple bookcase he made me for my birthday. Michael Jordan coming back to the NBA, wearing the peculiar number 45. Alas, it was clear to both of us that after graduation he would be hitting the road despite these positives.

He gave me this tape a few nights before he left. Two Disney stories—*Pinocchio* and *Snow White*—with the same music and characters as the record I listened to as a child, except all in Spanish. (Another name for Jiminy Cricket, by the way, is *Pepe Grillo.*) He put the tape in the (embarrassing to call it this) jam box and we listened together to part of *Blancanieves y Los Siete Enanitos*, then Francisco fast-forwarded to the end, where he had recorded a surprise track—"Ashokan Farewell," from Ken Burns's Civil War documentary. This song features a violin in lament, accompanied by a reading of the letter soldier Sullivan Ballou wrote to his wife several days before he died:

> *Forgive my many faults, and the many pains I have caused you. How thoughtless and foolish I have oftentimes been! . . . But, O Sarah! If the dead can come back to this earth and flit unseen around those they loved, I shall always be with you, in the garish day and in the darkest night . . .*

It was hot and the windows were open. We sat upstairs on the bed in my new apartment, leaning against the van Gogh poster, our hearts aching for poor Sarah and Sullivan Ballou. Not long after, we kissed good-bye in the parking lot next to Time Out Chicken. Francisco got into his new Subaru, headed west. That fall, we called each other often. He told me he was teaching seventh grade and dating an earthy fashion model. I told him I was taking a very light course load and dating a depressed actor. When Francisco came back to town for a visit before Christmas, he took me to his brother's fancy wedding. We dressed up, slow-danced, whispered in each other's ears—how weird marriage was, how weird his brother was, how weird the world was.

A year later he phoned to tell me he was engaged. I said something like this: "Oh, ha, well, that's rather surprising, I hope it works." He never called me again, which makes sense, given the fact that the next three times I left messages on his answering machine, I was drunk.

Meanwhile, the truth about this tape is that I never listened to it, not even once, after the night he gave it to me. I am sad and ashamed to admit it, because in that small example of nonlistening, I detect the larger emotional patterns of my inattentive, unhappy college self; that girl with the funny boots non-listened a whole lot. Its taken me thirteen years to notice the psychological relevance of Francisco's sophisticated mixtape work, and to consider what he might have been trying to communicate; only now do I hear in it the stories we told each other about our families, the sadness we carried, the things we didn't know. How simple it is from here to make the connection between fairy tales *en español*, and young Francisco, who showed up in American kindergarten without speaking a word of English. ("Apple," he remembered the teacher saying, terrorizing him with the strange, relentless sounds, cheerfully, like Snow White's evil stepmother. "Apple, Francisco, honey, this is an AP-PLE.") And what a cinch to see that we, two Spanish speakers lost in the American South, used the plight of a poor Yankee soldier to say our sad but necessary farewell.

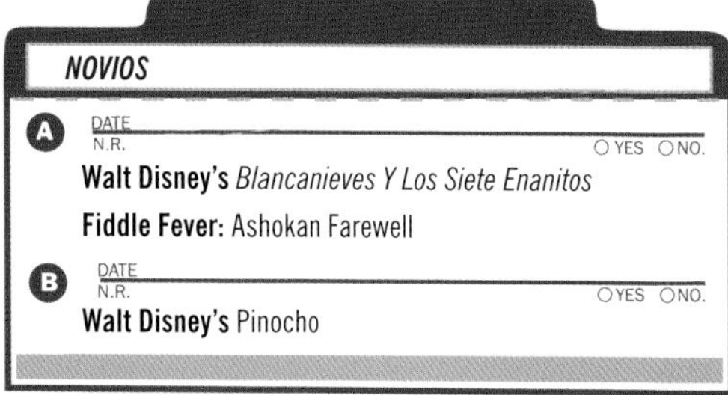

NOVIOS
A
DATE
N.R.
YES NO.
Walt Disney's Blancanieves Y Los Siete Enanitos
Fiddle Fever: Ashokan Farewell
B
DATE
N.R.
YES NO.
Walt Disney's Pinocho

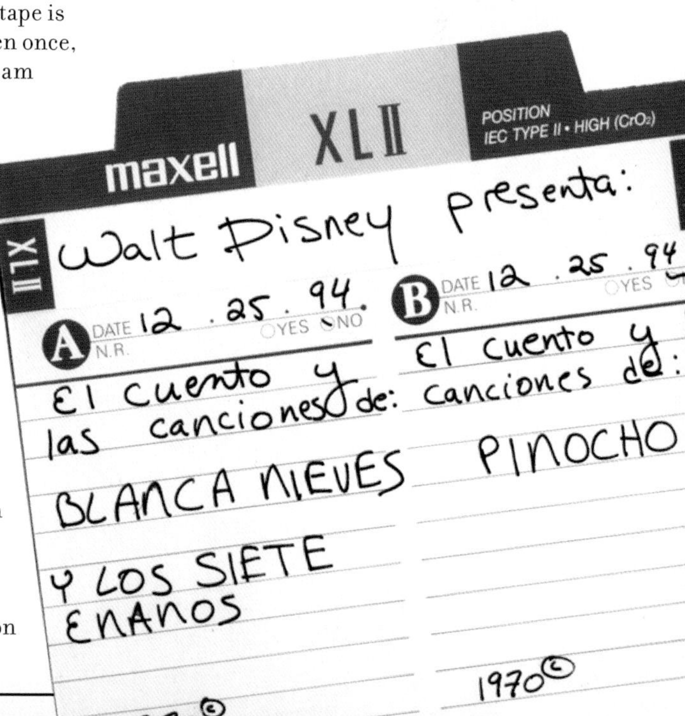

maxell
XL II
POSITION
IEC TYPE II • HIGH (CrO2)
Walt Disney presenta:
A DATE 12 . 25 . 94.
N.R.
YES NO
B DATE 12 . 25 . 94
N.R.
YES
El cuento y las canciones de:
BLANCA NIEVES
Y LOS SIETE
ENANOS
El cuento y las canciones de:
PINOCHO
1970©

Me now Me next Wednesday 7/16/91

I miss you! Lots!

Hey Sweetie,

This is going to be a short one because its very late and I'm very sleepy. I finally got this tape made, and I hope it's okay, because if it's not, tough. Just kidding. Seriously, though, I tried not to be very sappy (with a few obvious lapses), because I'd rather have you think of me when you're happy and boogie-ing around than when you're moping around, listening to some dreary song. Some of the songs have no relevance to anything - I just liked the way they sounded (as in, don't go trying to figure out the significance of "Octopus's Garden" to our relationship - there isn't any. Although I'm sure you could come up with some interesting theories.) I left some room on Side B, and I'd really like it if you could put "Crazy Love" at the end. That's the only song I really regretted not being able to put on (it's on your Moondance album). Give yourself a really big hug for me, I love you,

- BIG hug

Meredith

Reality Bites With a Clan of Winonas

By Robert Lanham

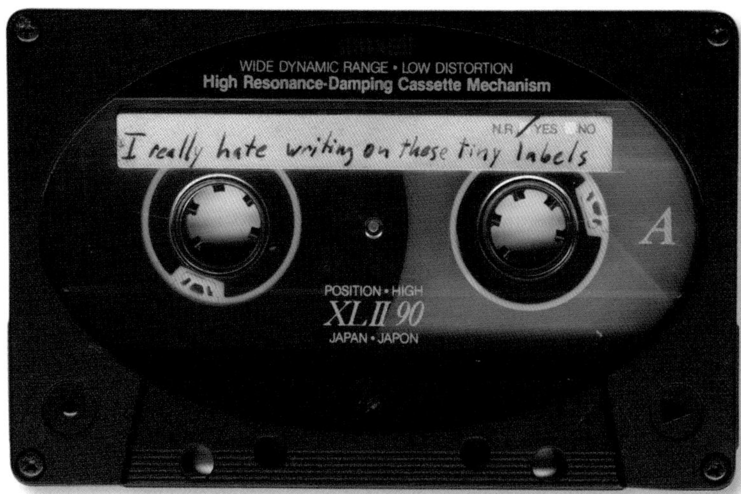

WIDE DYNAMIC RANGE • LOW DISTORTION
High Resonance-Damping Cassette Mechanism
N.R. YES NO
I really hate writing on these tiny labels
A
POSITION • HIGH
XLII 90
JAPAN • JAPON

Like most freethinking heterosexual males who came of age during the Reagan era, Winona Ryder was my Aphrodite in black eyeliner. She was the thinking teen's Audrey Hepburn. *Beetlejuice* was our *Love in the Afternoon.* From 1986 (*Lucas*) to the winter of 1990 (*Edward Scissorhands*), I serial-dated girls with dark hair and brooding temperaments who rolled their eyes at the slightest of irritations. Normal boys longed for golden-haired girls in stonewashed jeans. Not me. I was turned on by pale-skinned women who talked about death and would likely grow up to shoplift.

When I was a senior in high school (*Heathers*), I swore my devotion to a glossy two-dimensional photo of my tempestuous muse, ripped from the pages of *Rolling Stone,* and taped to my bedroom wall. Surely it was our destiny to meet. The cruelty she endured, my beloved princess, stuck to my wall with beaming eyes locked open, at the site of my indiscretions. I hoped she found solace in seeing that she'd defined my ideal. The few girls I sneaked into my bedroom always had the same ebony hair. The same coal-black eyes. So fated were we, I knew she'd intuit my guilt.

By the time I entered college (*Great Balls of Fire!*), I found myself accumulating a long line of Winona-inspired exes. There was Tiffany, who smoked clove cigarettes with black silk gloves and blamed me for her affair with my best friend. ("Well, *you* introduced us!") And then there was Elisabeth, a stickler for precise grammar, who returned my love notes copyedited with a crimson highlighter. And I won't even get into Krista, who feigned schizophrenia (I think) whenever I caught her taking money out of my wallet. The one thing they all had in common—other than

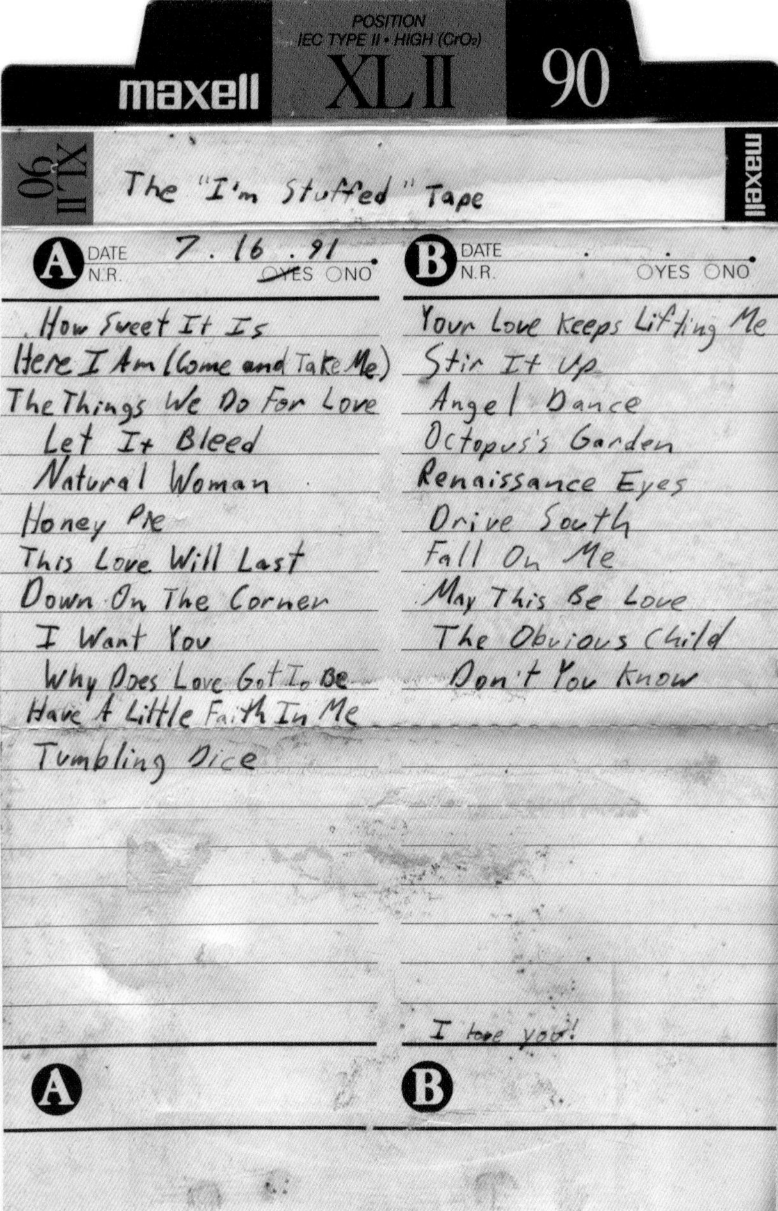
POSITION
IEC TYPE II • HIGH (CrO2)
maxell
XL II
90
The "I'm Stuffed" Tape
A DATE 7.16.91
N.R. YES NO
B DATE
N.R. YES NO
How Sweet It Is
Here I Am (Come and Take Me)
The Things We Do For Love
Let It Bleed
Natural Woman
Honey Pie
This Love Will Last
Down On The Corner
I Want You
Why Does Love Got To Be
Have A Little Faith In Me
Tumbling Dice
Your Love Keeps Lifting Me
Stir It Up
Angel Dance
Octopus's Garden
Renaissance Eyes
Drive South
Fall On Me
May This Be Love
The Obvious Child
Don't You Know
I love you!

each owning at least a dozen pairs of black tights—was a deep sense of sadness. And it was contagious. Anyone who's dated a brooding Winona knows that they can take their toll. Their dark, sad mysteries are enticing as a teen, but will engulf you as you grow older.

I met Meredith when I was a sophomore in college and we were introduced by a friend at a New Year's Eve party as 1990 (*Mermaids*) came to a close. Meredith read Wordsworth, not Plath. She loved *Annie Hall* instead of *Harold and Maude.* She wasn't too cool to wear scrunchies in her wavy blond hair. There were no black tights. As the calendar turned to 1991 (*Night on Earth*) we found ourselves alone and drunk from champagne at my apartment. We sang Deee-Lite's "Groove Is in the Heart" together in a drunken falsetto and waited for the year's first sun. She became my post-Winona girlfriend.

Months later in my cramped apartment, Meredith made me dinner, never once complaining about my kitchen, which was essentially a closet with a hot plate. After we'd eaten, she told me she loved me. I'd known all along that I felt the same way. And then, interrupting that warm silence that often accompanies moments of intimacy, I looked at her and said something stupid:

"Wow, Meredith. I'm stuffed."

She looked at me as if I was insane. But instead of being irritated by my oafishness, we laughed until we were breathless. "I'm stuffed" became our own private joke, a phrase that we'd whisper to one another cautiously should someone say something heartfelt.

The next week, Meredith traveled out of town but she mailed me a mixtape. It was called the I'M STUFFED tape. There's no

Souxsie and the Banshees. No Cure. Nothing particularly "cool." God knows, the Winonas would have rolled their eyes at the inclusion of CCR. It's just a collection of sweet songs filled with emotion, minus the brooding. My favorite thing about the "I'm Stuffed" tape is the note that's attached.

Today, whenever I hear "Crazy Love"—which I managed to record at the end of the mix—I'm reminded of our short-lived romance. We only dated for about a year, but Meredith got me out of my Winona rut, and showed me a life less bleak. Even if I still feel a little jealous when I see Johnny Depp.

THE "I'M STUFFED" TAPE

DATE
N.R. ○ YES ○ NO.

Marvin Gaye: How Sweet It Is (To Be Loved By You)
UB40: Here I Am
Gregson and Collister: The Things We Do for Love
The Rolling Stones: Let It Bleed
Aretha Franklin: Natural Woman
The Beatles: Honey Pie
Chris Isaak: This Love Will Last
Creedence Clearwater Revival: Down on the Corner
Bob Dylan: I Want You
Buckwheat Zydeco: Why Does Love Got to Be so Sad
John Hiatt: Have a Little Faith in Me
The Rolling Stones: Tumbling Dice

DATE
N.R. ○ YES ○ NO.

Jackie Wilson: (Your Love Keeps Lifting Me) Higher and Higher
Bob Marley and The Wailers: Stir It Up
Los Lobos: Angel Dance
The Beatles: Octopus's Garden
Arrogance: Renaissance Eyes
John Hiatt: Drive South
R.E.M.: Fall on Me
Jimi Hendrix: May This Be Love
Paul Simon: The Obvious Child
NRBQ: Don't You Know
Van Morrison: Crazy Love

SUCK IT, LOU BARLOW!

BY JULIE GERSTEIN

Collage from a zine by Walter X. Pierce

Todd and I developed a bond over sexually repressed indie rock bands and handmade fanzines. Even before we dated, I sort of knew he might have a thing for me. For my sixteenth birthday he orchestrated an elaborate scheme that involved wrapping himself in a large refrigerator-size box and "delivering" himself in my parents' foyer. Awkward. Sweet. Maybe a little creepy. Very Todd.

He would frequently send me mixtapes when he was away at college, fraught with gross lovesick meaning. There were often Sebadoh songs on those mixes, where singer Lou Barlow would croon endless withering songs about how his girlfriend was just so disappointing. This was when I learned never to date a guy who said he could "relate" to Lou Barlow.

After several months of hanging out at rock shows and the local Taco Bell, Todd ultimatum-ed his way into a relationship: Either we date, or we don't hang out. I was sixteen and really afraid of losing one of my best friends, so I agreed to make him my boyfriend. It was terrible.

This was the era before cell phones, before the Internet pervaded everything—and he made me call him every day from the pay phone at my school. He hated when I hung out with other guy friends, hated anything that took time and attention away from him. It was a gently creepy, possessively weird relationship and after three months I couldn't take it anymore. One day, while my parents ate dinner downstairs, I called him from the phone in my sister's room and broke up with him. He told me I was

breaking his heart and he never wanted to talk to me again.

Several months later, I was over at a mutual friend of ours' house and she brought up Todd. There was a new issue of his fanzine out, had I seen it? She handed me the thick sheaf of photocopied pages. The issue featured an interview with indie rock darlings Superchunk. It also included thirty-five viciously worded pages devoted to me. My stomach dropped into my toes when I saw it. I had no interest in how Todd had put his college-level English classes to use, but I paged through the xeroxed sheets anyway. In them, Todd detailed his every grievance with our faux relationship—and graciously included my picture and address, inviting his two thousand or so readers to contact me.

And they did! I got letters from a few angry and extremely bored fanzine readers demanding to know why I broke Todd's heart. I never answered (duh), but I did spiral into an angst-y panic (perceived mass humiliation will do that) and proceeded to do a bunch of depressed teen-girl crap like cutting my hair weird, throwing everything out that reminded me of him, and getting a new, totally stupid non-indie-rock boyfriend. It wasn't so much that I was broken up over our breakup—I just felt completely out of my skin—as if everyone everywhere knew that I was the girl who had broken this stupid boy's heart.

But I did hang on to a couple of Todd's mixtapes. This one was indicative of Todd's signature style—a seemingly innocuous mix of songs filled with not-so-hidden messages.

You only need to read the track titles to get the idea: "Brand New Love," "Friends," "I Only Have Eyes for You," "The One I Want." Not very obtuse, but at least he knew what he wanted.

SUCK IT, LOU BARLOW!

DATE
N.R. ○ YES ○ NO.

Blake Babies: Boiled Potato
The Mr. T Experience: I Love You, But You're Standing on My Foot
Superchunk: Brand New Love
Tiger Trap: Super Crush
The Wedding Present: Click Click
Small Factory: Friends
Eggs: It's Hard to Be an Egg
Sleepyhead: DCC
Helium: XXX
The Wedding Present: Dare
Ween: Don't Laugh (I Love You)
Grenadine: I Only Have Eyes for You
My Bloody Valentine: Soft as Snow (But Warm Inside)
Boyracer: That's Progress
Lois: From a Heart

DATE
N.R. ○ YES ○ NO.

Small Factory: The Bright Side
Dinosaur Jr.: Just Like Heaven
The Partridge Family: Girl, You Make My Day
Tiger Trap: Words & Smiles
The Mr. T Experience: Love American Style
Junebug: You Are Wet
Green Day: The One I Want
The Cocktails: The Penguin/Powerhouse
The Spinanes: Hawaiian Baby
Bunnygrunt: Gi2k
Six Cents & Natalie: Boyfriends
The Karl Hendricks Trio: Beergasm
Bubblegum Thunder: Describe the Symptoms
The Karl Hendricks Trio: She's the Shit
Tuscadero: Mount Pleasant

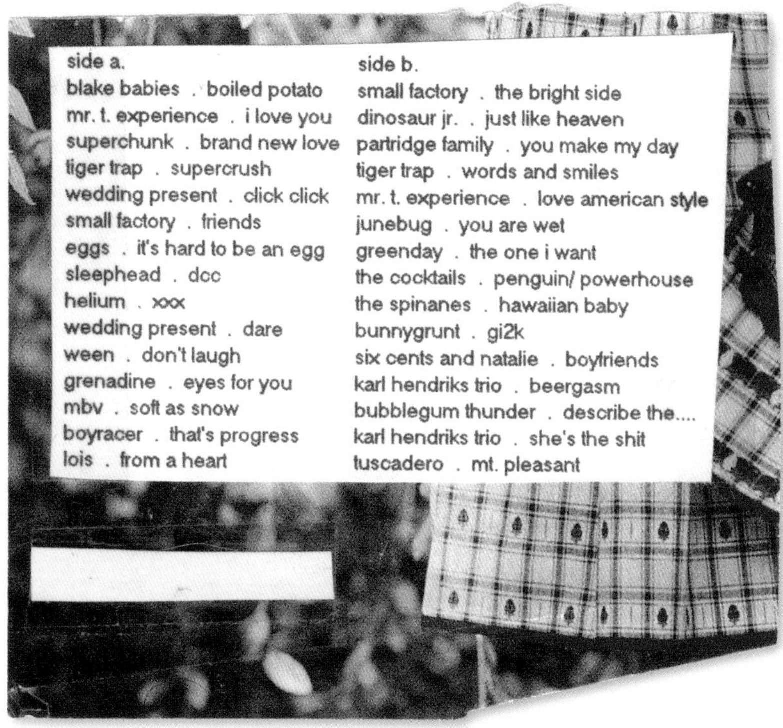
side a.
blake babies . boiled potato
mr. t. experience . i love you
superchunk . brand new love
tiger trap . supercrush
wedding present . click click
small factory . friends
eggs . it's hard to be an egg
sleephead . dcc
helium . xxx
wedding present . dare
ween . don't laugh
grenadine . eyes for you
mbv . soft as snow
boyracer . that's progress
lois . from a heart
side b.
small factory . the bright side
dinosaur jr. . just like heaven
partridge family . you make my day
tiger trap . words and smiles
mr. t. experience . love american style
junebug . you are wet
greenday . the one i want
the cocktails . penguin/ powerhouse
the spinanes . hawaiian baby
bunnygrunt . gi2k
six cents and natalie . boyfriends
karl hendriks trio . beergasm
bubblegum thunder . describe the....
karl hendriks trio . she's the shit
tuscadero . mt. pleasant

YAZ in OUR HEARTS
B
A
Yaz: Only You
Tears for Fears: Mad World
Depeche Mode: Everything Counts
Yaz: In My Room
Duran Duran: Save a Prayer
Wang Chung: Dance Hall Days
Dead or Alive: You. Spin Me Round
Yaz: Too Pieces
Visage: Fade to Gray
Paul Young: Come back to Stay
Yaz: Only You
BY MATT CASPER

At first, I thought she was an alcoholic lesbian. Not that I immediately suspect others of being such, but the lesbian alcoholics used the same room of the church basement as our theater group. And since Mandy had not been to the theater group's first couple of meetings, I thought maybe she was looking for support from other hard-drinking lesbians and had gotten her days mixed up. But no. She was merely a latecomer.

I, too, was a latecomer. Most boys generate their first orgasm themselves circa age eleven, but my first time was in Mandy's hand at the age of fifteen.

And that was probably my plan, though I couldn't possibly have articulated it at the time. My articulation went as far as "boobs." So once I learned she was to join our acting troupe, I became energized and focused as I knew I would now get the opportunity to look at her boobs once a week and possibly even attain them for my own purposes.

One thing led to another—expeditiously, as I was determined to say and do what was necessary to attain those boobs—and soon, we were "in love." I don't remember saying so, but according to Mandy's mom—who would allow us to sit unsupervised in the rec room—we most certainly were.

And we did the things that teenage lovers do: make out and fondle each other in said rec room (my idea/plan all along), have a playful soapy waterfight as we washed the station wagon (her mom's idea, which she also photographed like some Abercrombie spread: "Now Matt! Take the sponge like you're about to throw it. Mandy, throw your hands up like you're hiding! Hold it . . . hold it . . . and . . . Perfect!"), and make mixtapes.

Glorious mix tape; dated, timeless analog love.

Three minute novenas, secrets written for us alone.

Let heartache ring through the mix tape, the beginning of the end,

when we learn love is worth about 90 minutes of corporate rock.

Alas, the soundtrack to our passionate affair topped out at about forty-five minutes, as Mandy deemed only one side of the tape necessary to capture our love. But each song had bottomless significance.

We spun round and round, dancing for days in her room (Dead or Alive, Wang Chung, Yaz).

We felt the nihilism of the world in our bones, knew it was mad, yet also knew that all that we did counted for something—even the smallest actions were writ large (Tears for Fears, Depeche Mode).

We were cursed, too. We knew we were destined to fade into that gray night, knew the prayers we put aside would not save us (Visage, Duran Duran).

Most of all, we knew we were not meant to last. No matter how our hearts desired to stay for good this time, we must have known we were two hearts and destined to fall to pieces (Paul Young, Yaz).

In spite of this painful knowledge—sung in fey male voices and one belting female voice—we were very, very, very, and way serious about each other. The depth of our six-week commitment to each other is evidenced by the forty-five-minute tape opening and closing with an eternal dedication: There will be no one else. There will be "Only You."

(Had I been a little more intuitive at the time, though, I would have better understood our destiny. The tape's title said it clearly: ONLY YOU, SUMMER 1985. That is, only you during the summer of 1985. Come next summer or even as soon as fall, only someone else.)

The rest of the tape, well, Mandy may not have been all that hip—unlike a friend of hers who clearly saw something else in me when she gave me her MY WAR cassette (thank you, Lori!)—but she was meeting the basic requirements to live in a John Hughes world.

So why all the Yaz? Well, it was our make-out music. They sang "our song." And it was more than fitting that Mandy gave the gift of a Yaz-centric mixtape as it was "Only You" playing when she put her hand down my pants allowing me to give her the gift of yaz, too; a whole handful of yaz.

Mandy, where are you now? For whom do you string together songs of love, hope, despair, and regret? Who is your "only you" now? Whose yaz dirties your hands? I may never know, but so long as there are maudlin songs backed by drum machines,

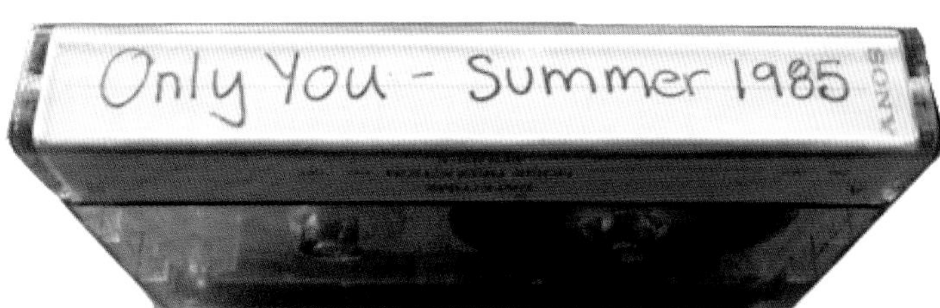

synthesizers, and keytars, I will always remember.

(Note: This was a hard choice. In the mid- '90s, a male coworker I wasn't all that close to gave me a mixtape letting me know he felt pretty darn close to me. It was filled with Sarah McLachlan—stuff from the CD with the song that goes, *I'll take your breath away.* He even included a lyric sheet. Yeah, that's right. A dude I worked with and barely knew gave this to me. Clearly, another story for another time and place . . . perhaps in a courtroom alongside my dental records.)

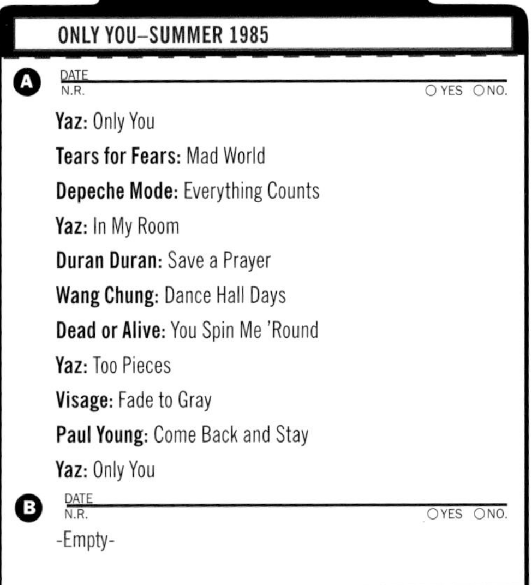

ONLY YOU–SUMMER 1985

A DATE N.R. ○ YES ○ NO.

Yaz: Only You
Tears for Fears: Mad World
Depeche Mode: Everything Counts
Yaz: In My Room
Duran Duran: Save a Prayer
Wang Chung: Dance Hall Days
Dead or Alive: You Spin Me 'Round
Yaz: Too Pieces
Visage: Fade to Gray
Paul Young: Come Back and Stay
Yaz: Only You

B DATE N.R. ○ YES ○ NO.

-Empty-

BRINGING YOUR TAPES BACK FROM THE DEAD

The simplest way to listen to an old cassette is with your cassette deck. You still have one, no? We didn't have one, so we borrowed a friend's tape deck and plugged it into a computer. All you need to create digital backups is a cassette player, an adapter cable (RCA to stereo mini plug, or maybe mini to mini, depending on your setup), and some audio recording software on your computer. If you don't have ProTools or Cubase or Acid or Sonar, there's plenty of free software out there—just search online and you'll find a ton of options. Plug your cassette player into your computer's soundcard and get started. With this software, you should be able to either record or export your audio files as mp3s. It does take a while—cassettes play in real time, so there's nothing quick about the process. When you're finished recording, pop them into your iPod and relive your glory days!

THE ONLY LIVING BOY

BY STARLEE KINE

I recently saw a French film called *A Christmas Tale*. It starred Catherine Deneuve and also Mathieu Amalric, who is the actor in *The Diving Bell and the Butterfly* and he's also in the new James Bond movies. Depending on the kind of person you are, you can choose which reference to go with. He has the kind of face that must look the same now as it did when he was six. In *A Christmas Tale* he plays the brother who forever disappoints. He was conceived in the hopes that his bone marrow would save another brother who was dying of cancer, but his marrow turned out to be just as big a screwup as he is. His family is so frustrated with him, for stealing their money and getting in fist-fights, but I found it hard to see their side. In the hospital he wore a long wool coat over his hospital scrubs, lending the outfit a bit of panache. At home he scampered down the brick facade instead of taking the stairs. Sure, he was drunk all the time, but he said such funny things that made me laugh. When he wasn't on-screen I was hoping that he hadn't wandered very far, that he'd be back soon. It never once occurred to me to regard him as a complicated creature. I thought the actual plot of the movie was to fall unequivocally in love with him on sight. (It's what I'd always done in real life, and what is a French film after all but your life with wallpaper?)

I met Dave in my college dorm's cafeteria. We were wearing the same sneakers. The first thing he asked was my name, followed by, "Starlee? Are you from California or something?" Later he told me he already knew I was from there, that he'd asked his friend about me before we ever met. It made me so happy to think our relationship had started before I'd known about it. It was like getting paid back money that I'd forgot I lent.

He was scrawny and still had pimples left over from high school. The first time we made out was after we watched *Manhattan* in his apartment. I saw it in the theater for the second time ever last year and the combination of creepiness of plot, coupled with the realization that Woody Allen's physical gestures were identical to that of Dave's, caused me to see the film with my hands over my eyes, peeking through the cracks of my fingers, as though I were watching a horror movie.

There's a spot in Washington Square Park, near the southwest entrance, that I can't walk on without my stomach feeling like it's about to take a test. It's where he wrote his number on the inside of a matchbook and then handed it to me. I bought a new sweater last week and I've already left it behind at a party, but it's been fourteen years and I still have that matchbook. If I were to try and burn it up, an unlit matchstick would blow the lit one out. The same with the mixtape he made me. When I went to look for it in the suitcase in my closet where these things are kept, I was sure it'd be gone. Once I found it, I was sure it'd be the wrong tape inside or that it wouldn't play. It wasn't and it did.

Inside that same suitcase is also a fourteen-year-old bottle of perfume. It isn't cool-looking, it doesn't have a little glass stopper. It is from the mall and the perfume inside smells too strong. My mom got it as a free sample and gave it to me. I used to wear it because I didn't know any better, and then Dave decided that it was my scent and there was nothing I could do but keep wearing it. He used to hold my wrist against his nose as if it were an oxygen mask. Then they discontinued the line and I tried to ration it out as best I could. I thought if I could keep the stuff from running out our relationship would never really die. Like a genie in a bottle, I could summon it whenever I wanted just by removing the cap. And in a way, all these years later, it does function like that. The sense memory that hits me whenever I dare inhale the perfume is as close to time travel as I'll ever get. I breathe in and I can remember perfectly what his shadowy room looked like at four in the morning while he was sleeping but I was sitting upright against the wall, not wanting to miss anything. I can remember the exact shade of green of his bath towel and even that makes me nostalgic, because when you are young almost everything you do is a first in your life and thus equally meaningful and exciting, even taking a shower in a guy's crappy apartment, even using his two-in-one shampoo and conditioner to wash your hair.

He broke up with me every couple of weeks, each time in a more dramatic fashion. He invited me home with him to St. Louis for Christmas, broke up with me on the last morning as I was waiting on his front lawn for a cab, and had already called to patch things up by the time I'd landed back in New York. We watched *Days of Wine and Roses* one night and as the credits rolled, he tucked a lock of hair behind my ear and said, "I hope we're like that one day." He equated passion with dysfunction, love with heartbreak, stability with death. The more we broke up, the crazier I got. It was like jumping back and forth from a hot tub to a pool. You just can't do that and then act surprised when you get pneumonia. I once poured an entire bottle of wine over his head in front of all our friends. His brother wrote a poem about it.

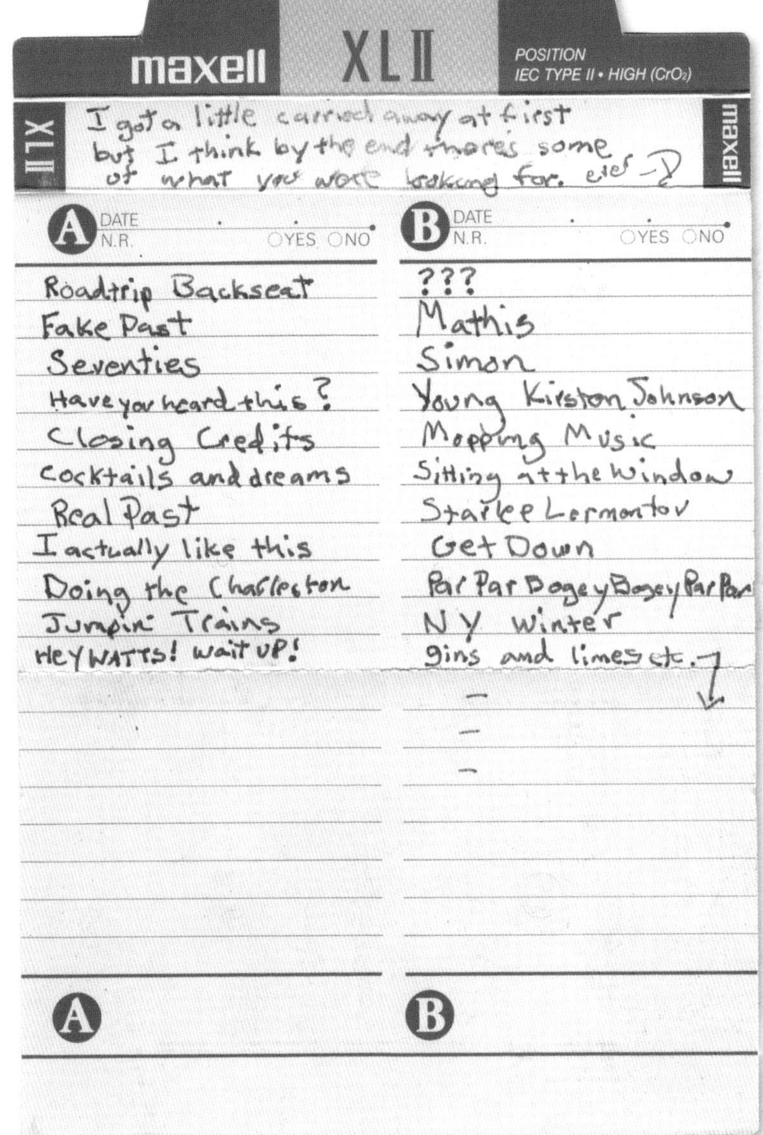
maxell
XL II
POSITION
IEC TYPE II • HIGH (CrO2)
I got a little carried away at first
but I think by the end there's some
of what you were looking for. eve -?
A DATE
N.R.
YES NO
B DATE
N.R.
YES NO
Roadtrip Backseat
Fake Past
Seventies
Have you heard this?
Closing Credits
Cocktails and dreams
Real Past
I actually like this
Doing the Charleston
Jumpin' Trains
HEY WATTS! wait UP!
???
Mathis
Simon
Young Kirston Johnson
Mopping Music
Sitting at the Window
Starke Lermontov
Get Down
Par Par Bogey Bogey Par Par
NY Winter
gins and limes etc.
A
B

That first summer, I signed up to go on a study-abroad program in Italy. He, of course, broke up with me before I left. I sat on his futon and cried, and he looked at me like I was letting him down. He wanted me not to care, to go to Italy and sleep with cheesy Italian guys and throw it in his face. Finally he opened the door for me to leave, and as I did I turned to him and said, "Good-bye for real this time. I hate you so much. I wish you were dead."

The night before I flew out, I got a call from his best friend. Dave had cancer.

My summer abroad was spent writing him letters on every scrap of paper I could find. I would buy bread and jam at the market just so I could use the receipt to scribble sentences. I never sent them, just stuffed them in my pockets and textbooks. My handwriting was so crooked and sloppy that it canceled out any authentic sentiment that I managed to achieve. One night I got up the nerve to call him and the first thing out of his mouth was, "Remember the last thing you said to me?" I told him I knew he wasn't going to die because he could haunt me more if he were alive.

He didn't die. He got a bone marrow transplant from his brother, who was a screwup just like in the film but whose marrow was reliable and mature, it paid its bills on time and went to sleep at a decent hour. He sent me pictures of himself with no hair, so frail inside his sweatshirt, and I Scotch-taped them above my bed. I flew to St. Louis to take care of him for a week. I went to an actual travel agent and paid for the ticket in cash. In my mind, the stack of bills is so high, as though I laid out the money entirely in one dollar bills, as though every quarter ever found between the couch cushions was used to get me there. There were posters of tropical beaches covering the walls but I couldn't imagine wanting to go anywhere else but the chilly, gray Midwest. If there had been a big poster of his house on her wall, I would've thought, "That seems about right."

It may sound awful, but that week was the best time we ever had together. He was too weak to be mean and I was too grateful he was alive to be neurotic. He'd lay his head in my lap and when his mom called me his girlfriend, he didn't fight her on it. I slept in a pair of his blue hospital pants, way too big, falling off my hips even when I cinched them as tight as they would go. He was so skinny that it felt as if he could just climb in with me and we'd be set for a while. We watched movies and talked about living together. We both agreed it didn't matter where the place was as long as it was filled with blankets and pillows.

I flew back to New York and the tape came in the mail a week later. It was the first mixtape I'd ever gotten from a guy. His handwriting was still shaky. It was supposed to serve as a soundtrack to my first apartment, which I had just moved into. I was to listen to "Ease on Down" while cleaning the oven and mopping the floors. "Starlee Lermontov" was because I was taking clarinet lessons at the time, from a teacher whose number I'd gotten off a flyer (he'd show up at my door once a week asking, "Ready to jam?"). "The Only Living Boy in New York" was from when Dave first moved to New York to go to college. His plane touched down at the same moment the song came streaming through his headphones.

Dave broke up with me shortly after my visit to St. Louis, cutting me out of his new life. The gentleness he'd shown while he was getting better was replaced with a strange, self-destructive cockiness. Postcancer he went on a several-years-long bender that involved drugs and girls and also a considerable amount of basketball playing. We barely ever spoke again, except for a disruptive resurfacing once a year for a long while and then finally, nothing.

I thought that when I heard the mixtape it would be like the perfume. I'd become dizzy and woozy and only be able to listen in stops and starts. Perhaps it's because aural memory isn't the same as scent. Perhaps it's because the songs themselves have their own lives, they exist, even the weird ones exist, somewhere outside of that tape. Whatever the reason, I was able to listen straight through, with only the occasional faint tug in my chest.

I GOT A LITTLE CARRIED AWAY AT FIRST...

A DATE N.R. ○YES ○NO.

The Oh Papas!: Sod House
The Church: Under the Milky Way
Simon and Garfunkel: The Only Living Boy in New York
They Might Be Giants: (She Was a) Hotel Detective
Tommy Makem and Liam Clancy: The Garden Song
Brandford Marsalis Quartet: Mo' Better Blues
John Wesley Harding: Things Snowball
Ray Lynch: No Blue Thing
Leon Redbone: Diddy Wah Diddy
Woody Guthrie: Worried Man Blues
Lick the Tins: Can't Help Falling In Love

B DATE N.R. ○YES ○NO.

Sulhassii: Varttina
Johnny Mathis (with Ray Conniff and His Orchestra): When Sunny Gets Blue
Carly Simon: Coming Around Again
Howard Jones: No One Is to Blame
The Wiz Ease On Down the Road
Nina Simone: Ev'ry Time We Say Goodbye
Sidney Bechet: Shake It and Break It
Aretha Franklin: Spanish Harlem
Chet Baker: My Funny Valentine
Ella Fitzgerald: I've Got My Love to Keep Me Warm
Fats Waller: The Joint Is Jumpin'
Sidney Bechet: Sweetie Dear
Sidney Bechet: I Want You Tonight
Sidney Bechet: I've Found a New Baby

A BROKEN TAPE DOESN'T HAVE TO LEAD TO A BROKEN HEART: *WHEN YOUR CASSETTE FAILS*

Tapes are breakable, erasable, meltable, and water-damagable. Fortunately, many of these issues can be repaired with spare parts and a little ingenuity. Before you toss out your damaged mix, try one of the following to revive your compilation.

Problem: Busted cassette shell.

Solution: The clamshell case is easily swapped out.

Get yourself a fine-tipped Phillips head screwdriver and unscrew the remaining screws, paying close attention to make sure the magnetic tape stays spooled on the cheap plastic hubs. Carefully set the tape aside and find an unused or unwanted tape. Remove the screws from this intact cassette and open up the housing. Toss out the magnetic tape from the donor housing and swap in the tape from the broken shell. Reassemble the case, screw together, and you're back in business.

Problem: You accidentally record over your favorite tapes.

Solution: Pop the tabs!

Those little tabs up on the top of the cassette shell aren't just for looks. Everyone knows you need to pop those tabs to keep tape decks from accidentally recording over your bootleg copy of Queen's *Live at Wembly*. Tragedies often take place with the tabs still intact—with the Record button sitting perilously close to the Play button—leading to dreaded "holes" in the audio. Immediately after checking your recording, poke them out with a flathead screwdriver or ballpoint pen and relax, knowing your cassette will be in your collection forever. This, of course, is a preventative measure—doing this after the fact won't bring back your lost audio, so get in the habit of doing it as soon as you finish recording side B.

This procedure is reversible, however, with a small piece of Scotch tape. This is also useful for when you want to tape over that store-bought tape you picked up for that one single, which you're already tired of.

Problem: While rewinding/fast-forwarding, your tape deck pulls the tape out of the spools.

Solution: Break the momentum! Use the Stop button before the tape runs out.

Sometimes tape decks are too good for their own good; those ultra-fast fast-forward and rewind features can often lead to cassette injury. As the take-up reel gathers additional magnetic tape, it gains size and power over the supply reel, causing the leader tape to be pulled right out from its hub.

For this procedure, all you'll need is a small Phillips head screwdriver. Start by removing each of the screws in the cassette housing, followed by the top half of the cassette. Next, remove the empty reel and pop out the tiny piece of plastic that pinches the magnetic tape into the hub. Lay the tail end of the magnetic tape into the gap and reconstitute the hub, pinching the tape into the joint. Carefully align the two plastic covers back together and screw back into place. You did it!

Problem: Poor audio quality from your tape deck.

Solution: Clean the heads!

After a significant amount of use, you may notice the quality of the audio coming from your boombox speakers is starting to sound a little crappy. Don't fret, help is on the way. The best thing to do is to dip a cotton swab into some rubbing alcohol and then rub away the grime that's collected on the tape heads in your player. A couple quick swabs should take care of the problem.

Some manufacturers came up with a tape head–cleaning cassette, but those things are bunk. Avoid 'em!

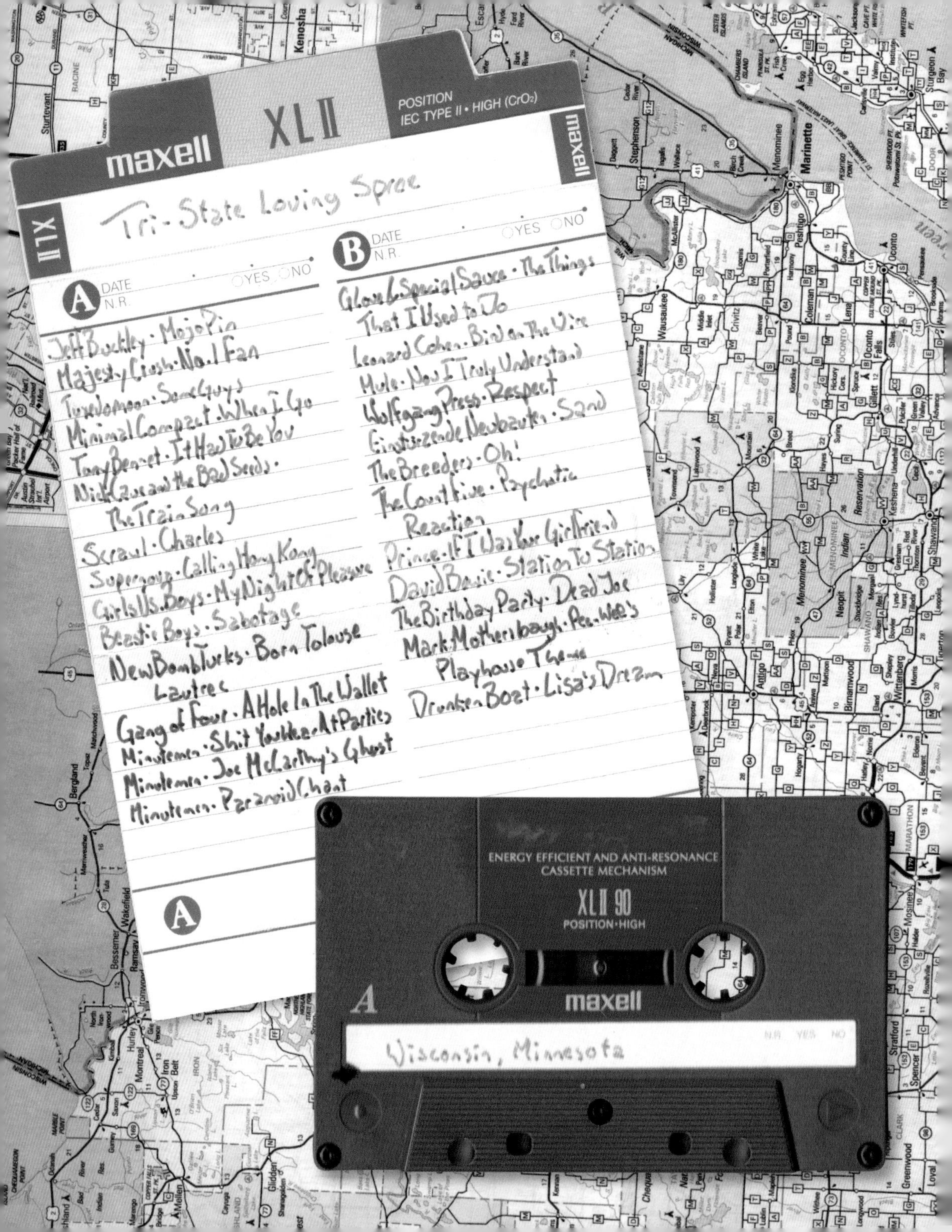

maxell
XL II
POSITION
IEC TYPE II • HIGH (CrO2)
Tri-State Loving Spree
A DATE N.R. YES NO
Jeff Buckley · Mojo Pin
Majesty Crush · No. 1 Fan
Tuxedomoon · Some Guys
Minimal Compact · When I Go
Tony Bennett · It Had To Be You
Nick Cave and the Bad Seeds · The Train Song
Scrawl · Charles
Supergrass · Calling Hong Kong
Girls Vs. Boys · My Night Of Pleasure
Beastie Boys · Sabotage
New Bomb Turks · Born Tolouse Lautrec
Gang of Four · A Hole In The Wallet
Minutemen · Shit You Hear At Parties
Minutemen · Joe McCarthy's Ghost
Minutemen · Paranoid Chant
B DATE N.R. YES NO
Glove & Special Sauce · The Things That I Used to Do
Leonard Cohen · Bird on The Wire
Mule · Now I Truly Understand
Wolfgang Press · Respect
Einstürzende Neubauten · Sand
The Breeders · Oh!
The Count Five · Psychotic Reaction
Prince · If I Was Your Girlfriend
David Bowie · Station To Station
The Birthday Party · Dead Joe
Mark Mothersbaugh · Pee-Wee's Playhouse Theme
Drunken Boat · Lisa's Dream
ENERGY EFFICIENT AND ANTI-RESONANCE CASSETTE MECHANISM
XL II 90
POSITION · HIGH
maxell
Wisconsin, Minnesota

Something I Still Feel Bad About

By Anne Elizabeth Moore

My most renowned story relating to mixtapes is actually not so much a story about the tape as it is the story of how Jeff Buckley, college radio star, died—which, by the way, is something I still feel bad about.

In the mid-1990s, I was dating a boy who worked in the music industry, who was all gaga over this swoony singer-songwriter type, Jeff Buckley. He would make me mixtapes chock-full of Buckley's melodic falsetto, expecting my panties to fly off whenever he sang another "hallelujah." (Which they did.)

So as one does when one is in one's mid-twenties, once I had fallen in love, I fled the country. I went to hike a volcano in Nicaragua where, as one does when one travels alone and ignores the dictums of both hygiene and common sense, I fell ill. With cholera, in my case, which, if I had known you could still get, would have caused me to think twice before drinking from that stream and accidentally ingesting human feces. Which is how one contracts cholera. Apparently.

Anyway.

Soon I was sick and unable to move from my dirt-floored motel room, having gone without even water for four days. I could not speak the language. *What the fuck was I thinking?*, you are surely asking yourself and I am saying to myself; well, you have a pretty good point there. Honestly, the only thing I could do was listen to mixtapes. Somehow, though, I received on my deathbed a letter from the boy who had made them, and he had asked Jeff Buckley to write me a cute note on the back. *Jeff Buckley!* I thought. *There's so much to live for!*

When I read the letter, I was racked with guilt. It seemed that my rapidly impending death would sadden my boyfriend, who had, after all, put Scrawl, Prince, and the New Bomb Turks all on the same tape for me, even though he named it after a sexual experience he'd had with another girl. But still. He didn't ask Jeff Buckley to write a note to *her*.

So I clambered out of bed in an attempt to drag myself to a phone to call the boy and say good-bye and he could have my stereo, except luckily I was not twenty feet outside the door when the only doctor in town strolled by and demanded I go back to bed immediately, where he would return in a few moments with some penicillin. Which he did. I got better. I went home.

After his next concert in town, I waited to meet Jeff Buckley, to thank him. "I mean, part of it was you and part of it was him"—here I gestured to the boyfriend—"but the bottom line is, that note on the back made me get up and that's when the doctor found me, you know? So, umm, I don't really know how to thank you for saving my life."

"That's OK," said Jeff Buckley, in the voice that I had listened to on tape on my deathbed.

"Maybe someday you can do the same for me."

I agreed. I agreed to save Jeff Buckley's life. Of course I did.

Then, of course, he died a few years later. He drowned in Memphis, waded into the river with all his clothes on. And I didn't do anything about it.

TRI-STATE LOVING SPREE

A DATE
N.R. ○ YES ○ NO.

Jeff Buckley: Mojo Pin
Majesty Crush: No. 1 Fan
Tuxedomoon: Some Guys
Minimal Compact: When I Go
Tony Bennett: It Had to Be You
Nick Cave and the Bad Seeds: The Train Song
Scrawl: Charles
Supernova: Calling Hong Kong
Girls Against Boys: My Night of Pleasure
Beastie Boys: Sabotage
New Bomb Turks: Born Toulouse-Lautrec
Gang of Four: A Hole in the Wallet
Minutemen: Shit You Hear at Parties
Minutemen: Joe McCarthy's Ghost
Minutemen: Paranoid Chant

B DATE
N.R. ○ YES ○ NO.

G. Love and Special Sauce: The Things that I Used to Do
Leonard Cohen: Bird on the Wire
Mule: Now I Truly Understand
Wolfgang Press: Respect
Einstürzende Neubauten: Sand
The Breeders: Oh!
The Count Five: Psychotic Reaction
Prince: If I Was Your Girlfriend
David Bowie: Station to Station
The Birthday Party: Dead Joe
Mark Mothersbaugh: Pee Wee's Playhouse Theme
Drunken Boat: Lisa's Dream

THE MIXTAPE VIRGIN

BY DAVID NADELBERG

By Amy
OBLITERATION
For Dave
Curve : Horror Head
Ned's : Saturday Night
New Order : Liar
Pet Shop Boys : Go West
The Magic Dragon : Splash
Toad T.W.S. - Is It For Me
Peter Murphy - Cuts U Up
Ween - Don't Get 2 Close
Depeche Mode - But Not Tonight
New Order - Procession
Sugar - Walking Away
Ride - Taste
The Cavedogs - Leave Me Alone
Replacements - Torture
Mock Turtles - Can U Dig It?
Lloyd Cole - Chelsea Hotel
Pixies - I Can't Forget
Opus III - Fine Day (It's A)
2 Unlimited - Get Ready For This
New Order - All The Way
Juliana Hatfield - Feelin' Massachusetts

As a teenager, I was mystified by that guy who got to make out with a stranger on the dance floor. On one hand, I envied him. He was a suave, sexual magnet who lured the ladies by the sheer power of his machismo. On the other hand, he was creepy.

And then one night in college, thanks to several red plastic cups of beer and a girl in a tight white top, I magically became, well . . . that guy.

We were at a rave in Ithaca, New York. I was drunkish. She was stoned-ish. Despite our inebriated vision, it was lust-at-first-sight-ish.

With no regard for the social codes of PDA, we began groping one another during a song that involved heavy BPM, a highly repetitive chorus, and lots of whistle tweets. After twenty minutes of electronic thump and grind, I decided to do the chivalrous thing and introduce myself.

This was the start of my relationship with Amy, a short-lived affair that, from that moment on, was defined by music. Not surprisingly, during one of our first sober conversations, Amy and I discussed our mutual love of making mixtapes.

We shared an appreciation for the artistry involved in coming up with mixtape titles, artwork, and, of course, the perfect set list. To me, mixtapes were more than mere compilations. They were expressions—portraits of personalities, feelings, or relationships.

So when I revealed that despite my years of making tapes, no one had ever given one to me, Amy made it her mission to pop my mixtape cherry.

A few weeks later, Amy handed me a decorative, yellow cassette. It even had a title. OBLITERATION, the spine read. OBLITERATION was to be the soundtrack of our relationship.

That night, I put OBLITERATION into my roommate's stereo, climbed onto my bunk, and waited to feel obliterated. After all these years, I was finally about to discover what all the fuss was about.

Forty-five minutes later, side A was complete. I lay in bed spent from the experience. But in the hours that followed, a sense of disconnect emerged. I liked it. But it didn't consume me. It felt like it could have been made for anyone.

Truth be told, OBLITERATION was inconsistent with what I needed out of a mixtape relationship. It featured songs from bands I liked (Ned's Atomic Dustbin, the Pixies), bands I kinda liked (Depeche Mode, Juliana Hatfield), bands I disliked (Toad the Wet Sprocket, 2 Unlimited), and bands I still to this day have no clue about (Dub the Magic Dragon, Mock Turtles). As much as I appreciated it, the tape seemed thrown together. Kinda like two strangers making out on a dance floor.

I spent so many years building up the idea of receiving a mixtape from someone, that I failed to consider one key possibility: What if I didn't love the cassette as much as I loved the gesture? Can a mixtape with such a buildup ever live up to its expectations?

Then again, maybe the lukewarm feelings weren't exclusive to me. Reading the liner notes, I now notice a curious theme of emotional distance in her song selections: "Don't Get 2 Close," "Leave Me Alone," "Walking Away," "Go West, Liar," . . . and "Torture." Hell, even the mixtape's very title implied dissolve.

I had to face the music—it wasn't meant to be.

Eventually, Amy and I dated others, lost touch, and grew up. Then last year, we reconnected. This time, we did not meet in a loud, sweaty dance club but rather in a loud, air-conditioned strip-mall chain restaurant. En route, I remember wondering if we might feel some sort of renewed attraction or spark, as if our relationship had a B-side, and all we had to do was wait a decade to flip it over.

We sat down, ate our combo meals, and reminisced. I told her I still had OBLITERATION, and I've always cherished its unique place in my life. She barely remembered it, though abruptly apologized about the Mock Turtles. The meal didn't end with any groping, but with a warm hug—the kind you give to old friends.

Looking back, I'm not sure what we had. But she popped my mixtape cherry. And you never forget your first. Or, to quote a song she placed in the middle of side B, *I can't forget . . . but I don't remember what.*

OBLITERATION

A DATE
N.R. ○ YES ○ NO.

Curve: Horror Head
Ned's Atomic Dustbin: Saturday Night
New Order: Liar
Pet Shop Boys: Go West
Dub the Magic Dragon: Splash
Toad the Wet Sprocket: Is It for Me
Peter Murphy: Cuts You Up
Ween: Don't Get 2 Close
Depeche Mode: But Not Tonight
New Order: Procession
Sugar: Walking Away

B DATE
N.R. ○ YES ○ NO.

Ride: Taste
The Cavedogs: Leave Me Alone
The Replacements: Torture
The Mock Turtles: Can You Dig It?
Lloyd Cole: Chelsea Hotel
Pixies: I Can't Forget
Opus III: It's a Fine Day
2 Unlimited: Get Ready for This
New Order: All the Way
Juliana Hatfield: Feelin' Massachusetts
Depeche Mode: Mercy in You
Lenny Kravitz: Believe

PARADISE BY THE DASHBOARD LIGHT

BY ARTHUR JONES

Amy was the first girl I met at college, in late August of 1993. She was a senior leading a campus tour and I was in the group of freshman boys shuffling obediently behind her. We attended a tiny liberal-arts school in Nowheresville, Kansas, which didn't have college-town luxuries like pizza parlors, coffee shops, or traffic lights. Students drank beer in the Conoco parking lot and the nearest movie theater was an hour away. It was a windswept desolate place, surrounded by miles of prairie grassland, and I felt like I had just enrolled in the last college at the end of the earth.

Over the next few months, I kept a wandering eye on Amy. She had tousled blond hair, a raspy voice from years of high-school cheerleading, and a crinkly smile that gave her a vague Meg Ryan quality. She was popular, but different from the terrifying, stuck-up, big-haired blondes she hung out with. She was sweet, down-to-earth, and unlike them, she didn't wear sweatpants with her name across the butt or wear makeup to the cafeteria for breakfast. Amy's usual outfit was a ratty, knee-length sweater worn over tights and she always looked like she had just rolled out of bed. Her boyfriend, Anders, was the school's one authentic badass. He was a rail-thin, bearded slacker who dealt weed and acid. Several of the campus buildings were named after his grandfather, which is probably all that kept him from getting expelled. He and Amy were notorious. They partied hard and fought often. They threw things from open dormitory windows and screamed at each other from moving cars. They were our Bobby and Whitney, our Kevin and Britney, and I found them exotic and fascinating.

Second semester, Amy and I ended up in a Shakespeare class together. The course culminated in a performance of *Twelfth Night.* She was the lead, Lady Olivia, and I was Sebastian, who Olivia accidentally marries believing him to be Cesario, his cross-dressing identical twin sister. Like many of Shakespeare's comedies it's a play of mistaken identity and so, too, became my relationship with Amy. As Sebastian I was a passionate, swashbuckling man of mystery but as Arthur I was a shy, non-swashbuckling bundle of nerves. I felt so awkward around Amy I could barely speak. As a result I ignored her, was rude to her, and often disappeared after rehearsals without saying good-bye. Despite all of this, Amy found my aloofness intriguing, she mistook my shyness for confidence, and we developed an unlikely spark on- and offstage.

Twelfth Night opened the last week of school and Anders was strangely absent from the performances. Amy seemed happy and carefree. The night the show closed she flirtatiously tackled me backstage. At the cast party she danced with a beer in each hand while a band from Kansas City played a train wreck of covers—"Closer to Fine" by the Indigo Girls, "We Built This City" by Starship, and "Beds Are Burning" by Midnight Oil. When it was time to go home she insisted that I walk her back to her dorm.

"Shit, I lost my sandals," she said, staring down at her feet, just then realizing she'd walked across campus barefoot.

"No you didn't," I replied, producing them from my backpack.

She squealed as though I'd performed the most amazing magic trick she'd ever seen. Then, to my shock, she leaned in and gave me a big sloppy kiss.

The next night Amy and I made out under a blanket while her roommate watched TV. At one point the phone rang and the machine picked up. It was Anders.

"Amy, where the fuck are you?"

Amy threw off the blanket and ran across the room, hitting the top of the answering machine with her fist as his voice grew angrier. "We were supposed to—" CLICK. She smiled at me and then hopped back under the covers. I was officially the other man. It felt amazing.

A few days later, Amy picked me up in her Cutlass Ciera and drove us out to a secluded field. The sun was setting and the horizon was so flat and unencumbered that the car felt like an island on an endless grassy sea. We were undressing in the front seat when Amy handed me something from her purse.

"I made this for you."

It was a cassette labeled PJ 4 AJ, in loopy handwriting. I figured it was a mixtape but had no idea what "PJ 4 AJ" meant. I was "AJ," obviously, but what was "PJ"?

Party Jams, perhaps? Pretentious Jazz? Prune Juice? The possibilities were endless.

"Let's listen to it!" Amy said as she snatched it back and shoved it into the stereo.

My heart sank as the music kicked in. It was "Once," the first song on Pearl Jam's grunge-era-defining album *Ten*.

"Oh, I get it!" I yelled, feigning a smile. "Pearl Jam for Arthur Jones!"

Amy cranked up the volume and shrieked, "I love this song!"

She pushed me hard against the passenger seat and climbed on top of me. After that things got a little crazy. It was as if Eddie Vedder had sabotaged our quiet, romantic moment by putting a drop of Spanish fly under her tongue. The cassette wasn't a mixtape. It was a dub of *Ten*, a record full of grunty, monosyllabic songs about murder, depression, and teen

suicide, making it perhaps the worst sex album ever. For instance, it's really hard to get a blow job while listening to that song "Alive," and it's even harder to go down on someone during "Jeremy," especially at the end of the song when Vedder sings the words *Jeremy spoke in* over and over again like a bleating goat. But that's what happened and that's what I did.

History is full of lonely freshmen who never got the opportunity to nail a smoking-hot ex-cheerleader. I recognized the magnitude of my situation and wasn't about to let a guy who sang like Foghorn Leghorn ruin my moment of destiny. So, I maintained my composure, focused, and made love with the spastic enthusiasm of someone who had won the sexual lottery. I blew on Amy's neck and massaged her forehead. I kissed her ankles and rubbed her shoulders and while we were doing it, I mentally referenced at least three porno movies and one episode of the *Red Shoe Diaries*.

When we were finished, Amy put her head on my chest and sang along quietly as the tape played out. It was dark and a full moon hung low in the sky. We rolled down the windows and a cool breeze drifted in. It was one of the few singularly perfect moments in my life, so naturally, I fucked it up by saying something stupid.

"I just want you to know . . . " I said, pausing to lift her chin and look her in the eyes. "I've never done that before."

She jerked up. "Done *what* before?"

"You know, go all the way."

The phrase hung awkwardly in the air and I could tell Amy wasn't thrilled by the news. Whatever illicit thrill we had just shared was over and now she was stuck in a car with a freshly deflowered nineteen-year-old boy.

We sat in silence as I hunted for my socks and she buttoned up her shirt. I briefly considered flinging open the car door and running away but decided not to, thinking it might make things more awkward if Amy had to chase a half-naked man across an empty wheat field in her car. Eventually she sighed and smiled a wide, crinkly smile.

"Well, I didn't notice."

Amy and I had sex a few more times but eventually she went back to Anders. She joined the Air Force after graduation and I transferred schools. After a handful of letters we fell out of touch. Pearl Jam continues to make not-very-good records and I'm sure people continue to lose their virginity to those not-very-good records—that's the way things work.

PJ FOR AJ
A
DATE
N.R.
YES NO.
Pearl Jam: Once
Pearl Jam: Even Flow
Pearl Jam: Alive
Pearl Jam: Why Go
Pearl Jam: Black
Pearl Jam: Jeremy
Pearl Jam: Oceans
Pearl Jam: Porch
B
DATE
N.R.
YES NO.
Pearl Jam: Garden
Pearl Jam: Deep
Pearl Jam: Release

LIVE FREE OR DIE

JODYNE L. SPEYER

My first kiss ended in bloodshed. His name was Jonathan and the kiss was the result of a mixtape he made me. He was a Deadhead, I was a Goth. An unlikely match, but we weren't the ones who chose each other, our classmates did. They decided we should be a couple based solely on the fact we were the only Jewish kids in my small-town New Hampshire school.

We were hanging out on his bed minutes before he threw what turned out to be the biggest party my town had ever seen. Knowing that besides breathing and black eyeliner, music was the most important thing in my life, Jonathan spent hours making me the perfect ninety-minute tape. He popped it in his Onkyo deck, put his arm around me, and after two seconds of hiss it was The Cure, Joy Division, The Smiths, and Echo and The Bunnymen. With each song, I fell deeper and deeper in love, so when he leaned in for a kiss I decided to meet him halfway, a decision I regretted since his braces ended up splitting my bottom lip wide open. Horrified, I raced to the bathroom, refusing to let him see me like that.

By the time the swelling subsided and I found the courage to open the bathroom door, the party was in full swing. My

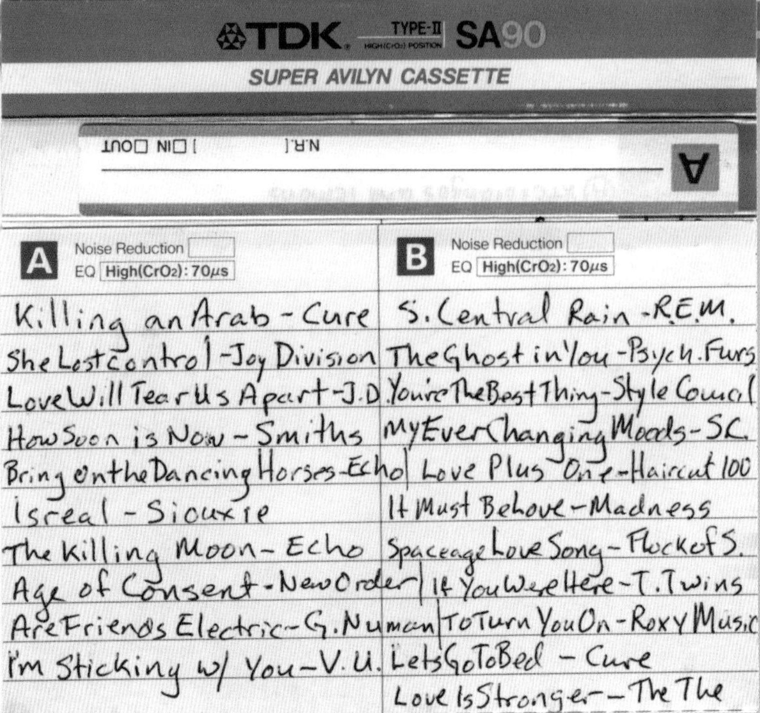

mixtape was now blaring on the loudspeaker and was such a big hit that it made it into the school yearbook under the heading: "Remember Jonathan's Killer Mixtape?" I pushed my way through the crowd looking for Jonathan. My Jonathan. And then I found him. He was in his dad's Jacuzzi making out with this girl Chrissy. Fat-lipped and heartbroken, I left without my boyfriend or my mixtape. Two days later Jonathan was expelled from school for smoking pot, and the following week his father sent him to boarding school upstate.

TDK
TYPE-II
SA90
SUPER AVILYN CASSETTE
A
Noise Reduction
EQ High(CrO2): 70μs
Killing an Arab - Cure
She Lost Control - Joy Division
Love Will Tear Us Apart - J.D.
How Soon is Now - Smiths
Bring on the Dancing Horses - Echo
Isreal - Siouxie
The Killing Moon - Echo
Age of Consent - New Order
Are Friends Electric - G. Numan
I'm Sticking w/ You - V. U.
B
Noise Reduction
EQ High(CrO2): 70μs
S. Central Rain - R.E.M.
The Ghost in You - Psych. Furs
You're The Best Thing - Style Council
My Ever Changing Moods - SC
Love Plus One - Haircut 100
It Must Be Love - Madness
Spaceage Love Song - Flock of S.
If You Were Here - T. Twins
To Turn You On - Roxy Music
Lets Go To Bed - Cure
Love Is Stronger - The The

As time passed, it was the tape I'd miss, not Jonathan. Often I tried to recreate it, but since I couldn't remember all the songs, or their order, it paled in comparison. But then something happened. A year later I came home and spotted a brown Trans Am parked in my driveway. Inside was Jonathan talking with my mother, who was giggling like a schoolgirl. It turned out he was hoping to take me to his dad's ski house in Loon Mountain for the weekend. There would be a number of kids coming, but no parents. I knew there was no way my mother would say yes. A parentless weekend? Pleeeze.

"Of course I said it would be just dandy. Your father and I have always loved Jonathan." I pulled my mother into the other room.

"Are you crazy? This is the same boy who cheated on me and got kicked out of school for drugs. You won't even let me stay overnight at a friend's house for fear a boy might be there."

"This is different."

"How so?"

"He's Jewish." Then she shoved a suitcase at me, and off I went. I was surprised I

didn't find condoms or the wedding ring passed down by my grandmother inside. I'm not even sure why I got in the car. The first ten minutes were filled with awkward chitchat. But then there it was. Sitting in the compartment between us was the mixtape. "Surprised?" he asked. I nodded my head and excitedly asked if I could have it back, but he pretended not to hear me.

When we arrived, much to my surprise, the condo was empty. "Where is everyone?" Jonathan said nothing. The next minute we heard a box spring squeaking and moans coming from the upstairs bedroom. "Who's that?" I asked. "Fitzy and Heather," he said. Then it all clicked. No one else was coming. This was a double date and he expected me to put out. "You didn't invite anyone else, did you?" Still nothing. "Did you think I was going to have sex with you?" He couldn't even look at me. "You're an asshole." And with that, I went to his car, popped my mixtape out, and got the next bus back to Manchester.

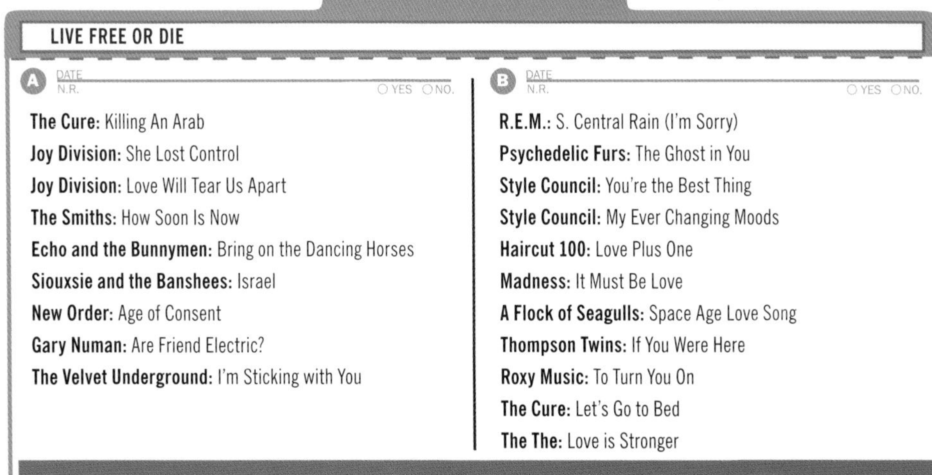
LIVE FREE OR DIE

A
DATE
N.R. YES NO.

The Cure: Killing An Arab
Joy Division: She Lost Control
Joy Division: Love Will Tear Us Apart
The Smiths: How Soon Is Now
Echo and the Bunnymen: Bring on the Dancing Horses
Siouxsie and the Banshees: Israel
New Order: Age of Consent
Gary Numan: Are Friend Electric?
The Velvet Underground: I'm Sticking with You

B
DATE
N.R. YES NO.

R.E.M.: S. Central Rain (I'm Sorry)
Psychedelic Furs: The Ghost in You
Style Council: You're the Best Thing
Style Council: My Ever Changing Moods
Haircut 100: Love Plus One
Madness: It Must Be Love
A Flock of Seagulls: Space Age Love Song
Thompson Twins: If You Were Here
Roxy Music: To Turn You On
The Cure: Let's Go to Bed
The The: Love is Stronger

When I think about Ben, it's like watching an old Super-8 movie: The focus is fuzzy but the feeling is sweetly nostalgic, and I am an unreliable narrator if one ever existed. No matter how hard I try to fill in the missing details of our teenage crush, memories come forth only in staccato bursts. A few things I know for sure: I remember ruffling his peach-colored hair while we watched the sun sink over Lake Michigan, and I know we shared a Coke at a matinee of *Matilda*, and we walked along abandoned railroad tracks in Kalamazoo. I like to think that we held hands at a punk show, but more than a decade has passed since I've talked to him, and I can't be sure whether our fingers intertwined or that I just wish that they did. The rest is lost.

I wish I could say that Ben was the love of my teenage life, but truthfully, I just wanted him to be. In reality, we were two punk kids who barely knew each other. He was sixteen, beautiful, gifted with lips that looked as though they were stained with Kool-Aid. When I first saw him, I assumed he wouldn't notice me, and for a while, I shrunk into myself with the belief that I was right. When he finally approached me, shoving his hands in his pockets and awkwardly stammering, I was stunned and giddy. We bonded in the way teenagers do, quickly and intensely, and parlayed a shared interest in obscure punk seven-inches into a summer romance that played out to the screamed songs and octave chords of touring hardcore bands.

Because all good punk romances begin with a mixtape, we exchanged ours early. Ben had used an X-Acto knife to carve my name and stars into the gray Maxell cassette, and I'd listen to its contents during the drive from my house to his. We both lived in touristy resort towns on the lake—him in Grand Haven, me near South Haven. Door to door, it was about a ninety-minute trek that synced up nicely with the tape; even if the landmarks were to disappear, I would have been able to measure how far I'd driven by which song I was on. And of course, I listened obsessively to deconstruct every song, every lyric, to fill in the blanks of what I didn't know about him. Including queercore band Team Dresch meant that he was down with the lesbian struggle, while including "Mr. Eliot"—complete with misquoted *Prufrock* stanzas—made him a poetic soul by association.

Maybe he was both of those things, but I never found out. Like all perfect summers, ours was too short, and we split before we could figure out what to do with our infatuation. In August I left to start college in Ann Arbor. Ben and I promised to write to each other, and I even mailed a few earnest letters before realizing that a reply would never come. The strange thing is, I wasn't heartbroken or even all that surprised. If I'm honest with myself, I knew even then that it was better to preserve the memory of our blissed-out summer than to try to force its unnatural extension. If I listened to Ben's mixtape long after I should have moved on, it's only because listening to it resuscitated a sliver of teenage joy. It's not that I've been hung up on the guy or anything—I went on to have greater loves and lasting relationships—but I'm not sure I'll ever recapture the rush of pressing his lips to mine for the first time.

Nor, as it turns out, will I ever hear the tape again. A few years ago, heavy rains filled my basement with dirty water, swallowing up the souvenirs of my youth. Ben's tape was destroyed in a filthy swirl of sewage, leaving me to reassemble the tape by tracking down digital copies of the songs. I've managed to piece together almost half of it in the following years, but my spotty memory leaves it incomplete. Even if I do manage to hunt down that rare Rye Coalition B-side in some file-swapping service, it lacks the warm analog crackle of vinyl transferred to tape.

Technically, I could ask Ben for help. I found him online last year; a little sleuthing reveals that he's living in Portland and singing (OK, screaming) in a punk band. I thought about emailing him for old times' sake, asking him if he remembers the details that I cannot, finding out what kind of life he's created for himself. But I think I like to remember things as they were, or at least as I like to think they were. Otherwise, it's like stitching together a decade-old playlist without the original recordings: The songs haven't exactly changed, but there's no way they'll ever sound the same again.

SUMMER PICK-UP

A DATE N.R. ○ YES ○ NO.

Texas Is the Reason: Blue Boy
The Promise Ring: E. Texas Ave
Lync: Heroes and Heroines
Team Dresch: Freewheel
Liz Phair: Fuck and Run
Car vs. Driver: Summer Pick-up
Car vs. Driver: Without a Day

B DATE N.R. ○ YES ○ NO.

Sicko: The Sprinkler
Weston: New Shirt/Heather Lewis
Chisel: Red Haired Mary
Karate: Cherry Coke
Sunny Day Real Estate: Pheurton Skeurto
Rye Coalition: Baby Puts out Old Flames
Spanakorzo: Ghost Dance
Bleed: Mr. Eliot

XSTRAIGHT-EDGEX HANGOVER

BY JEN HAZEN

We Meet

He smelled like a bagel—a garlic bagel with vanilla nut raisin cream cheese. As he handed me a napkin with his phone number scribbled on it, I bashfully stared down at his flour-crusted Vans. "Call me," he said. Then he wiped his hands on his apron and went back to work.

Scott was a baker at Klein's Deli in Kalamazoo, Michigan. That's where I met him in 1996. I worked as a barista/bagel shmearer in the front of the deli. Sometimes I'd check him out through the swinging door's square windows while frothing milk for stupid lattes. So hot—about six feet two inches, emaciated, white blond hair (a decent dye job), a large nose like Adrian Brody, and slightly crooked teeth. Virtually all fetishes of mine were covered.

The first time we hung out at Scott's shit-hole apartment (which also smelled like a bagel) we bonded instantly based upon four criteria.

1.He showed me lots of pictures of himself. Some were of him posing nearly naked in a jockstrap for his roommate Kim's feminist theory class—mocking contorted poses of fashion models to prove how ridiculously sexist fashion magazines are. (He's a feminist, like me!)

2.Scott had a tattoo that circled his right wrist and explained that four friends from his hometown Detroit shared the same one. (We both have tattoos . . . with profound meaning!)

3.He was born on July 31. I was born on August 1. (Oh my god, we're both Leos! We're twins!)

4.Scott listened to records and coveted music. (Soul mate!)

Scott gave me his blue Dickies coat to wear that day—with his last name stitched on the breast pocket. Like a punk-rock varsity jacket, I wore it with pride. It was official.

Oh, I forgot to mention one important thing.

Scott also proudly showed me photos of his first girlfriend, Tara, on that first date at his apartment. Tara—who he had "lost his virginity to" just a couple of months earlier. He looked like a punted puppy as he filed through the pictures slowly, pausing on one in particular where she smiled while sitting on the couch. It looked a lot like the couch that I was sitting on. I should have run from his apartment that day. Instead I stayed . . . on and off for about ten years.

Siamese Twins

In the beginning, everything was perfect. Scott and I ate tons of veggie burgers and bags full of free day-old bagels from the deli. We watched Woody Allen films, listened to the tragic bastard music of Palace Brothers, and had too much sex while listening to Spiritualized, Fleetwood Mac, Jawbreaker, The Rolling Stones. We never stopped listening to music, actually. We studied together and Scott even helped me create a newsletter for my Computer Media class project at Western Michigan University. ARGH! STOP SOFTWARE PIRACY! the newsletter's headline read.

And we watched too much porn. Afterward Scott would usually end up in front of his computer playing *World of Warcraft* or *Marathon*, while scarfing down potato chips and I'd read in his bed, laying on sheets that probably hadn't been washed since he'd moved out of his parents' house. Life was good. But then the band got back together.

Crusade

When Scott's hard-core band, Crusade, got back together later that year the vegan, straight-edge, soapbox politipunk, testosterone scene in Kalamazoo went ape shit. And so did his ego. A shiny new star named Scott was born.

Aside from howling like he was being dipped in flesh-burning acid when he sang, Scott's stage theatrics revealed some intriguing attention-seeking behavior that I hadn't been privy to in our first few months of dating. For instance, I often wondered why Scott's male friends always made jokes about his "huge cock." It all made sense, however, when he whipped it out in between songs during a set, wrapped it around his wrist, and shouted, "Anybody know what time it is?"

The sea of adoring TVP-sausagefest kids went wild and Scott was obliged to give them more. Meanwhile, I wondered what the hell was wrong with me for loving this guy. Dick tricks? Really? Why is the male version of *moi* stooping to such a level?

When the applause died down after many nights of shows in college kids' basements and other crusty punk dive bars, Scott would find some house party where he'd most likely be the entertainment. And then I'd get a drunk dial in the middle of the night, "Will you come pick me up?" And I did. Because I knew a side of him that no one else did. And I was in denial. And the sex was good.

I know what you're thinking. There are perks to dating a guy in a band. Here they are:

1. My name in the liner notes and it was in the top five. Rank matters.

2. An abstract photo of my boob on the cover of a seven-inch record—currently available on eBay for twenty dollars, thank you.

3. Being invisible. In Kalamazoo's hardcore

scene, women were just appendages of dudes who oddly resembled the "Can you hear me now?" cell-phone guy—all Dickies coats and Buddy Holly glasses. Women couldn't possibly go to shows on their own because, hey—girls don't like music.

Doppelganger

As Scott's ego swelled, I spied a roving eye and that consumed me with jealous rage. To think that he would crane his neck to check out the ass of some patchouli-dipped hippie in spandex as we walked to class together. The nerve. The attention-seeking. The cock-wielding ways. Dear God, what was I doing with this guy? It was love.

And don't think that I wasn't just as awful. The doppelganger and I truly brought out the worst in one another. Take, for example, a cruel phone prank we pulled on some random guy who was trolling a sex chat website. I don't remember how we got his phone number, but I called and got this stranger off on a pay-phone call in the company of Scott and his buddies while they listened in, unable to contain their bursts of laughter.

Scott followed up the money shot by grabbing the phone, and shouted into the receiver, "Hey, hope you know a bunch of dudes are sitting around listening to you." Sadly, I sought approval from Scott and he sought approval from his peers. It was a nauseating vicious cycle. And, looking back, I disgust me.

In true Woody Allen fashion, Scott and I split up several times over the next two years, yet the "sincere sensation" of drama continued. He usually did the dumping, but we were both guilty of dial-a-fuck at 2 A.M., leaving notes on car windshields like stalkers, and making mixtapes for each other to keep the neurosis alive. And until 2005, we called each other every year on our birthdays—because we're Leos with huge egos who can't stand the thought of someone forgetting our birthday.

Brooklyn vs. Chicago

After Scott graduated from college, I received a random call from him. "I'm moving to New York. Can I see you before I go?" A couple days later he picked me up in his gray Escort and we drove to a department store to buy him a suitcase. We sat in the car and held hands. We called each other silly pet names and reminisced about old times. Then I went home and snuggled on the couch with my new boyfriend. Did I mention his name was also Scott?

Until I left Kalamazoo in 2001, I would drive over to Scott's old apartment. Often. I didn't even know anyone who lived there anymore. I just sat in my parked car on his street, listening to music. Built to Spill ("Perfect from Now On"), Radiohead ("The Bends"),

Jawbreaker ("Dear You"), and Luna ("Slide EP"). No Crusade. And no audience—because I didn't need one.

In summer 2001, I went to visit Scott, now a graphic designer, in Brooklyn. I had recently moved to Chicago to attend grad school and we were still talking on the phone. Still emailing. Still sending mixtapes. Would this ever end? When I arrived at Scott's Brooklyn doorstep, he seemed a bit sullen, yet that healthy ego quickly surfaced.

He showed me pictures of himself posing with the Fanta girls (from the TV commercial, "Wanna Fanta, Don't You Wanna?") smashing their boobs in his face during some photo op in Manhattan. He had also started playing in a new band: Fillet Show and the Titty Committee. Guess who was Fillet Show?

When I left Brooklyn to return home, I felt a million miles from Scott as soon I set foot outside of his apartment. I purposely called a cab early to take me to LaGuardia.

A few days later, the first tower burst into flames on the morning of September 11, 2001. I frantically called Fillet Show. Jesus, what if he was dead? I was crying when he answered his cell. "I'm OK," he said, in a confused daze. "I was supposed to go for an interview downtown today. There's paper in the air everywhere, Jen. I'm on the roof and the air is just filled with dust." Two weeks after 9/11 I wrote Scott a letter which said, "Either we are together or we're not, because life's too short." And he decided "not" by not responding to that letter.

I met my husband, Dave, in 2005. When Scott contacted me after I first met Dave, I told him that it had to stop. He continued to call once in a while. I ignored him. He emailed. I ignored him—until May 19, 2006, the last time.

The E-mail

May 19, 2006

> Scott wrote:
>
> If you don't want to talk to me at least you could say that. Things are always complicated but at least I always responded . . .

Jen wrote:

I guess I just don't understand why we keep doing this . . . sure, the "we're friends" thing is an easy one to fall back on. But are we really friends? Doesn't seem like it. Nothing is really complicated. I just don't want to live in the past.

X STRAIGHT-EDGE X HANGOVER

DATE
N.R. ○ YES ○ NO.

Coldplay: Yellow

Teenage Fanclub: Everything Flows

The Ropers: Waiting

Guided by Voices: Teenage FBI

Brian Jonestown Massacre: (David Bowie I Love You) Since I Was Six

The Velvet Underground: I Found a Reason

Luna: Kalamazoo

Bob Dylan: Final Theme

DATE
N.R. ○ YES ○ NO.

Billy Bragg & Wilco: Remember the Mountain Bed

Townes Van Zandt: No Place to Fall

Dinosaur Jr.: Water

Sam and Dave: I Got Everything I Need

Otis Redding: Remember Me

Billy Bragg & Wilco: Secret of the Sea

Guided by Voices: I am a Scientist

Mercury Rev: I Collect Coins

Bizarre Love Octagon

By Jennifer Brandel

Our lives began their overlap at the UW–Madison during my senior year. I wouldn't say my college experience was necessarily lonely before then, but in the three years prior I hadn't managed to find my people. So I stopped looking, and instead took one credit short of losing my mind each semester. Perhaps that's why when I was asked to codirect a play—I agreed, despite having zero experience with the stage and not really even liking plays. I needed a shake-up.

I smelled him before I first saw him. He was sweating through the pits of his baby-blue T-shirt—a shirt he made himself that read on front: Who Farted? On back: Me. He was murmuring, pacing the hallway, waiting to be called in to try out. Being rather dryness-challenged myself (I had to place towels under my hands on exam days to keep from destroying the ink, paper, desk, my self-esteem), I felt for him as he stood before me—vulnerable and soaked.

He was going for the part of a martini-swilling lawyer and patriarch of a hyper-dysfunctional Jewish family. He is not Jewish. He is 100 percent Wisconsin. He nailed it. I can count on one hand the number of times that I've released a pig-snort while laughing. His tryout accounts for three of those. I whispered to my new friend/codirector as he walked offstage, "I don't know where the hell that guy came from, or who the hell he is, but I want to be his friend." She grinned hard and nodded hard.

But it was messy; so messy that thinking back to how I managed to disentangle the web of people that kept us apart leaves me equally impressed and ashamed. The cast and casting rivaled the incest of *90210*, and I stepped on the scene completely oblivious. Turns out the other director knew Sweaty Boy, and she had briefly dated him, as well as his roommate, the year before. In the early rehearsal days I became ensnared with this aforementioned roommate—who also happened to be playing the part of Sweaty Boy's coke-addled brother, and who in real life was also Sweaty Boy's best friend. And for a short while during the getting-to-know-everyone phase, she

I'm horrible at flirting so I started working him the only way I knew how. He'd make up a song; I'd jump in with a new verse. He'd toss out an offensive joke; I'd one-up it. He'd look at me sideways; I'd cock an eyebrow, flare my nostrils. I spent months trying to subtly convince him that I was his person. Though perhaps it started off a little too subtle. Early on in the game I actually

(the director) was flirting with me. I realized this only after I had already agreed to go with her as lesbian high-school gym teachers for Halloween.

As complicated as it all was, I had found my people. But in spying Sweaty Boy riding around town solo on his old tandem bicycle that he'd outfitted with speakers and handlebar streamers, and jogging to and from class in racquetball goggles and an iridescent, 1980s purple-and-red woman's tracksuit, I began to realize he was my person. He let his freak flag fly; mine was folded and ironed and tucked safely away.

helped him deliver a flower and yes, a mixtape to another hurdle. I mean, woman. This woman he was crushing on just so happened to be the director's best friend and roommate. I believe my thinking was that if I let Pit Stains figure out on his own that his crush was (1) just not that into him (I'd done reconnaissance), and (2) that I was always there for him, he'd eventually start looking around at other options, namely me. Except that I wasn't an option quite yet.

So I did something about it. The play had ended; his crush went cold; my codirector seemed to be back into men. The actual moment of reckoning came less than a week after I'd ended the wrong relationship with his roommate/best friend/pretend drug-addict brother. It was at their house during an end-of-finals-beginning-of-winter-break boozedown. And all the major players were there, but my conscience wasn't.

Three too many hot toddies yielded a kaleidoscope of spinning Christmas lights, leading to words uttered, gestures gestured, then oh lord blur blur kiss blur, and then me, escaping the party by jumping out of his bedroom window, high-kneeing it through the snow back to my apartment, coatless and shoeless. Two hours later he rang my doorbell. He kissed me again and passed out in my bed. And thus it began.

During our first month together, for reasons still unknown, we only spoke to each other in Russian accents. The only time we spent apart was in the bathroom and going to class; but from time to time we made exceptions to that, too. We tumbled so entirely, so deeply in love that two months in we decided we needed to do community service. No two people should be allowed to be *this* happy. So during spring break he went to South Carolina to rebuild a hurricane-ravaged home, I went to South Dakota to run an elderly center on the Cheyenne River Reservation.

He designed this mixtape for me for that drive to Dakota. Listening to it now after many years, it's a perfect snapshot of that goofy, gleeful era and our quirky, novel love.

maxell
HIGH BIAS
XLII
POSITION
IEC TYPE II • HIGH
XLII
maxell
A DATE N.R. YES NO
1. Heat
2. I think We're Gonna Be Friends
3. No Rain
4. Herbie - Watermelon Man
5. MosDef - Ms. Fat Booty
6. Femme Fatale
7. Ween - Mr. Would you Please Help My Pony?
8. Bjork - Joga
9 Caetano Veloso.. Ilê Ayê
Paranoid Android - Meldau
B DATE N.R. YES NO
1. Look-a-py-py - Meters
2. 5 Years - Bowie
3. Rain Beatles
4. Time has Told Me
5. Rollerskates
6. Baby - Os Mutantes
7 Pollo Asado - Ween
8. Slo Crostic - Fugazi
10. Plenty - Badu
Lovage - Dan the Automator

From Wisconsin we moved to Washington, D.C., and decided it was too buttoned-up (our internships expired). Then we moved to Montreal and decided it was too cold (our work visas expired). Then we moved to Hobart, Tasmania (because these grapes aren't going to pick themselves), before moving to Chicago (grapes all picked) and breaking up.

It couldn't last. We were dating our mirror images—and grew dependent on, then tired of, and ultimately stifled by, our own reflection. But we had a mighty memorable time making faces at ourselves for a while.

11. Waiting For A Superman - Lips
12 God's Child - Byrne & Selena
13 GOT - Mos Def
14
10. More Lovage
12. The Teen Thing
13. Feel the Power of RockN Roll
14. Matzoh Balls - Slim & Slam
15. Don't Worry Be Happy
16. Fish N' Whistle
17
DATE
N.R.
YES
NO
maxell
XLII
POSITION
IEC TYPE II • HIGH

BIZARRE LOVE OCTAGON

 DATE N.R. ○ YES ○ NO.

John C. Reilly and Mark Wahlberg: Feel the Heat
The White Stripes: We're Gonna Be Friends
Blind Melon: No Rain
Herbie Hancock: Watermelon Man
Mos Def: Ms. Fat Booty
Nico: Femme Fatale
Ween: Mr. Would You Please Help My Pony
Caetano Veloso: Ile Aye
Björk: Joga
Brad Mehldau: Paranoid Android
Flaming Lips: Waiting for a Superman
David Byrne and Selena: God's Child
Mos Def: Got

B DATE N.R. ○ YES ○ NO.

The Meters: Look-Ka-Py-Py
David Bowie: 5 Years
The Beatles: Rain
Nico: Time Has Told Me
Melanie Safka: Brand New Key
Os Mutantes: Baby
Ween: Pollo Asado
Fugazi: Slo Crostic
Lovage: Strangers on the Train
Dan the Automator: Pit Stop
Erykah Badu: Plenty
The Young Fresh Fellows: The Teen Thing
Wesley Willis: Feel the Power of Rock & Roll
Slim and Slam: Matzoh Balls
Bobby McFerrin: Don't Worry Be Happy
John Prine: Fish n' Whistle

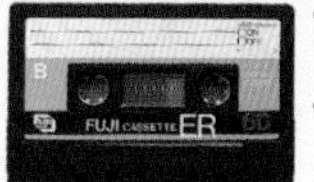

TYPES OF MIXES

The mixtape serves a dual purpose: First, it's an expression of your own personality and musical taste. Second, it helps craft an image you'd like to portray through your perfect compilation of tracks. Nerds write poems, mixtape makers get the love.

Have a plan. Get out your records, tapes, and CDs, remind yourself which songs you love, and which tracks you want to share. Before you touch the Record button, determine what kind of tape you will be creating. Is this a love tape? Is this a new music sampler tape? With the amount of recorded music currently available, there's a nearly infinite number of ways to craft your mix. Make sure to pay close attention to the technical aspects too. Some general ideas are listed here to help create a roadmap for your song collection.

CRUSH TAPES

Crush tapes serve as a proxy first date; let your intentions be known! If you're not well acquainted with the tape's recipient, they will have scant information to go by and they will have to read into your song selection. These tapes tend to have songs and titles which are leading and flirtatious. You will want this tape to be fun and energetic, with a few songs showing your softer, gentler side. (Don't go too hot or too deep with the emotions, however—you don't want to skeeze out your crush).

Perhaps you'd like to promote a cosmopolitan and worldly image (perhaps some Serge Gainsbourg and Caetano Veloso), or show your "anything goes" attitude (Decendents, Nick Drake, Sabbath), or maybe you'd like to expose your island-stoner 'tude (Marley, Peter Tosh, etc.). Crush tapes are all about image and promoting your ideal self. Show your crush what to expect of you by choosing representative and telling tracks.

MUSICAL JOURNEY (AKA MY STACKS ARE DEEP) TAPES

From Coltrane to Philip Glass to Bad Brains to Minnie Riperton, show off your eccentric taste. Norwegian metal? Check. Early Folkways ethnographic collection? Check. Ethopiques #6? Check. Share your vast knowledge of classical and jazz and highlight your expansive collection (and/or creative use of the Internet). This is your opportunity to impress and share a side of yourself that you keep under wraps.

"Rock block" tapes can be another useful "musical journey" tape solution. On these mixes, you will share two songs per artist, with the tracks being pulled from different source albums. This will help share music from a variety of artists, but also give a deeper sense of the group's sound and development. This is clearly an exception to the one-song-per-artist rule, and your audience will appreciate the extra effort.

AUDIO POSTCARD TAPES

Sometimes known as the "Trans-Atlantic-pen-pal-maybe-we'll-meet-one-day," or the "help-carry-us-through-the-long-distance" tape. Audio postcard tapes may be similar to a Crush Tape or a Musical Journey tape, but they're made special with the addition of the creator's recorded words.

Often these tapes will lead side A with a spoken introduction acquainting the recipient to the sounds of own voice ("so now you know what my voice sounds like . . .") or describing their longing ("I miss you so much since you relocated to Sri Lanka!"). No matter which stage of the relationship, the added effort can make this musical gift even more personal. We recommend for added intimacy and emotional depth.

CONCEPTUAL TAPES

Art students! You're itching to create a conceptual mixtape. While mixtape making is an art form in itself, you should make a conceptual tape under only one condition—the recipient is also an art student. We have heard reports of one creator who made an avant-garde collection with exactly 4'33" between songs, as a nod to John Cage. There are very few people who will tolerate this kind of whack job. Let's be clear: this is a novelty stunt and the tape will be intolerable for one listen, much less repeated takes. Keep the Art in the gallery and away from this populist medium.

ERA-DEFINING TAPES

While some would argue that every mixtape defines the era in which it was received, this category describes compilations heralding the music of a particular year or period. These compilations are often titled after the era, such as "Senior Prom Mix" or "Summer of '92," and they contain the greatest hits of the time.

BREAKUP TAPES

The Breakup Tape is rarely created, but reports have sprouted up. These are created less frequently due to the additional effort needed to craft cassettes. When a relationship is over, sending a message through an audio medium may be less satisfying than writing a scathing letter or destroying the belongings your ex left behind. That is, unless the tape reminds the recipient how awesome the creator is, in which case it may act as salt in the wounds.

THEMED TAPES

Theme tapes make great special-occasion gifts. Perhaps a friend recently gave birth? Present her with a tape filled with songs that include the word "baby" in the title. Or your boyfriend is embarking on a month-long road trip? Present him with a Memorex loaded with "Drive" titles and he'll be sure to come home with with a gift for you.

POSITION
IEC TYPE II • HIGH (CrO2)
UD II
60
maxell
For Larry
Because I love
you so much,
and because
you are there
for me when things
are at their
worst.
My Valentine Baby
UD II 60
maxell

3000 MILES AWAY, KIND OF BLUE

BY LARRY SMITH

Marianne was a grad student getting a master's degree in communications at Penn when I was an undergrad. She arrived by way of Harvard and was the teaching assistant in a class called History of Pop Culture—even more of a waste of an Ivy League education than it sounds, if that's possible. She was exalted by some (my family) and misunderstood by a few (primarily my animal male friends). She was best understood by me in the very beginning and only years after it was all over.

Our courtship was, appropriately, a textbook thing. I came wagging around her office fairly often as I was tapping out, on my Apple Classic, a final paper about the media's coverage of AIDS (the year: 1990; the coverage: quite bad). I don't need to dig out those pages to recall, verbatim, her notes: "Try as I might, I cannot find a single thing wrong with this paper—A+."

Claiming that "a bunch of us want to take you out, because you're the coolest T.A. ever," I asked her if she might like to get a beer before the Christmas break. She answered with an eager "Sure!" I neglected to invite my pals. A few hours (and quite a few beers) later, I walked her home to her place in funky West Philly. At some point during the chilly walk home, I slipped my hand in her jacket pocket to keep warm, and got no discernable protestation. I still can't believe I kissed her.

Not long afterward, I graduated, with plans to move to San Francisco. The economy was lousy, but back then the Bay Area was still a place where you could arrive and find a dumpy 3BR for $900 and start your life. That's what I did. I got a job at Pizzeria Uno, where I huffed whippets in the walk-in freezer with fellow waiters and hoped for my big writing break. Life was good, by and large, and much to my surprise my smart, hot, and (slightly) older girlfriend announced that she was going to join me.

On the night before her arrival, while bowling with some buddies I had a mild panic attack: The next day, five feet five inches of commitment was coming on a jet plane, and I wasn't ready. My friend Eric—the only one of us with a live-in girlfriend—caught me descending into a dark place, pulling at my hair and staring down, deep into the floor. (In hindsight, taking mushrooms before hitting the lanes wasn't the best plan.) "Larry and I are going to step outside and have a little talk," Eric said, after which I was more or less fine. Marianne arrived eighteen hours later. She got a job as communications director of a domestic-violence nonprofit. I started getting writing assignments. We were off.

The Valentine's Day tape that Marianne made for me two years later still holds up today. Not as a masterwork, or even

close. Marianne's inclination toward pre-Beatles, doo-wop-y rock ("Lollipop" by the Chordettes? "Let the Good Times Roll" by Shirley and Lee?) gets grating in a hurry. It's much too sentimental even for a softy like me (Joan Armatrading's "Willow," anyone? "Bookends" by Simon and Garfunkel?). Salt-N-Pepa's fuck-me-feminist, 1991-airwaves-ruling anthem, "Let's Talk About Sex," is such an obvious beginning that I can hear those coldhearted *High Fidelity* clerks chuckling. But fuck 'em. Our songs are a time capsule of who we were: old souls, goofballs, a young couple recently out of school wondering if we had found our partner for life.

As if she was gaining confidence, the B-side is pure Marianne—the girl I fell in love with despite such obstacles as her vegetarianism, her love of colored jeans, and her willingness to announce to a roomful of people at an Oscar party that Clint Eastwood should not win a Lifetime Achievement Award because, after all, it really was a woman's turn. On the B-side are Madonna, a riff from Rob Base & DJ EZ Rock, Steve Winwood, and—God love her—Bobby McFerrin.

So. My Valentine Baby, as the label reads, offers a public proclamation that any silly couple could make ("Stand by Me," "When I'm Sixty-four," . . .), along with the notes particular to us (the Roches' "Older Girls"). In the static between Rob Base & DJ EZ Rock's "It Takes Two" and Eddie Murphy's all-but-forgotten single, "Boogie in the Butt," I hear hundreds of private jokes and personal moments that exist only between us.

If there's a theme apart from the message behind any mix—"Me to you," "This thing of ours," "Where do we go from here?"—it's pleading. Pleading for an emotional suite of services I did not possess, and wouldn't for many years. I refused to move in with Marianne. I refused to go to couples' therapy. I refused to grow up. I refused all this because I did not want to accept *us* despite how good she was for me, and how in so many ways I was for her.

"Express Yourself" opens side B—but we didn't need Madonna to know which way the wind blows. We broke up on my twenty-seventh birthday. It wasn't ugly, or really so tragic, simply time to shut 'er down. My path took me to Burning Man,

New York City, and then on to professional magazine-making. Marianne was on her own way to Russia, the White House, and to big jobs in notable nonprofits.

Some of my male friends mocked Marianne because of her ban on the music of alleged wife-batterer Miles Davis in our house. I didn't agree with her precepts regarding the artist and his life, but I respected her conviction—not to mention her willingness to debate my asshole friends about such things. "The airwaves are free!" my pal Dave crowed into my answering machine a few days after Marianne and I broke up, him with *Kind of Blue* playing in the background. He was right, and I was mainly glad. Yet in many ways I was jealous of Marianne's earnestness, her possession of a self-confidence that's hard to find in a girlfriend, or anyone at all.

In the years that followed, I have gorged on Miles, and Clint, and wild-boar ragu, and sundry other things that certainly haven't added years to my life. I later married a woman who I also met in San Francisco and knew my ex just well enough to remind me of this whenever her name comes up: Marianne made me a better man.

M6 V-DAY MIX

A DATE N.R. ○ YES ○ NO.

Salt-N-Pepa: Let's Talk About Sex
The Silhouettes: Get a Job
The Chordettes: Lollipop
Steel Pulse: Your House
Joan Armatrading: Willow
The Fleetwoods: Come Softly to Me
Simon and Garfunkel: Bookends
Joan Armatrading: Show Some Emotion
Ben E. King: Stand by Me
Shirley and Lee: Let the Good Times Roll

B DATE N.R. ○ YES ○ NO.

Madonna: Express Yourself
Steve Winwood: The Finer Things
The Roches: Older Girls
Salt-N-Pepa: Let's Talk About Sex
Mister Señor Love Daddy: (interlude from *Do The Right Thing*)
Perri: Feels So Good
Gipsy Kings: Volaré
Rob Base & DJ EZ Rock: It Takes Two
Eddie Murphy: Boogie in Your Butt
Bobby McFerrin: (Being Bobby McFerrin)
The Beatles: When I'm Sixty-four

XMAS CASSETTE BY VINNIE ANGEL

Cute, nonconformist behavior and lo-fi rule-breaking had always been big turn-ons for me. We'd met before, when she was still dating a friend of mine, but when I crossed her again a year later in his kitchen, walking in as she was whipping mashed cauliflower balls at his dog with an ice-cream scoop and laughing uncontrollably, I was slightly smitten. As I said, cute, nonconformist behavior and lo-fi rule-breaking had always been big turn-ons for me. When I left my friend's house after midnight she was still hanging out, so I simply assumed that they were back in the saddle. A mile later, having walked three quarters of the way back up the hill to my mom's house, a white Mercedes slowed to a crawl beside me. The automatic passenger window scrolled down and I bent my head sideways to look inside. All I could make out in the dark interior, in the reflected moonlight off the hood, were her glistening teeth silhouetted into the shape of a flirty smile.

She taught me probably my most important feminist lesson—how to give a woman an orgasm. It was on our first date, in my mom's house, in my old room, with the poster of a life-size Debbie Harry in a sexy backlit dress over the bed. At least the beds were no longer set up as bunk beds. We'd gone to a Red Hot Chili Peppers show that night and the next day she was off for Varanasi, India, for two months, to begin a Fulbright documenting the Varanasi tradition of ephemeral urban exterior wall paintings. Mmmm. Sexy, geeky, independent. My fave.

At that fragile and unstable, freshly postcollege transitional juncture in my life, this chance-ish encounter with a whip-smart, focused, and soon-to-be worldly woman was perfect timing. The inspiration I'd glean from laying next to her would sling me headlong into a certain future and I would skip over my anticipated period of wayward floundering and binge drinking. But sadly, I gleaned the bare minimum. Irrational fears, cowardly apprehensions, and a false confidence inflated by punk rock and macho posturing with my brothers rebuffed what she had to offer. Not to mention my distraction whenever she talked as I imagined that her full lips were a pair of banana slugs doing "the bump."

The steady string of letters she sent me from India were stream-of-consciousness riverboat tours of her strangest experiences in Varanasi. The letters were funny, sweet, and personal but not particularly intimate, which was fine for my noncommittal self at the time. I wasn't looking for love.

We'd see each other in the months that she'd be home, avoiding India's scorching summer heat and then the monsoons. We got along for the most part, sharing a similar appreciation for full-contact teasing, but the longer the stretch she was back from India the more she expected an evolving commitment. It wasn't coming. I was coasting in our relationship and she knew it. She began to resort to ridiculous ways to snap me into a greater consciousness and to induce better conversation (mixing dangerous amounts of hot sauce into my drinks whenever I left the table and purposely running red lights in her Mercedes). She risked death simply to see me risk an emotion. But I never did.

Her Fulbright ended and she moved back to town for good, getting a full-time job at PBS. I, of course, abruptly moved far away from my mom's house, never to return. She was over my shit anyway. It was for the best.

The cassette she made for me the Xmas before I split was a cunning stunt. It was dastardly but ingenious. It was the

mixtape equivalent to Columbus delivering smallpox blankets to Pocahontas—a slow-release virus that, at each listen, would diminish my pathetic obstinacies. Her calculated assemblage of songs and their linked messages of revolution, independence, sexual and racial equality, and half-breedism equated a summer college intensive at a small liberal arts college that she had attended and I, obviously, had not. Innocently, like Pocahontas, I assumed it was a loving gift. My ears, those undiscerning, lyric-ignoring, nonlobed little fuckers, fell for the trap.

She cleverly salted her bait with rap songs she knew I liked, but even these rap songs were infected with not-so-subtle directives that could have saved me years of egg sucking and time wasting, if I had only listened to the words then. She knew what she was doing. She knew she wouldn't be with me for long but that her cassette would. As the years went by, and as I opened up to the world, every time I innocently played the cassette a sensation of being pelted with mashed cauliflower balls intensified until I swear I had bruises. Listen now. You'll feel it, too. But don't worry, it's therapeutic.

XMAS CASSETTE

A DATE N.R. ○ YES ○ NO.

Meat Loaf: You Took the Words Right Out of My Mouth
Wild Cherry: Play that Funky Music
Etta James: W-O-M-A-N
Bob Marley and The Wailers: Trenchtown Rock (live)
Jungle Brothers: Doin' Our Own Dang
The Jimi Hendrix Experience: Crosstown Traffic
Salt-N-Pepa: Express Yourself
C. W. McCall: Convoy
The Untouchables: FBI
Cher: Half-Breed
Tone-Loc: Funky Cold Medina
Pop-O-Pies: The Catholics Are Attacking
Kool & The Gang: Get Down on It

B DATE N.R. ○ YES ○ NO.

Lulu: To Sir, With Love
John Mellencamp: Pop Singer
Bonnie Raitt: My Little Runaway
Bonnie Raitt: What I'm Listening to Tonight
Sam the Sham & The Pharaohs: Wooly Bully
A Tribe Called Quest: Bonita Applebum
A Tribe Called Quest: Can I Kick It?
Carl Douglas: Kung Fu Fighting
Al B. Sure!: Missunderstanding
Nancy Sinatra: These Boots Are Made for Walking
The Afros: Afros in the House
Steve Miller Band: The Joker

TAKE A LOOK... CHILDHOOD NOW... AND THE FUTURE

BY LEAH DIETERICH

This cassette predates my driver's license. It predates my loss of virginity. It predates my first boyfriend, my first kiss, my first drink. It does not, however, predate my first love.

TAKE A LOOK is a mix given to me by my best friend Kelly, in or around 1994. (Date confirmed by a cursory search of Wikipedia to find out when the second and worse of the two Cranberries albums came out.)

In 1994, I was in eighth grade, and Kelly and I were entering our fifth straight year of being attached at the hip. We were a duo: Kelly and Leah, like some kind of vaudeville act. In school you'd never speak of one of us without the other. I recall being aware that everyone at school saw us as exclusive and exotic, and probably thought we did all kinds of illicit things together. I always kind of wished that we had, if even to just confirm their suspicions. But at the same time, I couldn't have been happier just doing the things we were doing, like video-recording each other dancing around in weird thrift-store outfits and drinking giant bottles of no-calorie flavored seltzer water.

Kelly and I were mirror images, except she was blonde and I was brunette. I'd always envied her blondness and the fact that her parents had let her get a perm back

in the day. But by the time she gave me this mixtape, the perm had long since grown out, and we were sort of on par, hairwise, which was strangely comforting to me.

Nothing was half-assed with this tape. The front cover has a giant green eye, with clouds running through the iris, likely cut from an ad for colored contacts. Above the eye, in her curlicue script is the title Take a Look. Below that: Childhood, now and the future . . . Odd to speak of childhood that way at age thirteen or fourteen, but I guess we thought we were really mature. Funnier still, is that none of the songs feel like "childhood" anyway. It's filled with Dire Straits, and Queen. Hers was the childhood of someone born outside of time, outside of a generation and an era. And it inspired me even then.

On the inside cover, she'd cut out the eyes from various photos of herself, her older sister, and her two dogs. There's even one where her eye is swollen shut, the result of an insect bite. I think it impressed me at the time that she was willing to show me herself at her ugliest. At that age, I didn't feel I could be that revealing. I don't know that I feel that way even now.

I listened to this tape in my bedroom, on a giant stereo. Never in the car, since I didn't have a license yet, and it definitely wasn't something I wanted to share with my parents as they carted me to and from my various obligations.

Song one on side A is pretty standard for a friend-to-friend mix: James Taylor's "You've Got a Friend." A bit expected, sure, but a nice sentiment.

Then it moves on to hits like "Tammy" by Debbie Reynolds, and a Marilyn Monroe/ Jane Russell duet called "When Love Goes Wrong."

There's "I Don't Know How to Love Him" by Helen Reddy, a title that would prove a bit ironic later in life. And continuing on the "love" theme, there's "Road to Lovin'," "Love Shack," and late on side B, a song called "Love Changes Everything." It's from some Andrew Lloyd Webber musical, I think. I hated that song. But sometimes I'd listen to it anyway. Because love does change everything. Did change everything. Did make me listen to that song, even though it sucked. At the time, I'd have given almost anything a chance for her.

There are two songs from an album that model/actress/fashion designer Milla Jovovich came out with during that era. The first one is called "Charlie" and I remember liking it at the time. But I was a pretty big sucker for female singer-songwriters back then. Especially pretty ones. The final song is another of hers, called "Don't Fade Away," and it's the perfect song to end the mix with. Because no matter what the willowy and beautiful Milla wished for us, we did fade away. But unlike most love stories, ours had no abrupt or dramatic ending. No breakup. It had no words exchanged that we regretted later on. It simply faded away with the help of distance, college, and age. And that's the way it should've been. Had to be. Was.

TAKE A LOOK...CHILDHOOD NOW... AND THE FUTURE...

(A) DATE ____ N.R. ○ YES ○ NO.

James Taylor: You've Got a Friend
Milla Jovavich: Charlie
Debbie Reynolds: Tammy
The Cranberries: Ode to My Family
***A Chorus Line*:** One
Helen Reddy: I Don't Know How to Love Him
Dire Straits: Where Do You Think You're Going?
Weezer: Undone–The Sweater Song
Marilyn Monroe and Jane Russell: When Love Goes Wrong
Faith No More: Epic
Dave Binder: Road to Lovin'
Simon & Garfunkel: The Sound of Silence

(B) DATE ____ N.R. ○ YES ○ NO.

The Beatles: Here Comes the Sun
The Cranberries: No Need to Argue
Michael Jackson: Ben
The B-52's: Love Shack
Counting Crows: Einstein on the Beach
The Samples: Little Silver Ring
***Hair*:** Aquarius
The Beatles: Ob-La-Di, Ob-La-Da
Queen: Another One Bites the Dust
Michael Ball: Love Changes Everything
Milla Jovavich: Don't Fade Away

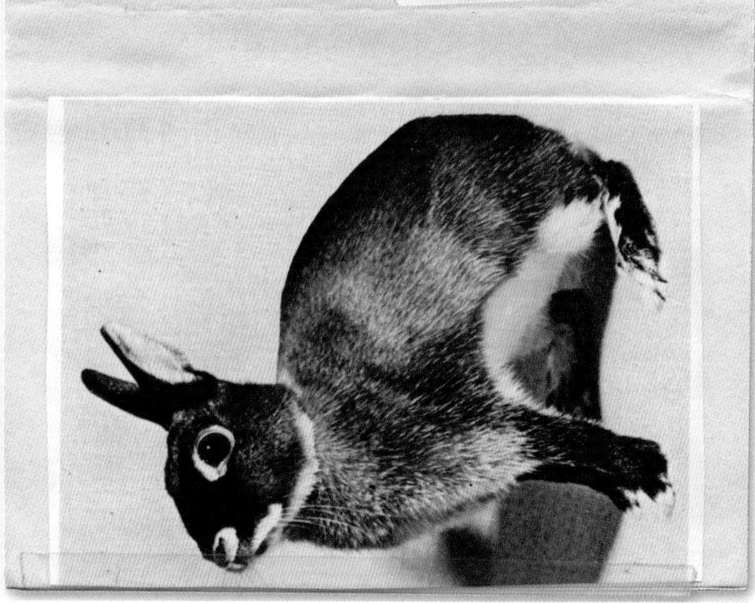

Most of the DJs at my college radio station were omnivorous in musical taste but socially we still self-selected along genre lines: the popsters, shoegazers, straight-edgers, and industrial/noise set (and just about everything else, but those were the main caucuses). We were all devoted to our little cliques but also reflexively made fun of our own stereotypes. The noise DJ recorded a promo for his show whining, "Where's my Nurse With Wound?" I had a show called Pop Smear. You can't tease each other about taste in college radio; everyone's taste is pretty silly when you get right down to it.

That's where I met Michelle. She was two years ahead of me, and in more of a Goth/industrial mind-set. Her hair was bleached in a professionally acceptable range, however, as she was also working in publicity for a decidedly *un*Goth label: the primarily folk-oriented Vanguard Records, part of the Welk (as in Lawrence) Music Group. This tape really summarizes her thing at that time. My 45s from proudly twee labels like Sarah Records by bands like Another Sunny Day and the Field Mice started to sound like kids' stuff. Michelle's music had gravitas; it was in this musical melancholia that we found each other.

We had planned on going out but it was mandated that we stay in on our first date—literally. We huddled inside watching on television as patches of the city around us burned; we broke curfew to try to get beer at a supermarket in Palms that was rumored to be open. A National Guardsman waved us away from the parking lot of the boarded-up store with an automatic rifle. Love among the riots, Los Angeles 1992.

I wasn't into all of these bands, but I associated them with her, and this tape symbolized that romance. Now the rhythms tend to sound tedious (like the "He Said" song, which I still don't like, from the bassist of one of my favorite bands, Wire), but part of what I liked about this music is the unusual and sometimes trippy production values. And though often too ponderous and groany, it was less these particulars than the sensibility that I still admire. What I and, I think, most other romantic personalities love about melancholy music (and other art) is that it's deep down somehow *happy*. It's not "depressing"—I don't revel in the concept of tragic love, love that is destined for doom. At least it's not that simple. We wouldn't normally admit it but melancholy people usually think of themselves as smarter, because we figured out the secret. The key to the secret is in being attuned to the darker stuff in life and art.

The spring before I graduated, we decided to move to San Francisco together; this cassette is from that time. We drove up to scout out the city one weekend in early summer. I was recovering from food poisoning and still in a febrile haze. At a rest stop I read the headline in the paper that the day before a guy had gone on a shooting rampage in a downtown San Francisco lawyer's office. The violence of California felt inescapable. Dark music helps you understand—and enjoy—if you survive.

SWEET SECRET DOOM

A DATE N.R. ○YES ○NO.

Wolfgang Press: I Am the Crime
He Said: Could You?
Clan of Xymox: Agonised by Love
Curve: Coast Is Clear
Red Lorry Yellow Lorry: You Are Everything
Breathless: Sometimes on Sunday

B DATE N.R. ○YES ○NO.

Beautiful Pea Green Boat: Nostalgia
Ultra Vivid Scene: Kind of a Drag
Levitation: It's Time
Nitzer Ebb: Ascend
Nick Cave & The Bad Seeds: The Weeping Song
The Jesus and Mary Chain: Don't Ever Change
A Flower Sermon: If God Is

PUNK AND NOT PUNK

PROPAGHANDHI - ANTI-MANIFESTO
THIS MIGHT BE SATIRE

CLOCKWISE - EMPATHY (DEMO)
SO TIRED

BOUNCING SOULS - I LIKE YOUR MOM
(THE GOOD, THE BAD AND THE ARGYLE) THESEARETHEQUOTESFROMOUR FAVORITE 80'S MOVIES
OLD SCHOOL

MIND OVER MATTER - NEW YORK, NEW YORK (security)
THE NEW BOMB TURKS - GROUNDED EX-PATRIOT
SOME VELVET SIDEWALK - LOCH NESS
WESTON - TATOO MONEY
MAN... OR ASTRO-MAN? - OF SEX AND DESIRE
(Destroy all Astromen) MADNESS IN THE STREETS (drunk on crack)
(your weight on the moon) → ELECTROSTATIC BRAIN FIELD
KING MISSILE - MARTIN SCORCESE (HAPPY HOUR)
CHEESECAKE TRUCK (MYSTICAL SHIT)
TAKE STUFF FROM WORK (FLUTING ON THE HUMP)
PRIMUS - JERRY WAS A RACE CAR DRIVER (SEAS OF CHEESE)

POP WILL EAT ITSELF - KICK TO KILL

PUNK AND NOT PUNK

BY MARIE HANSEN

By the end of eighth grade I had only had one real boyfriend and, subsequently, my first kiss. It took place in the woods on the outskirts of town and after it was done, I promptly threw up all over the guy's shoes. This event placed me in the realm of "loserville," a realm which all teenagers dread, for it leaves you indefinitely single for, perhaps, your entire grade school career. But that all changed when my older sister started dating Ash. Ash was a twelth-grade pseudointellectual and while he was wooing my sister with Nietzsche and red wine, I was hiding in my bedroom blasting the Sex Pistols. I dubbed him "The Ash-hole," and by this point, had turned my entire life over to punk rock. If something did not have a three-chord progression, I was not interested. I looked exactly like someone from the Bromley Contingent, completely unaware that the early '90s had its own brand of punk rock brewing: pop punk. On one rare day that I let The Ash-hole into my room, he stood staring at my Clash poster a while before announcing that he was going to set me up with his friend Justin. He told me that Justin was also punk and in the twelth grade. The prospects of not only a real-life punk-rock boyfriend, but also one that was a great deal older than me, was exciting and so, the morning that he was to arrive, I spent the day trying to look as unexcited as possible.

When the door to my room opened, I was expecting a Sid Vicious or at least an early Glenn Danzig look-alike to come storming in, singing the lyrics to the Ramones' "I Wanna Be Your Boyfriend." What I found instead was Justin, a gawky kid wearing an argyle sweater over a Weston shirt. I had thought that The Ash-hole had finally pulled a number on me but when I started talking to Justin, I realized that Justin actually did consider himself punk. We talked about music and I had never heard of any of the bands he talked about. He told me that next time he came, he would make me a mixtape. I told him that I would do the same, to teach each other what punk really was.

We talked almost every night on the phone and the next time I saw him, his hair was dyed red with Kool-Aid and he had a mixtape for me called PUNK AND NOT PUNK. We put it on and right away I said that the tape should just be called "not punk." I could not understand how the pop music coming from my speakers was anything like the 1977 punk I was used to. It even had Primus on it! We argued for hours about music and eventually settled down by taking a walk to the cemetery by my house. I was surprised when he leaned in to kiss me; I hesitated a moment but then went with it, surprised that this time, I didn't even throw up on his shoes.

The following week we talked on and off but as summer came closer, Justin stopped calling. I asked The Ash-hole what happened to him and he told me he went away for the summer. Mid-July, I received this weird postcard from him. On the front was a picture of the Misfits album *Walk Among Us* (one of the only bands we agreed on) and on the back it said he was away for the summer studying marsupials. I asked my sister what that meant and she told me, "Him and Ash go to weird camps for smart kids." The strangest thing was the postcard had no stamp! By August with no other word from Justin, I decided to annoy The Ash-hole again about his whereabouts. He told me that Justin had moved to Israel and I immediately sensed something fishy.

Realizing I was dissed, I forgot all about Justin. There was no sign of him until the twelfth grade. I was at a show and my

PUNK AND NOT PUNK

PRIMUS - NATURE BOY (PORK SODA)
DMV

Nine Inch Nails - WISH (BROKEN)
HAPPINESS IN SLAVERY
MARCH OF THE PIGS (DOWNWARD SPIRAL)

VOODOO GLOW SKULLS - INSUBORDINATION
HERE COMES THE SUN
1st 20 seconds of COUNTRY PHUCK
(W/ THIS IS)

MORPHINE - BUENA (CURE FOR PAIN)
HONEY WHITE (YES)

JANE'S ADDICTION - PIGS IN ZEN (NOTHING'S SHOCKING)
STOP! (RITUAL DE LO HABITUAL)

RAGE AGAINST THE MACHINE -
BULLET IN THE HEAD (CUT OFF)

boyfriend at the time was friends with the headlining act so naturally, I got in for free. I was standing by myself at the coat check when all of a sudden someone tapped me on the shoulder. I turned around to find Justin. The only thing I could think to say was, "I thought you moved to Israel." He told me that he had told Ash to lie to me, too. Noticing my annoyance, he said, "I thought you didn't listen to any punk from after 1977, what are you doing here?" I told him the best thing I could possibly say, the truth. "I'm with the band."

PUNK AND NOT PUNK

A DATE
N.R. ○ YES ○ NO.

Propagandhi: Anti-Manifesto
Propagandhi: This Might Be Satire
Clockwise: Empathy (demo)
Clockwise: So Tired
Bouncing Souls: I Like Your Mom
Mind Over Matter: New York, New York
New Bomb Turks: Grounded Ex-Patriot
Some Velvet Sidewalk: Loch Ness
Weston: Tattoo Monkey
Man or Astro-man?: Of Sex and Demise
Man or Astro-man?: Madness in the Streets
Man or Astro-man?: Electrostatic Brain Field
King Missile: Martin Scorsese
King Missile: Cheesecake Truck

B DATE
N.R. ○ YES ○ NO.

Primus: Nature Boy
Primus: DMV
Nine Inch Nails: Wish
Nine Inch Nails: Happiness in Slavery
Nine Inch Nails: March of the Pigs
Voodoo Glow Skulls: Insubordination
Voodoo Glow Skulls: Here Comes the Sun
Morphine: Buena
Morphine: Honey White
Jane's Addiction: Pigs in Zen
Jane's Addiction: Stop!
Rage Against the Machine: Bullet in the Head

SOMETHINGS BORROWED, SOMETHINGS SCREWED

BY TODD BACHMANN

"Todd—here are what I consider to be the best cover tunes in my collection! Enjoy, let me know what you think and please keep in touch!"

Phil passed me this mixtape at the end of summer before I took off for college. The phrase "Keep in touch!" was an empty gesture for sure, but giving me this mixtape wasn't. Phil was the older brother I never had.

Actually, I did have a biological older brother but he was a dick. Our interactions usually involved him kicking the shit out of me, flailing odd insults like "douche lips," or administering some other ridiculous torture. But Phil, he was my real gateway to quality rock' n' roll. He led me out of the hair-metal-haze, which captured the suburban Midwest in the late '80s and guided me toward The Velvet Underground. The Pixies, Mudhoney, The Orb, and house music. My friends Luke and Andy and I all embraced him as our avatar, helping us escape Busch Light house parties and endless hours hanging in the McDonald's parking lot. It was through Phil that we learned about the great rock clubs of Chicago and the burgeoning underground party scene called raves.

We first met him when we all landed the same dream job at a local CD-only "record" store wedged into a strip mall surrounded by farmland. The store had brass railings, which we had to shine with a noxious cleaner every other day, and a dedicated room for new age music. Our manager even hung a Patrick Nagel portrait in the back stockroom. It was the record store for the late '80s yuppie.

Our assistant manager, Phil, was tall and lanky, with a distinctive Italian nose and

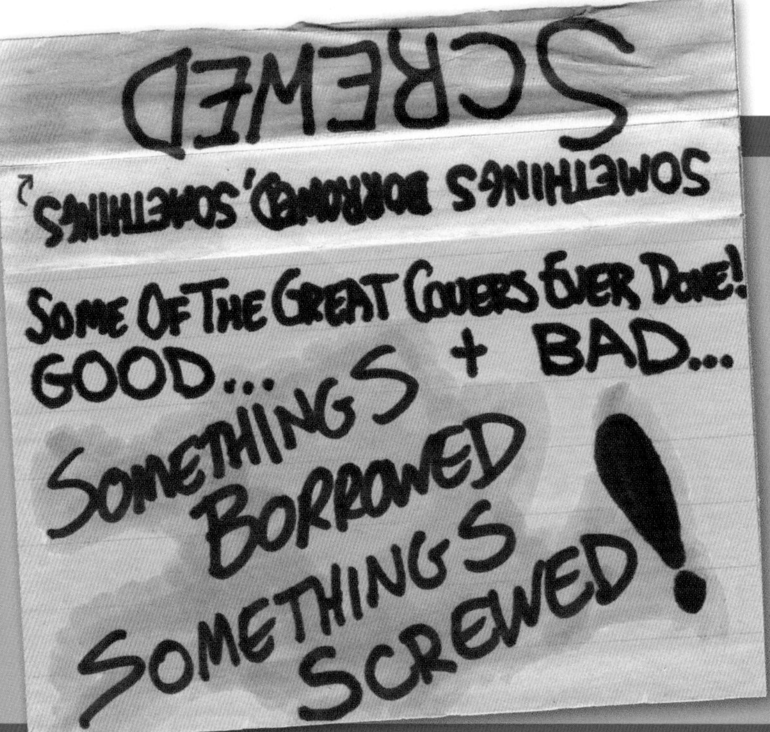

a mop of blond hair. Phil gave a mild punk rock "FU" to the record store's mandatory tie-and-slacks dress code by frequently wearing a piano or bolo tie and wearing dress pants that were just an inch or two too short.

Phil was actually pretty aloof to us. He liked having us around so he could play the role of sage, or musical pied piper, and to give his opinion, for instance, on the awesomeness of John Wesley Harding's cover of Madonna's "Like a Prayer."

Phil had this habit of exaggerating stories about his mingling with musicians or authors or actors. We initially ate up his tales, but then quickly caught on. In hindsight, I realize that these were tales that made him feel like he was somebody—that he mattered. One time Phil told us that a record-industry friend of his called him up on the phone to taunt, "Guess who's in the room with me? It's Lou Reed." He then claimed Mr. Reed (one of the most notorious curmudgeons in rock) got on the phone to chat with him. I often wondered what Phil imagined they talked about. "Phil, do you think my album *New York* is on par with *Transformer*? Is my tribute album to Andy Warhol, *Songs for Drella*, an OK record? Andy Warhol meant so much to me, you know." There was also Phil's "time" spent with Hunter S. Thompson in a bar in Chicago. We'd just let him tell us his lies and played along.

That said, he'd occasionally throw us a curve that forced us to reconsider our assumptions. There was also this time my friend and I had planned to see the Violent Femmes play during their *Why Do Birds Sing?* tour. Phil was going, too, but he bragged that he'd be going with Richard Butler of the Psychedelic Furs. We simply nodded and bit our tongues. We figured he'd just lie to us the next day cheating

TODD -
HERE ARE WHAT
I CONSIDER TO BE THE
BEST COVER TUNES IN
MY COLLECTION! ENJOY,
LET ME KNOW WHAT YOU THINK.
AND PLEASE KEEP IN
TOUCH!

SONG LIST

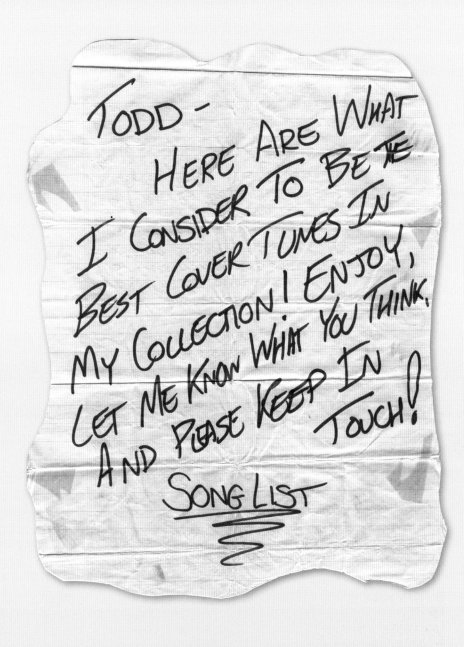

details about the show and go on about how he and Richard shared vodka gimlets together and chatted about the origins of "Heartbreak Beat."

Later that night at the show, after the opening act, Phil came by to say hello. He was with a local record label rep and . . . the man himself. "Richard—these are my friends." It was actually Richard Butler. We played it cool and said a meek hello to Richard. He amicably said hi back. We were too uncomfortable and moved to another part of the theater for the rest of the show.

After moving away from Phil years later, I did follow through with his Sharpie-written request in his mixtape liner notes to "please keep in touch." We connected every once in a while, but only when I reached out to him. I realized we had a finite friendship that was only meant to last during a specific period in our lives. It started to wane rapidly as we both moved to different cities and grew into different people. I also got tired of our one-way-street friendship. I no longer needed to orbit around a guide to jump-start my culturally myopic point of view. I could guide myself. Although, he did help me get there.

SOMETHINGS BORROWED SOMETHINGS SCREWED showcases Phil's dedication to mixtape craftsmanship—it's as if he would create his own record-store-quality compilation from a blank tape. This one came with a specially cut song list folded up in the tape case. The list is complete with annotations for each song like, "Way Better than Pseudo Echo's version!" for World Domination Enterprises' cover of "Funkytown," or "Madonna probably wet herself when she heard this" for Ciccone Youth's* cover of "Into the Groove."

The songs don't really reflect anything about our friendship; it's simply his favorite cover songs.

***Ciccone Youth was an experimental band comprised of members from Sonic Youth and Mike Watt from the Minuteman.**

SOMETHINGS BORROWED, SOMETHINGS SCREWED

DATE
N.R. ○YES ○NO.

Scatterbrain: Down with the Ship
World Domination Enterprises: Funkytown
Ciccone Youth: Addicted to Love
Devo: Are You Experienced?
Living Colour: Should I Stay or Should I Go?
The KLF: Burn the Beat
The Chipmunks: My Sharona
The Wonderstuff: Get Together
The Beautiful South: Girlfriend
Rights Of The Accused: Do You Love Me?
Social Distortion: It's All Over Now
Killdozer: Take the Money and Run
The Lemonheads: Step by Step

DATE
N.R. ○YES ○NO.

The Eat: Summer in the City
Celebrity Skin: S.O.S.
Inspiral Carpets: Gimme Shelter
U2: Unchained Melody
Walter Murphy: Fifth of Beethoven
Poison Idea: We Got the Beat
The Replacements: Cruella DeVille
Big Drill Car: Surrender
Chemical People: Getaway
John Wesley Harding: Like a Prayer
Ciccone Youth: Into the Groove
Goo Goo Dolls: Down on the Corner

DOUBLE EX, 1982 BY ANNA DOMINO

There's a ritual that certain young men perform for one other, driven by some ancient urge. The purpose is to strengthen and burnish those famous male bonds. The role of sacrifice (ritual does require an offering) falls to the alpha bitch, lover of the dominant dog, the one in the way.

As a girl it can take a while to spot the pattern as there are endless subtle variations to the theme but after a few replays, you learn to step aside.

It runs something like this:

> You meet a beautiful, magnetic, genuine boy with skin smooth as milk. You really like each other. Weeks are exhausted in inseparable companionship at his freezing loft while he paints and you make coffee, share cigarettes, turn up the music, and spill histories—sleep together, dream together . . . The hours spent away from him aren't real. His presence is more vivid than whatever trivial task you've got to get through before you can return to him. He calls in the middle of the night, you listen to each other breathing for hours. Everything is funny, aglow, a secret. No sleep required, just whispered code, dancing and walking the cavernous avenues till dawn.
>
> As time goes by you become part of his life, are introduced to his friends, fan club, and even family (if they're speaking). And there is always one special comrade in this posse. They may not seem that close but they obviously admire each other, so you admire the guy, too.
>
> Months, even whole years can go by in mutual tenderness and bliss but one evening you get a call. Surprisingly, it's the guy, the good friend, the admirable sidekick, assistant,

accomplice. He's very nice and wants to meet up. He's concerned about your boyfriend, got some spare tickets, and thought you might like to go, he's offering to help you paint your apartment, he just drove back from California in your boyfriend's car and wants to show it off. Who can resist a '41 Packard? And he's your boyfriend's good friend so of course you go along and he, eventually, begins to lament . . .

Turns out he's been in love with you himself all this time! It's flattering but a little unexpected, not to say inexplicable, though the car is cool. But, he doesn't give up. He's around all the time now, or calling all hours. You brush him off/you don't want to offend. You don't take him seriously/he doubles his suffering. He's gracious and charming and takes you to meet his papa. He laughs at your commentary and loves your music . . . and so, one day you stumble into his waiting arms.

A few days pass, one or two more, and you pick up a call from your true love. He's heard all about the whole damn thing and he's furious and hurt and doesn't ever want you crossing his path again. You've destroyed his trust and the unique and intense love you'd shared with your senseless, depraved betrayal . . . the March wedding is definitely off. In confusion and in grief you raise the issue of his recent liaison with some girl called Madonna and he says it's not at all the same thing because your indiscretion involved his best friend. You feel awful, ashamed, sick with guilt and call the "best friend" to find out who could've spilled and why. He responds coolly that he has discovered his great friendship for your lost love to be stronger and more meaningful to him than his dissipating passion for you and, therefore, he owed it to his new soul mate to tell him the awful truth.

And voilá, the deal is sealed. Your ex-suitor, in confessing his offense, has offered you up as an example of the seductive power of perfidious females, begged forgiveness, and pledged eternal loyalty. Your ex–true love now sees the error of his affections and the strength in this greater bond between honest men and wonders if he ever really did love you. They laugh, they cry, they vow to never let a woman come between them.

As a consolation prize your ex-love sends a drawing and the scheming catalyst in this catastrophe cobbles together shards of music from record and radio for you to study if you are ever to learn what real music is. The drawing is powerful, the cassette is wacked and you just learned a priceless lesson in human nature. Well, almost . . .

. . . After twenty-five years I unwrapped the drawing to have it framed and found that he had rolled it up in a map of England with the town of Wedding circled. And listening to the cassette again, after all this time, I hear a lot more in it. Neither boy did anything without thinking it over from all sides. At the time I thought all the hurt was aimed at me, now I'm not so sure.

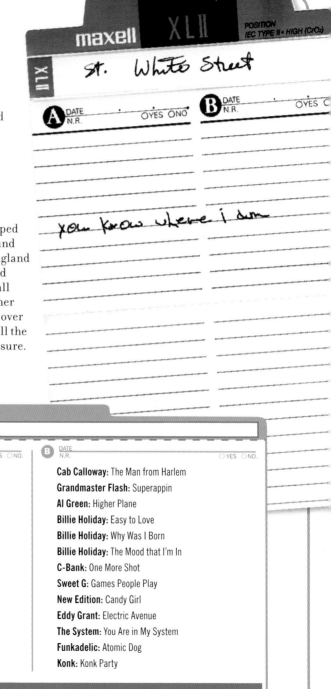

ST. WHITE STREET

DATE
N.R. ○ YES ○ NO.

Planet Patrol: Play at Your Own Risk
Bootsy Collins: Body Slam
Cheryl Lynn: Got to Be Real
Bob Marley: Rat Race
Grandmaster Flash: Flash to the Beat
Rockers Revenge: Walking on Sunshine
Al Green: Where Love Rules
Isaac Hayes: Theme from *Shaft*
Rockers Revenge: Walking on Sunshine
Freestyle Project: Pack Jam
Billie Holiday: Your Mother's Son in Law

B DATE
N.R. ○ YES ○ NO.

Cab Calloway: The Man from Harlem
Grandmaster Flash: Superappin
Al Green: Higher Plane
Billie Holiday: Easy to Love
Billie Holiday: Why Was I Born
Billie Holiday: The Mood that I'm In
C-Bank: One More Shot
Sweet G: Games People Play
New Edition: Candy Girl
Eddy Grant: Electric Avenue
The System: You Are in My System
Funkadelic: Atomic Dog
Konk: Konk Party

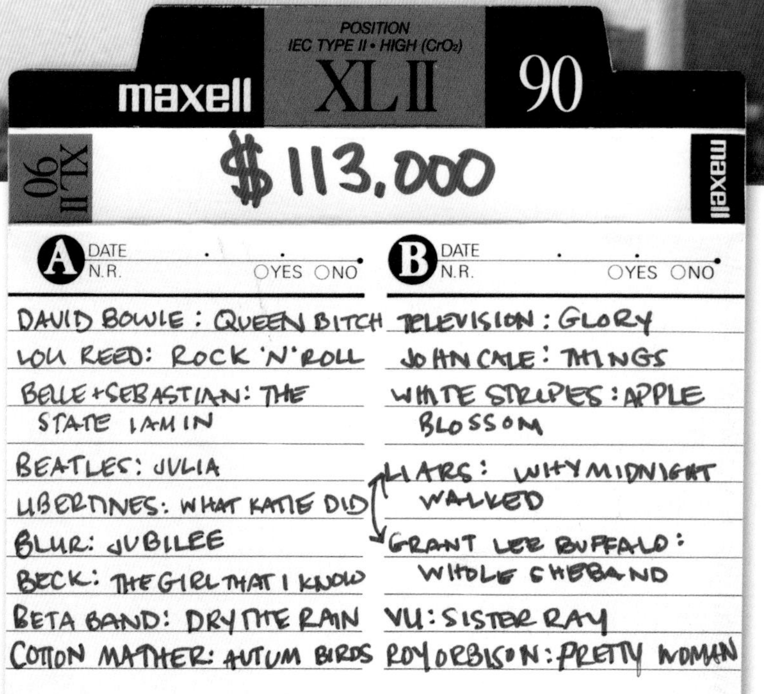

THE $113,000 MIX

BY JESSICA GENTILE

"I realize that this isn't worth $113,000, but I hope you enjoy it anyway," read the note in my mailbox.

I understood the significance immediately. That astronomical, and seemingly arbitrary dollar amount was the current eBay bid on an insanely rare and recently unearthed Velvet Underground record. The legendary band, you see, had played an instrumental part in us meeting. And not in the general, "Oh you like the VU, too—let's hook up!" kind of way (which could probably be said for a vast majority of collegiate couples on our liberal arts campus), but rather in an all-too-literal and tangibly concrete way.

At the time I was working as an office assistant for our school's media relations office, just an ordinary work-study gig, except for one minor detail. My boss was the widow of Velvet bassist Sterling Morrison. They met in high school—she the shy, bookish girl, he the prototypical, smokin'-in-the-boys'-room rebel—and following an introduction from a mutual friend, they soon became sweethearts who were inseparable since.

I knew of his classic rock infatuations from several marginally flirtatious conversations we'd had in class, and in general he seemed like a pretty cool guy, so I invited him to stop by the office one day. Martha loved to share stories. She was after all a firsthand witness of the Factory days, so she did have quite the stories to tell. And while more an observer then a

partaker in the debauchery, she spoke with fondness of the early days, hanging out with Lou Reed in a barren New York City apartment. "He only had a bottle of papaya juice to his name," she casually recalled. We listened, laughed, and geekily gawked, as rock history unspooled in a conversation held over a copy machine.

The following weekend he asked me out for dinner. And then, just one day following that first date, I found the $113,000 MIX in my mailbox.

Given our ultrabrief history, the Velvets heavily influenced the track list. In addition to solo numbers by Lou Reed and John Cale, the mix also included VU's epic "Sister Ray"—seventeen blistering minutes of squalling guitars and guttural sexual yearning—a bold inclusion in any mix, let alone one for a girl he'd only been on one date with. Apparently all it took was one dinner at a Vietnamese restaurant down the block for him to feel completely comfortable sharing a song about "sucking on a ding-dong."

On the same bold note, the mix kicked off with David Bowie's "Queen Bitch" and ended with Roy Orbison's "Pretty Woman." And over the course of the hour and a half that spanned those two polar binaries of femininity, I was treated to a marriage proposal courtesy of the White Stripe's "Apple Blossom" and even got compared to Pete Doherty's coked-up model girlfriend via The Libertines' "What Katie Did."

Sadly, not much resulted from what was probably one of the most blatantly awesome/romantic gestures I've ever received. For various untold reasons we remained in the "solely friends" category. And, of course, we were well into the throes of senior year, so graduation soon came and we went our separate ways. But to this day I still listen to his mix. And it turns out he was wrong; its worth has exceeded any price tag.

$113,000

A DATE
N.R. ○ YES ○ NO.

David Bowie: Queen Bitch
Lou Reed: Rock n Roll
Belle and Sebastian: The State I Am In
The Beatles: Julia
The Libertines: What Katie Did
Blur: Jubilee
Beck: This Girl that I Know
The Beta Band: Dry the Rain
Cotton Mather: Autumn Birds

B DATE
N.R. ○ YES ○ NO.

Television: Glory
John Cale: Things
The White Stripes: Apple Blossom
Grant Lee Buffalo: The Whole Shebang
Liars: Why Midnight Walked But Didn't Ring Her Bell
The Velvet Underground: Sister Ray
Roy Orbison: Oh, Pretty Woman

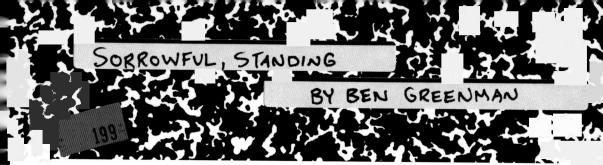

SORROWFUL, STANDING

BY BEN GREENMAN

199

1.

Long ago, in a city I will not name, I loved a woman, and she punished me for it. Later I learned the art of reversal and I punished a woman who loved me. Then I learned justice and punished a woman who punished me. Then I entered what I think is called adulthood and loved a woman who loved me. There are children to prove it. Some of them are even mine.

2.

The last sentence of that first paragraph is a joke. I joke because I feel safe. Long ago, in the city I will not name, the woman I loved asked me a question. "How come we don't get each other presents?" she said. "Why would you get a present for someone you hate?" I said. We both laughed, because we felt safe. We did not hate each other. We loved each other. When you pass a dog in the street and the dog growls, you look quickly for evidence of a leash or chain. Our laughter was the knowledge that we would not be bitten.

3.

In fact, we did get each other presents, often. We were poor but we were not actually poor: We had parents who were doctors and professors and they ensured that we would not, separately or together, perish. They ensured that we had roofs over our head and a bed beneath our bodies. They provided protected spaces in which we romantically, callowly, flourished. She had an apartment. I slept over frequently. Sometimes I came over after she was already asleep. "Are you here?" she would say, half-waking. "I'm not here," I said. "I'm gone, gone, gone." She would laugh, feeling safe, and roll toward me.

4.

No, no. We did not get each other presents. That misrepresents. We gave each other presents. For the most part, they were intentionally small things, creative works designed to serve as signs of something larger. She gave me a sketch she had drawn. I gave her a story I had written. There were doodles on Post-it notes that traveled in both directions. There were, above all, tapes that we made for each other. We were not the first young couple to do this but we may have felt as though we were. We were young and showed our love in ways that were both considerate and senseless.

5.

We made each other tapes because we believed that music articulated what we could not otherwise express. We may have been right about this: She was a painter (or maybe, given her youth, a prepainter). I was a prewriter. But if we were right about it, it was only by accident. We were confused about nearly everything—sex, money, responsibility, art—and whatever energy was not spent trying to bring things into focus was spent averting our eyes. If we did not look we could at least listen.

6.

I forget what tape I made her first. Prince? She knew everything about Prince. How could you not love a girl like that? No, it was Marvin Gaye and Talking Heads. I just remembered. In a moment of brave foolishness I put "Let's Get It On" on one side and "More Songs About Buildings and Food" on the other. "Thank you," she said. We made each other tapes because we believed that music articulated what we could not otherwise express. I made the second tape, too. I think it had Smokey Robinson on one side and Blondie on the other. "Thank you," she said.

7.

A third tape followed, then a fourth and fifth. These tapes were made when we were first dating. She would call late at night and tell me that she was listening to them. I could hear them in the background. "Guess what's next," I would say. Oh, that's another thing I just remembered: After that first tape, I didn't record complete albums, and I didn't list the songs on the label. The first required additional effort. The second seemed like it demonstrated a lack of effort. "Guess what's next," I would say. She would sometimes guess right. How could you not love a girl like that?

8.

After a little while she gave me a tape. She had written the songs on the label. "Unlike you," she said, "I care about information." This was another joke. There was little that I cared about more than information, but I was learning. The songs were written in her handwriting, which was distinctive to the point of strange. She indiscriminately mixed capital and lowercase letters within words. I would say that I recognized this as a sign of something larger—an inability to recognize what was important, a chaos of priorities—but the fact was that I loved it as I loved her. Sometimes in my journal I would write notes like this and feel I was closer to her: "fIrsT dAy of tEaCHinG toDay."

9.

The first tape she gave me thrilled me because it frightened me. It frightened me because it marked the distance between us. I had spent weeks with her, maybe even months. We had gone to bed together to confirm our closeness. But the first tape she gave me was a reminder of our difference. It had Pergolesi's *Stabat Mater* on one side and the Cocteau Twins album *Blue Bell Knoll* on the other side. I held the tape in my hand. I looked at the songs she had listed. There was a little drawing that was probably of Pergolesi. He looked like he was wearing a wig.

10.

I held the tape in my hands. I turned it over. "It's a present," she said. "It's customary to say thank you." I murmured something. Maybe it was "Thank you." I turned the tape over in my hands. Something about it affronted me and that, in turn, excited me. I did not know any of the music on the tape, any of it at all. It was as foreign to me as if it had been pipa music or mbaqanga or Malay folk songs. And yet, there it was, coming out of a woman I had taken to bed. It is possible that I should have thought about the reverse, how she thought when I gave her tapes of music she did not know, but it is impossible that I would have.

11.

When we spoke that night, or the night after, I expected her to ask me if I had listened to it. She did not. I started to wonder if I was supposed to volunteer the information. Remember, she cared about information. After a while, when she had not asked me anything about the tape and I had not told her anything about it, I started to wonder if the tape had ever existed. I checked the spot where I had left it, on top of my dresser. It existed.

12.

She made me other tapes. Those I listened to, diligently. One was a Prince tape. One had the Pixies on it. One had some Nick Lowe and some Dead Can Dance. That was a weird one. But that first tape never went into the cassette player. We continued to date. Things went well. We moved to another city together and moved in together. We went to sleep together every night and woke up together every morning. I loved her, but I was young, and I showed my love in ways that I am sure were both maddening and oppressive. She chose to punish me by moving out. I loved a woman and she punished me for it. I had it coming, but I was not prepared for the sting. I came home from a vacation and all my things were shoved into a heap in the closet and all her things were gone, gone, gone.

13.

Later I would get upset. I would cry a little. I would visit her mother and ask what she thought was happening, if she thought everything would be okay. At the time, though, I wasn't upset. I stood in the middle of the room for a while. Then I went to the closet and rummaged through the pile until I found what I knew I would find: the tapes she had made for me. I could have played the one with Pergolesi and the Cocteau Twins. Maybe I should have. But something stopped me: the knowledge that I had no knowledge. I didn't know what was on the tape. It could have been blank. It could have had a message on it, in her voice: "I will let you love me and then I will leave." It could have even had Pergolesi and the Cocteau Twins. I didn't want to know. I picked another one. Maybe it was the Pixies tape. I played it and stood in the middle of the room again. I laughed. My laughter was the knowledge that I had been bitten.

PERGOLESI STABAT MATER / COCTEAU TWINS

A DATE
N.R. ○ YES ○ NO.

PERGOLESI STABAT MATER

Stabat Mater dolorosa
Cuius animam gementem
O quam tristis et afflicta
Quae morebat et dolebat
Quis est homo, qui non fleret
Vidit suum dulcem natum
Eia Mater, fons amoris
Fac, ut ardeat cor meum
Sancta Mater, istud agas
Fac, ut portem Christi mortem
Inflammatus et accensus
Quando corpus morietur
Largo. Salve Regina, mater misericordiae
Allegro–Larghetto. Ad te clamamus exsules, fili Evae
Andante. Eia ergo advocata nostra iilos tuos
Largo. O clemens. O pia, O dulcis Virgo Maria, Salve.

B DATE
N.R. ○ YES ○ NO.

COCTEAU TWINS / BLUE BELL KNOLL

Blue Bell Knoll
Athol-Brose
Carolyn's Fingers
For Phoebe Still a Baby
The Itchy Glowbo Blow
Cico Bluff
Suckling the Mender
Spooning Good Singing Gum
A Kissed Out Red Floatboat
Ella Megablast Burls Forever

HEY BABE

BY JANCEE DUNN

I grew up in New Jersey in the '80s, in a town that was heavily preppy. My few high school boyfriends were Lacoste-clad, clean-cut types, until one summer in college when I met Russ. He bartended with my friend Melissa, and was decidedly not a prep. Unlike the guys in my town, Russ was good-looking but enticingly dipped in a light coating of scunge. Russ's tastes were simple: He liked beer, classic rock, and hanging out. I promptly joined him, and during that halcyon summer I ditched my prep-wear, got myself some gold chains, and repermed my perm for added volume. Soon I found myself spending my weekends driving my folks' secondhand light blue Buick LeSabre "down the shore," to Point Pleasant.

Russ and I would drink beers with his ever-present crew of dirtball buddies and then take a wobbly stroll on Jenkinson's Boardwalk ("Jenks," for those in the know). Then we'd cruise around town, blaring The Doors out the open windows. My hometown friends and I had more esoteric musical taste as well as carefully curated record collections, but I was a closet fan of the entire play list of WHDA, the Rock of North Jersey. With Russ, I could love it unabashedly.

Sometimes he would take me to parties at his sister Michelle's house. Michelle had the best collection of cheesy R&B songs—another one of my weaknesses. Give me a synth-heavy '80s R&B band with a subtle name like Klymaxx or L'Trimm and I am in heaven. I had asked Michelle a couple of times to make me a tape, but to my surprise, the normally recalcitrant Russ gave it a try. Our first—perhaps only—movie that we saw together was *The Lost Boys*, so he included a few songs from the soundtrack (hence Tim Capello and Gerard McMann). That was about as romantic

as Russ got, but at the time I was deeply moved and read all kinds of symbolism into the songs that did not actually exist.

I've since lost the tape's cover but his faint writing on the tape says HEY BABE, I remember at the time wishing that I had a cooler mixtape like some of my friends had, with songs from Wire or Big Dipper or something. I mean, you know, "Melissa"? I constantly tried to open his musical mind. Once I gave him a cassette of a New York City band I liked called Cruel Story of Youth. He put one of their songs on his mixtape to me but I guarantee he never gave it a listen beyond that. After a while I came to appreciate that he didn't try to be self-consciously hip. He just wasn't interested in alternative bands (nor, mercifully, the requisite William Shatner track that's funny the first time and thereafter fast-forwarded). And, of course, I played that tape to death. I finally got tired of driving him everywhere and paying for everything (he always had "money coming in," which I never saw) and I broke up with him in a parking lot of a 7-Eleven in Summit, New Jersey.

This is a shorter than usual list of songs, because Russ could only be bothered with a sixty-minute tape. He had some hanging out to do.

HEY BABE

A DATE N.R. ○ YES ○ NO.

The Rolling Stones: Can't Be Seen
The Doors: So Good Together
Cruel Story of Youth: You're What You Want To Be
INXS with Jimmy Barnes: Good Times
Cream: I Feel Free
Tim Capello: I Still Believe
INXS: To Look At You

B DATE N.R. ○ YES ○ NO.

The Doors: Moonlight Drive
Bob Marley: Slave Driver
The Allman Brothers Band: Melissa
Frank Sinatra: It Had to Be You
Frank Sinatra: The Way You Look Tonight
Prince: The Beautiful Ones
Gerard McMann: Cry Little Sister

Something To Say

By Andrew Huff

When I was sixteen, I went on a school field trip to Stratford, Ontario, for the International Shakespeare Festival. It was a long bus ride from suburban Chicago, and I didn't have a Walkman, so I spent most of the trip talking with my friends Mike and Suzanne and Suzanne's friends Kate and Christine. As the night wore on, it ended up being just Christine and me, giggling and flirting through the night. We continued to get to know each other throughout the trip, and by the time we got back to Barrington, we were a couple.

Not that we went out on many dates by ourselves; Kate and Suzanne or other friends were usually with us at whichever coffee shop we were hanging out at. Ah, high school.

Our relationship was not the easiest. Besides not getting a whole lot of privacy, she was a senior, getting ready to graduate and dealing with all the pressures of finding a college, etc. I was a junior, so all that was still ahead of me. Her home life was tense, and she dealt with it by clamming up. Mine was tense, too, but for once in my life I was trying to deal with it by talking about it with my friends. (My cassette of the Violent Femmes' first album became an invaluable part of my friends' and my frequent aimless drives, during which we would vent about our parents and scream the lyrics to "Add It Up" and "Kiss Off.") Her inability to open up to me was a constant source of strife as I pushed her to talk and she said she wanted to but couldn't. So I consoled myself by confiding in her best friend, Kate, talking about everything and anything. (We kept a jokey list of things we hadn't discussed yet, including such things as Civil Aviation and The Rutabaga.) Although I wasn't at all attracted to her (or maybe because of that), I became very close with Kate—closer, in fact, than I was with Christine. Needless to say, this was a source of increasing drama.

It was through Kate that I learned that Christine's relationship with her ex wasn't quite as complete as I thought. It had begun at a summer program at Harvard the year before, and ended the way most long distance relationships do—more from the circumstance than the loss of feelings. So my girlfriend was still pining for some other boy. It bothered me, but I was still smitten enough that I didn't want to end it.

When Valentine's Day rolled around, I got Kate to help me sneak a rose into Christine's locker (Kate knew the combo and when Christine would be away from it between classes). Meanwhile, Christine had done the same with one of my friends, and deposited a mixtape in my locker. On the cover it said, "twenty-six songs about LOVE, Relationships, and feeling SCREWED OVER. For Andrew, february 14, 1992 (to speak my mind whenever I CAN'T) Love Christine." It was accompanied by a long letter explaining the significance of each song. True to its rather long title, it covered emotions ranging

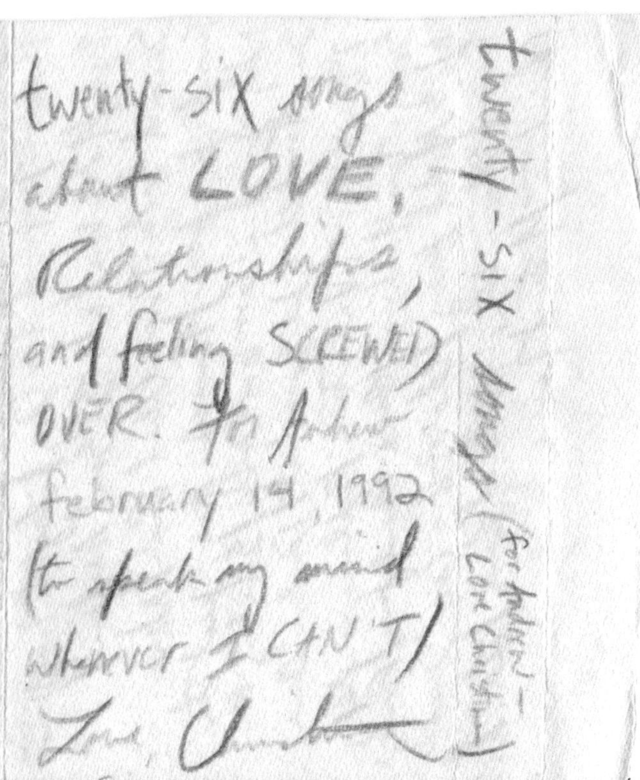

from romance ("There You Are," and "Just the Way You Are" by the Goo Goo Dolls), frustration ("Moving the Goalposts" by Billy Bragg), and even the triangle forming between her, Kate, and me ("We 3" by Soul Asylum). And as you'd expect from a mix with a title like that, the lyrics were deeply important—and I devoured them, thinking a lot about what each one might mean.

Unfortunately, the tape didn't really change things with our relationship, except perhaps stave off the inevitable. Christine broke up with me about a month before the prom, deciding instead to take her ex-boyfriend. I was heartbroken, but recovered and managed to stay friends with her, if only distantly. My friendship with Kate imploded soon after for a variety of reasons, some related to Christine, some not. I even crashed the prom, along with one of our other friends, Jill. I walked in under the pretense of looking for Jill, who'd gotten in already under the guise of taking photos for the yearbook. I was wearing khaki shorts, a blue shirt, and hiking boots, and through friends I managed to accumulate a full tux to blend into the crowd. We sat at Christine and Suzanne's table and had a great time.

The mix from Christine became a precious thing to me, one of my prized possessions, even after I'd moved on to other girls and new mixtapes. I played it so often that it began to get a little distorted and I started to worry that the tape would snap. So I retired it. It spends most of its time in an antique safety deposit box in my desk, along with my birth certificate, a few silver dollars, and other keepsakes from high school.

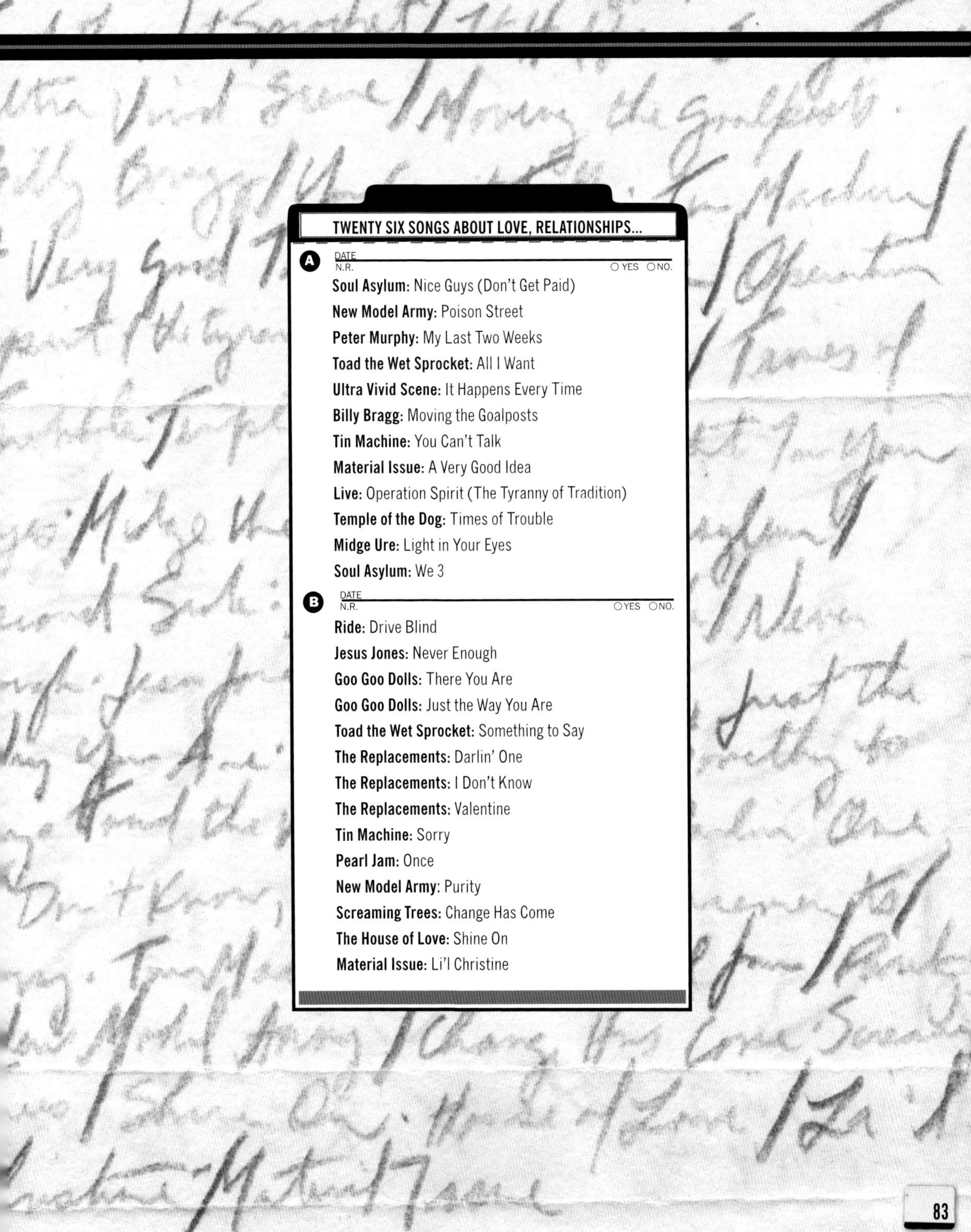

TWENTY SIX SONGS ABOUT LOVE, RELATIONSHIPS...

A
DATE
N.R. ○ YES ○ NO.

Soul Asylum: Nice Guys (Don't Get Paid)
New Model Army: Poison Street
Peter Murphy: My Last Two Weeks
Toad the Wet Sprocket: All I Want
Ultra Vivid Scene: It Happens Every Time
Billy Bragg: Moving the Goalposts
Tin Machine: You Can't Talk
Material Issue: A Very Good Idea
Live: Operation Spirit (The Tyranny of Tradition)
Temple of the Dog: Times of Trouble
Midge Ure: Light in Your Eyes
Soul Asylum: We 3

B
DATE
N.R. ○ YES ○ NO.

Ride: Drive Blind
Jesus Jones: Never Enough
Goo Goo Dolls: There You Are
Goo Goo Dolls: Just the Way You Are
Toad the Wet Sprocket: Something to Say
The Replacements: Darlin' One
The Replacements: I Don't Know
The Replacements: Valentine
Tin Machine: Sorry
Pearl Jam: Once
New Model Army: Purity
Screaming Trees: Change Has Come
The House of Love: Shine On
Material Issue: Li'l Christine

YOU GOT THE PEACHES, I GOT THE CREAM

BY ROB SHEFFIELD

The name of this Maxell UR-90? YOU GOT THE PEACHES, I GOT THE CREAM. Side A? "The Peaches." Side B? "The Cream." Our song? "Pour Some Sugar On Me," obviously. The summer? 1988, obviously. The girl? Not a damn thing obvious about her.

Peaches had long greasy black hair and brown eyes the size of hockey pucks, plus a denim jacket she would wear every day no matter how hot it was. She gave me my first taste of Jagermeister, mixed with Connecticut Cola for a truly revolting brew. She was a Southern Connecticut State University student, stuck in New Haven in the summer industrial-wasteland boredom. She did the reggae show on WYBC, which is how I met her, and I would hang out in the studio on Friday nights just to see her even though I couldn't stand reggae. Some nights she wouldn't show up and I'd get stuck doing her reggae show, which meant two hours of fumbling while fielding irate phone requests for "Now That We Found Love" and "No Woman, No Cry." Did I get mad? No. She was teaching me important stuff. Like *Girls don't show up for things*.

She *really* liked Def Leppard, and had it bad for Joe Elliott, who she always called Screamin' Joe. She loved Axl Rose, Johnny Depp, Joan Jett, setting off fireworks on rooftops, and me—except the me part. And yet her failure to fall for my beyond-obvious charms (explained only partially and meagerly by the artwork over my bed, a full-page ad for Morrissey's debut solo album *Viva Hate* ripped from *Spin* magazine, with the man's profile and the words MORRISSEY . . . ALONE) was just one of her many fascinating quirks. Her favorite Joan Jett song was "I'm Gonna Run Away," which maybe should have given me a clue.

We used to watch *Dial-MTV* together every afternoon over the phone, as she kept up a running commentary as Adam Curry (the VJ with the fantastic mousse-poodle hair) would count down the top-ten viewer requests, which was usually some mélange of "Nothin' But a Good Time," "I Hate Myself for Loving You," "Sweet Child O' Mine," Debbie Gibson's "Foolish Beat," Tiffany's "I Saw Him Standing There," all culminating in the inevitable "Pour Some Sugar on Me." She would howl along as Screamin' Joe intoned the mantra, "Red light, yellow light, green light, go." It was the highlight of my afternoon, five afternoons a week.

She was a tough punk-rock chick who loved pop music, the goopier the better. We argued over whether Tiffany was cooler than Debbie (she was), or whether Lita Ford was cooler than Joan Jett (she wasn't), or whether that guy Johnny Depp, on that new show *21 Jump Street*, heralded the dawn of a new golden age (obviously). I bought her *Bop* magazine faithfully. We went to see Debbie play the New Haven Coliseum.

One afternoon, around four, I called her up to watch *Dial-MTV*. Her housemate said she wasn't there, she left town. No, she didn't leave a forwarding number or address. Just gone. I never saw her again. Once more, she was teaching me important stuff.

I will probably listen to *Hysteria* once a year for the rest of my life, and it's all her fault.

YOU GOT THE PEACHES, I GOT THE CREAM

A DATE N.R. ○ YES ○ NO.

ABBA: The Name of the Game
Debbie Gibson: Between the Lines
Clancy Brothers: Bold Thady Quill
Van Morrison: Sweet Thing
Pet Shop Boys: Rent
Bob Dylan: I Dreamed I Saw St. Augustine
Finlan Tabor Bagpipe Band of Dublin: Bold Thady Quill
George Michael: Faith
Madonna: Angel
Lou Reed: The Heroine
Tiffany: Should've Been Me
The Vaselines: Dying for It
X-Ray Spex: Art-I-Ficial

B DATE N.R. ○ YES ○ NO.

Motörhead: Deaf Forever
Blondie: Dreaming
The Smiths: Ask
Michelle Shocked: Secret to a Long Life
The Dead Boys: (I Don't Wanna Be No) Catholic Boy
Bullet LaVolta: Dead Wrong
John Travolta and Olivia Newton-John: You're the One that I Want
Fastbacks: K Street
Television Personalities: Mummy You're Not Watching Me
J. Geils Band: Teresa
The Shangri-La-s: Give Him a Great Big Kiss
Debbie Gibson: Play the Field
Salt-N-Pepa: Idle Chatter
Bon Jovi: Livin' on a Prayer

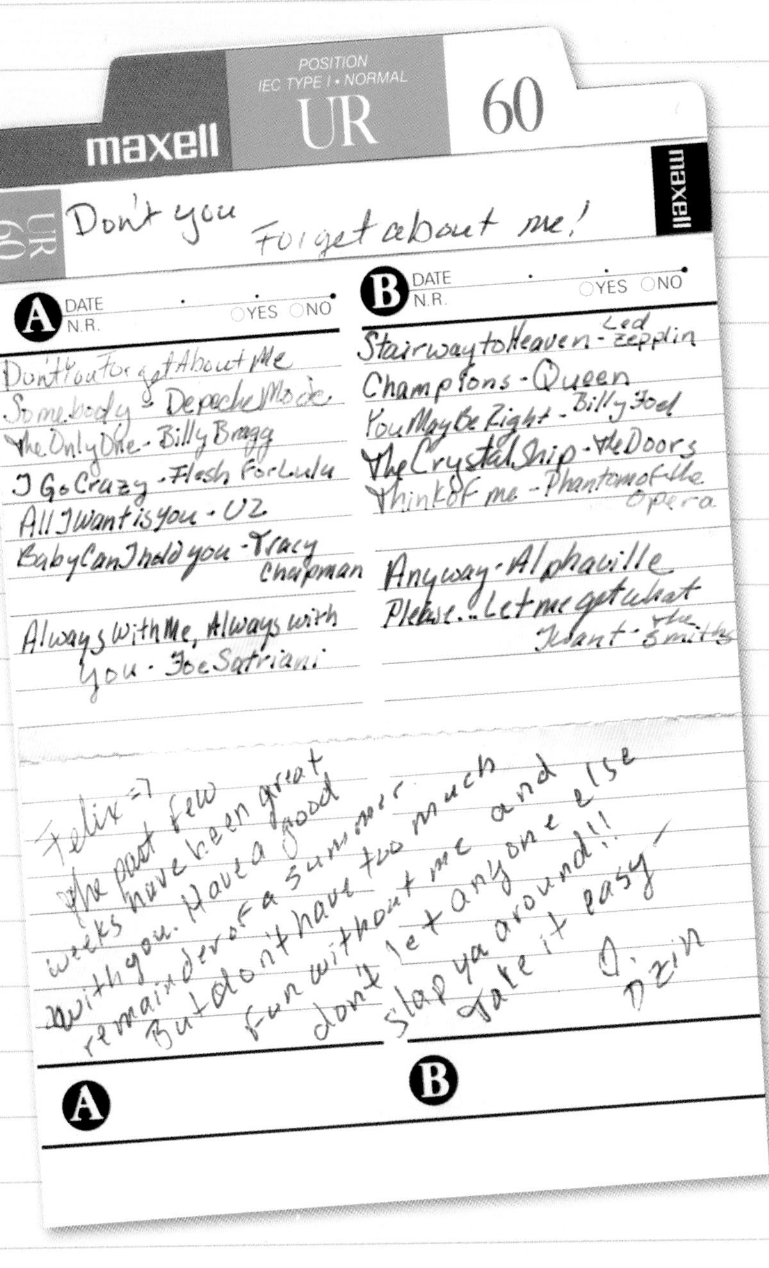
maxell
POSITION
IEC TYPE I • NORMAL
UR
60
maxell
UR 60
Don't you Forget about me!
A DATE N.R. YES NO
DontYouForgetAboutMe
Somebody - DepecheMode
The OnlyOne - Billy Bragg
I GoCrazy - Flesh ForLulu
AllIWantisyou - U2
BabyCanIhold you - Tracy Chapman
Always With Me, Always with You - Joe Satriani
B DATE N.R. YES NO
StairwaytoHeaven - Led Zepplin
Champions - Queen
YouMayBe Right - Billy Joel
The Crystal Ship - The Doors
Think of me - Phantom of the Opera
Anyway - Alphaville
Please...Let me get what I want - The Smiths
Felix—
The past few weeks have been great with you. Have a good remainder of a summer. But don't have too much fun without me and don't let anyone else slap ya around!! Take it easy!
A
B

Felix + Dzintra + Queensrÿche

By Felix Jung

I was an Asian guy with long hair who was into heavy metal; she was a Latvian dancer who chain-smoked Camels. We met in Mr. Dennis's orchestra class at North Central High School. We both played violin, and we both had unusual names: Felix and Dzintra.

The two of us lived fairly close to one another, in neighborhoods on the north side of Indianapolis, Indiana. Between our houses, at the bottom of a steep hill, there was a favorite graffiti spot everyone called The Wall. Kids would tag this stretch of wall mercilessly, and every so often some adult would get fed up and cover the entire thing in a coat of white paint.

One day in the spring of 1990, I drove by and saw that the entire wall had been wiped clean. While I wasn't a serious troublemaker, I knew an opportunity when I saw one. A few phone calls and a few nights later, under cover of darkness, my friends and I let loose on what was, essentially, a blank canvas.

In the movies, couples would take a knife and carve their initials into a tree to declare their love to the world. To me, I was doing the same, using spray paint and stone. I wrote out our names with large strokes: FELIX + DZIN, encircling everything within the sloppy outline of a heart. And then, in the blank square right next to our names, I spray-painted the name of my favorite heavy metal band: Queensrÿche.

Like me, I knew that Dzintra had to drive past that wall at least once or twice a day. The thing I forgot about was that, like me, she had parents who would also have to drive past that wall at least once or twice a day. At the time, there weren't a whole lot of couples named Felix and Dzin in the greater Indianapolis region. Or a whole lot of guys named Felix, for that matter. I doubt I won any points with the parents that year. . . hers or mine.

A few months later, in the summer, she went away for several weeks to a Latvian summer camp in Three Rivers, Wisconsin. We made promises to one another to send letters, and she left me with two things: her address and a mixtape.

During the days, I'd read the letters she sent and while away the time, keeping an eye out for the mailman. She told me stories about how hard it was to sneak cigarettes, and how she plotted with the other students to buy beer and wine coolers. The camp held a dance, she wrote me, but it was lame because she had no one to slow-dance with.

One of my favorite letters was signed with a bit of her lipstick, where she had kissed a space on the paper next to her name. Whenever I felt overcome with loneliness, I'd break out that letter and kiss the spot that she had kissed. By the end of that summer, it was a small miracle there was any lipstick left on the thing.

During the nights, I'd listen to her mixtape incessantly. In bed, with the kind of sadness and yearning that comes from being sixteen years old, I'd play each side in the pitch black and miss my girlfriend. When the tape stopped, I'd flip it over and play the other side. I'd repeat this over and over—play, flip, play, flip—until I fell asleep.

While the songs played, I imagined her in a dimly lit auditorium, sitting alone against a wall. And in the quiet spaces between the songs, I tried very hard not to imagine the many Latvian boys who lurked in the shadows nearby, waiting to ask her to slow-dance.

After her return from camp, things weren't quite the same between us. The extended absence had made things unfamiliar, had made us strangers to one another. A few weeks after she got back, she broke up with me.

The mixtape I had been given that summer stayed at my bedside, and my nightly ritual stayed the same. It would have been easier to burn the tape, or to throw the thing away. But listening to the songs, all I cared about was wallowing in my unhappiness. All I cared about was seeing how low I could get, to try sinking to the very depths of my sadness and to stay there as long as possible.

I spent the next year feeling heartbroken and sorry for myself. I filled an entire green notebook (complete with a Queensrÿche bumper sticker on the cover) with a volume of terrible poetry. Many of my poems were about love and loss. All of my poems rhymed.

It's been nearly twenty years since Dzintra gave me that tape. And though I no longer live in Indianapolis, I still visit my parents, who still live in the same house I grew up in. From time to time, I'll find myself driving along that stretch of hill, and always slow by The Wall out of necessity and nostalgia.

Rounding the curves, I remember the adrenaline of that night with my friends—the scruff of pavement underfoot, the headlights of oncoming cars cresting the hill, the smell and stain of the aerosol cans.

If you were to cut through that wall, you would see a small map of time, the handiwork of countless authors and signatures. Somewhere, underneath the rings of paint and names of couples long past, there's a thin layer that I helped create. Somewhere, for a brief moment of time, I made our names visible to the world.

To this day, The Wall is still sometimes clean, sometimes covered in tags. It is still victim to the whims of adolescents and adults. It's still standing in the same spot, on the north side of Indianapolis, near the bottom of a steep hill, as permanent and as fleeting as any tree.

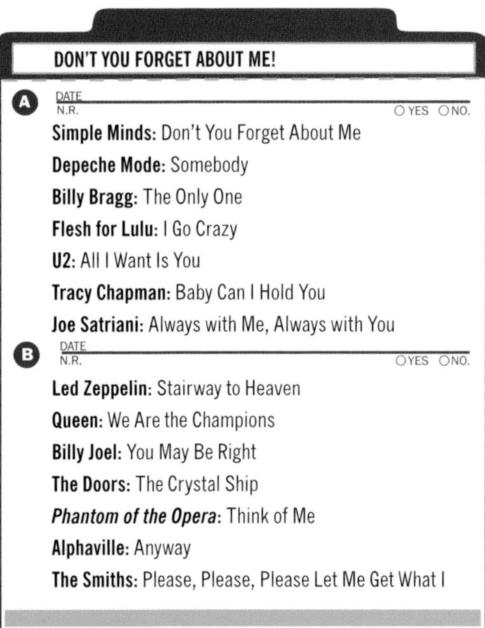
DON'T YOU FORGET ABOUT ME!

A DATE N.R. ○ YES ○ NO.

Simple Minds: Don't You Forget About Me
Depeche Mode: Somebody
Billy Bragg: The Only One
Flesh for Lulu: I Go Crazy
U2: All I Want Is You
Tracy Chapman: Baby Can I Hold You
Joe Satriani: Always with Me, Always with You

B DATE N.R. ○ YES ○ NO.

Led Zeppelin: Stairway to Heaven
Queen: We Are the Champions
Billy Joel: You May Be Right
The Doors: The Crystal Ship
***Phantom of the Opera*:** Think of Me
Alphaville: Anyway
The Smiths: Please, Please, Please Let Me Get What I

ODES TO ANGST

BY ABBY MIMS

Pat told me once that you can love someone in the moment, just for that moment and then it's gone. This was how he explained that he *did* love me that one time he said it, on a drunken New Year's in 1994, but once I'd moved to Seattle to be with him in the spring of 1995, he didn't so much love me anymore. I still like to harbor the idea that he did love me a little in the six or so months we spent together, yet my only proof of it lies in a few romantic poems and a long-lost mixtape he made me titled, ODES TO ANGST. The memory of it came back to me when Pat died nine years later, in a military plane crash. The tape was a shared piece of history that was just between the two of us, something that separated the guy I knew from this husband and father, a pilot and lieutenant in the Navy, who was a stranger to me. I hadn't seen or talked to Pat in nearly a decade, but I ached for the fact that he was gone.

I met Pat my senior year of college at Berkeley, while visiting a friend in Seattle over Thanksgiving break. She and her boyfriend and Pat and I went out one night in Pioneer Square. Pat was beautiful and hilarious, with eyes so blue it hurt and skin the kind reserved for Gerber babies. Add in his otherworldly dimples and I was just plain out of my league. But he brushed up against me as we walked from bar to bar that first night, and when he grabbed me by the shirt collar and kissed me on the dance floor in front of a cheesy New Orleans–style jazz band, I was in love.

We dated long distance for the next few months, talking for hours on the phone, writing letters, sending primitive emails with our college accounts. When he sent me ODES TO ANGST, it was funny and touching, given our nearly constant state of longing for one another. I'm sure I wore it out that winter, as it played on an endless loop in my Walkman. Oddly, for that much listening I can't remember many of the songs. What I do remember is that despite its title, the tape consisted mostly of tunes that had nothing to do with us. There was a Bing Crosby number, "Pennies from Heaven" Pearl Jam's early stuff, like "Alive" and "Daughter," which I didn't really care about, along with "What's the Frequency Kenneth" by R.E.M. There was "Fields of Gold" by Sting, which I liked, and also UB40's "Red, Red Wine," which I hated. In the end it was what was missing from the tape that stood out: Paula Cole's "I Don't Wanna Wait," Sarah McLaughlin's "Ice Cream," Sheryl Crow's "Are You Strong Enough to Be My Man," Counting Crows's "Anna Begins"—songs he knew I was obsessed with. But I listened to the thing anyway, over and over again, trying to decode its secret messages of love. This was mainly because soon after he sent it, Pat stopped calling as often and grew more distant as the months passed. Our subsequent visits lacked sex and romance but as my graduation neared, I talked of moving to Seattle so we could be together. He had little to say on the topic. In my twenty-two-year-old wisdom, I ignored this, along with all the other signs that we were falling apart. I moved to Seattle two days after graduation and six weeks later, we broke up.

Pat died in the summer of 2004, the same month I moved home from Los Angeles to Portland, Oregon. I was living back in my parents' house at the time, feeling at loose ends as I struggled to find meaning and direction in my life. I heard the story of his death through the grapevine, and looked up his obituary online. What I took in was entirely foreign, a story of a hero, of a husband who emailed his wife twice a day, who bragged of his love for her and sent flowers whenever he could; of a father who plastered his bunk with photos of his baby girl. This was a guy I couldn't get to buy me a beer or have sex with me a few months into our relationship, who let me go without looking back. So when I started to cry as I was reading, I wasn't sure who it was I was grieving for—his wife, his little girl, or myself. What I did want then was that tape, so I could've played it and remembered more clearly who it was that I had loved for those few moments in time, along with all the things that were and weren't between us.

GETTING THE UNWANTED MIXTAPE

The best solution for how to handle this potentially awkward situation: Make a mixtape in return with clear and obviously platonic song titles. Your message will be understood. Might we suggest this play list?

SIDE A

Amy Winehouse: Just Friends
Bobby Darin: Just Friends
Charlie Parker: Just Friends
Chet Baker: Just Friends
Coleman Hawkins and Sonny Rollins: Just Friends
Frank Sinatra: Just Friends
John Coltrane: Just Friends
Kool & The Gang: Just Friends

SIDE B

Maynard Ferguson and Big Bop Nouveau: Just Friends
Oscar Peterson: Just Friends
Pat Martino: Just Friends
Rapper Big Pooh: Just Friends
Sarah Vaughn: Just Friends
Sonny Stitt: Just Friends
Tony Bennett: Just Friends
Wilco: We're Just Friends
Wynton Marsalis: Just Friends

HERE'S A TAPE I MADE FOR YEZ

BY JULIE SHAPIRO

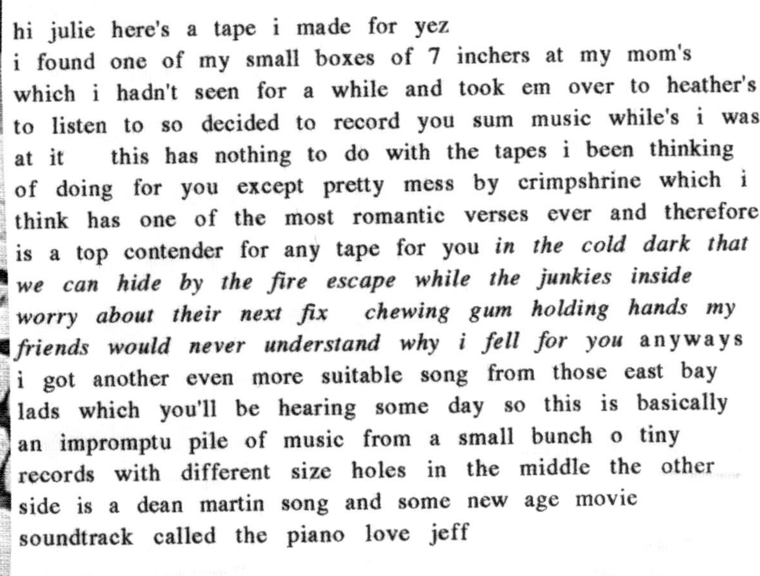

hi julie here's a tape i made for yez
i found one of my small boxes of 7 inchers at my mom's which i hadn't seen for a while and took em over to heather's to listen to so decided to record you sum music while's i was at it this has nothing to do with the tapes i been thinking of doing for you except pretty mess by crimpshrine which i think has one of the most romantic verses ever and therefore is a top contender for any tape for you *in the cold dark that we can hide by the fire escape while the junkies inside worry about their next fix chewing gum holding hands my friends would never understand why i fell for you* anyways i got another even more suitable song from those east bay lads which you'll be hearing some day so this is basically an impromptu pile of music from a small bunch o tiny records with different size holes in the middle the other side is a dean martin song and some new age movie soundtrack called the piano love jeff

When Jeff first walked into the record store, I took note from behind the counter because he was older than most of the undergrads slinking up and down the aisles, and because he seemed automatically sad. I broke the ice, inviting him to contribute to my zine, which meant filling in a blank sign (held up by two grinning white kids, straight out of the '50s,) with "whatever's on your mind these days." Jeff's returned sign depicted a frog, in profile, with some shading near the top of its head and the caption "Fig. 12–6. Frog, showing cut to remove fore and midbrain." The crush was instant, despite my vegetarian/animal rights inclinations. This was 1993, in Boulder.

For our first date we drove in a near-blizzard to Denver to shop for records and find some dinner, at which I remember babbling on about how little I knew about wine* beyond which color I liked, only to find out he'd been trained as a sommelier** in a small, fancy town in California, where he lived for optimal access to the coast, where he surfed whenever possible.

But Jeff was not such a surfing dude, with bulging muscles and sun-bleached hair and fluorescent, zinc-y sunscreen, and rowdy swimming trunks. Instead he was a writer of melancholy short stories and a collector of punk records and striped T-shirts. He had a soft voice, long arms and gentle, twinkly eyes.

Sooner than later came the mixtape. Forgoing excessive decoration, Jeff typed*** a short note on a slip of paper he wrapped around the cassette, and also inserted a list of the songs. One side was mostly a movie soundtrack, the other was com-

piled from a stack of 7 inches he'd recently rediscovered at his mother's house. The soundtrack was kind of boring**** and the other side just never really clicked. Except, that is, the one song Jeff had singled out in the typewritten note, and quoted from—"Pretty Mess" by Crimpshrine (see for yourself) which I agreed then (and still do) is one of the most romantic songs ever written.

I listened to the tape a few times before conjuring up these memories and still don't care for it much. The French song is kind of sweet, but the other novelty items (like the pot-smoking mom tune) wear thin quickly, and the Mecca Normal cuts are barely tolerable, though I was once a big fan.

Of course this got me wondering about Jeff, and what he's up to these days. We broke up eventually, he moved back out to California. I ran into him once, years later, at a used bookstore in Santa Barbara. He was standing under a ladder (the kind installed on a runner so you can read the titles on the highest shelves), which seemed ominous. It was an awkward moment, and we both may have wondered how it had ever not been. But thinking back now, I can appreciate a lot about that time spent with Jeff—a new sort of adventuring and my dog liked him so much—and I *have* relished having the "Pretty Mess" chorus stuck in my head for days.

*** Still don't know too much about wine.**
**** The first time I'd heard that word**
***** Actually quite radical for mixtape design**
****** Not anymore. It's alright, actually.**

HERE'S A TAPE I MADE FOR YEZ

A DATE
N.R. ○ YES ○ NO.

From the movie ***The Piano*** "dean martin song and some new age movie"

[note: see ** above]**

B DATE
N.R. ○ YES ○ NO.

Pooh Gets into a Tight Place
Ill Repute: Fuck with My Head
Juke: Kids Will Rock
Velocity Girl: I Don't Care If You Go
Courtney Love: Disappearing Lessons
Heavenly: So Little Deserve
Crimpshrine: Pretty Mess
Cringer: Understand
Jean Moreau: Le Tourbillion
Thee Headcoats: The Man I Am
Los Locos Del Ritmo: El Rey del Surfing
Mecca Normal: Follow Down
Rolling Scabs: Giuliano's Dream / My Mom Smokes Pot
Pegboy: Field of Darkness

1. poo gets into a tight place
2. ill repute: fuck with my head
3. juke: kids will rock
4. velocity girl: i don't care if you go
5. courtney love disappearing lessons
6. heavenly: so little deserve
7. crimpshrine: pretty mess
8. cringer: understand
9. jean moreau: le tourbillon (band orininal du film "jules et jim")
10. thee headcotes (i don't like) the man i am
11. los locos del ritmo: el rey del surfing
12. mecca normal: follow down
13. rolling scabs: giuliano's dream, my mom smokes pot
14. peg boy: field of darkness
15. brent's tv: what do you get
16. mecca normal: he didn't say, accidently

RIBBED... FOR HER PLEASURE

BY RICK MOODY + STACEY RICHTER

Dear Stacey,

What I remember is that there were these horrible five days in September of 1993 where my girlfriend and I had decided to break up, but neither of us had anywhere to stay yet. Five days of regret and not knowing if we are doing the right thing. Then when the days were through, I was to head off to one of those artists' colony places—to New Hampshire. But on the way out of town—not even out of Brooklyn, in fact—I scraped another guy's car on the BQE. Took his driver's side mirror clean off. I had to pull over, deal with the guy, call the Hertz people, etc. I was really nervous. I was nervous even *before* I hit the guy's car.

Eventually, I made it up to the artists' colony. There were a lot of really interesting people there. Some writers, some painters, a composer who loudly announced over dinner that he had heard the sound of one hand clapping and then proceeded to attempt to demonstrate this. And then there was this very spirited, alluring woman with dark hair who was kind of the life of the place. Dinner was more interesting at her table. I went to some kind of county fair with her and rode a Ferris wheel, even though I am scared of heights. I remember driving to a lake with her and listening to the new Nirvana album (*In Utero*), which, at the time, I thought was really whiny and bad.

Those colony things, I guess, are heady and concentrated, and she and I managed to get through a lot of *crush* pretty quickly, but then, as with many crushes, we didn't do such a great job adapting to regular life when it was time to return to it. And yet somewhere in the midst of this not-doing-very-well-at-returning-to-regular-life stuff, she (you) made me this mixtape. I guess we had talked a lot about music. That was one of the areas where I had been really impressed. And you made me this tape and it had some really good stuff on it. Stuff that I probably should have known about, but didn't. In the rush to go digital, I mislaid the cassette, and in the years since I have missed it, and it has begun to resemble, in recollection, the Platonic ideal of the mixtape.

Do you remember the story the way I'm remembering the story?

Love,

Rick.

Dear Rick,

Yes, I remember the story in the same basic way, though without the emphasis on your car wreck. And I don't remember being alluring. In fact, I believe I was avoiding you at first because you didn't talk very much and I thought you were boring. But eventually I did end up sitting with you at one of the endless artists' colony dinners, and when you finally began talking I immediately recognized that you had an odd, compelling charisma—an intellectual, offbeat charisma—and after that I thought you were totally adorable. So, my aim wasn't so much to allure you but more to shoot you with a dart and haul you in. It seemed like you weren't exactly in the mood for that, since you were in the middle of breaking up with someone else. You were a little bit in the mood, but not all the way.

As for the tape, I'm not sure exactly when I made it. Was the romance on, over, or a little of both? I know that was the last moment in my life when I liked music. Now I find music annoying, but it used to make me feel like I was in a movie and that something magical was about to happen to me. So, I remember basically what kind of things I liked to listen to at the time, and I even remember a few songs on the tape, but after that my memory starts to fade out.

Here are my nominations. I think some of them are wrong:

The Mekons: Wild and Blue

Patti Page: Tennessee Waltz

Some disco song—there was always a disco song on my mixtapes. Maybe "Super Freak"?

Young Marble Giants: Credit in the Straight World

Ed's Redeeming Qualities: Driving on 9 (I'm probably wrong about that one)

Something by Stereolab

The Velvet Underground: What Goes On

Mary Lou Lord: Lights Are Changing

Bikini Kill: Suck My Left One (I'm probably wrong about that one, too)

Does that ring any bells?

Love,

Stacey

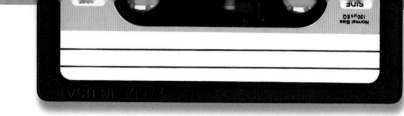

Dear Stacey,

That's a really interesting list of songs you sent. Some of them are right, and some of them are wrong, at least I think so.

Do you remember the little Hello Kitty sticker that you put on the cassette box? I was back in Brooklyn when I got it, and at some point you came to Brooklyn, and I think the romance was a little bit still *on* then, but maybe it was nearing its bitter end. Maybe you wouldn't have given me a tape after the bitter end, although a few years ago you sent me that Gillian Welch cassette, which I really liked, too.

There was definitely a Mary Lou Lord song on there. In fact, there were two Mary Lou Lord songs on the tape, which I really loved a lot, and then I went and bought her CD, when she made it, and it just wasn't anywhere near as good as those early songs. I know a guy now who used to be close to her back when she was a busker, and apparently he made out with her once. Maybe she made a cassette for him, too.

Related to the Mary Lou Lord aesthetic was the song from Girlysounds, or GirlySoundz—I can't remember how it was spelled. But it was she who went on to become Liz Phair. Before she was *Liz Phair*. Somehow you had one of those early songs, but I can't remember which ones, though I think she finally released some of them later on. Did I ever tell you how I tried to get Liz Phair to give me a blurb for *The Ice Storm*? I went to some sort of performance art night in New York where Liz was showing a short film she made, and I gave her my phone number and told her I wanted her to blurb my novel. Guess what? She never called!

I do think you had Young Marble Giants on there, but I had that record in college (and the song I loved was "Salad Days"), so "Credit in the Straight World" would not have been of surpassing interest. I don't know about the Mekons. I have always admired the Mekons more than I liked them, you know what I mean? I admire the project. The same goes for "Super Freak," which is not disco in my book. There were a few filler numbers on the cassette, so they might have included these, but if so, they made no impression.

What about Shonen Knife? I can't remember the title, but I remember that it was some sort of nonsense title that may have included the word "banana" or the word "cabbage." Maybe both. I loved the song, and the lyrics were inexplicable and weird, and the whole thing sort of sounded like the theme song from *The Banana Splits*, which probably makes sense because I know your favorite group, above all, was/is the Partridge Family. Correct?

Love,

r.

Dear Rick,

Wait—I'm starting to remember! Yes, Girly Sound was Liz Phair and a 4-track before she went on Lexapro—she was really good back then. I think the song was "Divorce Song," or the song to the tune of chopsticks that has the line, "I want to fuck you like a dog." Very daring. You did tell me that you met her in New York—I remember that. It's hard to get rock stars to blurb books. I wanted to get Donald Fagen to blurb my latest (which features some Steely Dan lyrics) but realized it was hopeless.

I think the Shonen Knife song was "Twist Barbie," or possibly the song where the whole chorus is just girls singing, "meow meow meow meow, meow meow meow meow." So supercute Japanese girl band! And speaking of supercuteness, though I don't remember that specific Hello Kitty sticker, I'm just finishing up a two-decade-long obsession with Hello Kitty, so that sounds about right. I have a few stickers left if you want some.

Also: Bettie Serveert, "Palomine"

And Carey's Problem: "Led Zeppelin" and/or "I Thought It Would Be Good Today"

Something by the electronica band Seefeel

If the romance was off, I might have put a Guns N' Roses song on there just to torture you . . .

Dear Stacey,

No Guns N' Roses on there, definitely not. Which I guess means the romance was still on. One thing I remember doing with the cassette a lot was taking it to the New York Sports Club I belonged to in Cobble Hill. There was a track by the Shaggs! I had never heard the Shaggs before, which is embarrassing, but you put "Philosophy of the World" on there, and I just absolutely could not believe the *singularity* of the Shaggs. In fact, I'm going to put them on right now, so as to recall, because after I heard this song, I had to get the re-released edition of the album. You, of course, were full of Shaggs lore, and I instantly became preoccupied with all the Shaggs lore. I can't believe how little communication there was between the various members of the band. It's like they were recorded in different rooms.

And you completely trumped me on Carey's Problem, because I was really looking forward to reminding you of them. I really loved, and still love, "I Thought It Would Be Good Today," and I heard "Led Zeppelin" the other day, too. Do you remember that we went to *meet* Carey when you were in New York? I was kind of intimidated because I liked "I

Thought It Would Be Good Today" so much, and we were in his apartment, and I was all intimidated, but he turned out to be this really shy, almost painfully mute guy, and when I was asking questions about how he got the idea to interpolate "Hey Jude" into that one song, he mumbled monosyllabic replies. I was really impressed that you were a *filmmaker,* and you knew guys who edited films and had bands like this on the side. What ever happened to Carey anyway?

And what about the Vaselines? I think there was a Vaselines song on the cassette, because you told me that Kurt Cobain said they were his favorite band. I can't remember what song, because I thought they were kind of a dull band, considering that Kurt liked them so much. He liked the Shaggs, too, though, so his taste wasn't all bad.

Love,

Rick.

P.S. The Blake Babies.

Dear Rick,

I don't even know who the Vaselines are anymore. Are you sure that wasn't on a tape from some other girl? And since you remembered Carey's Problem, are you holding back on anything else? I'm excavating the caverns of my mind here, I need all the help I can get. But I think I remember this: The Hello Kitty stickers were the little pink puffy kind. The tape was entitled SANITIZED . . . FOR YOUR PROTECTION.

So Carey Burtt, the brooding, talented filmmaker and musician, has disappeared from my life. He hasn't made any more records, even though that first one was so good. I think I might have lost him in the settlement of a breakup with a boyfriend, though I'm not sure about that.

I'm glad I introduced you to the Shaggs. That record is one of the best arguments both for and against homeschooling ever made. I don't listen to them anymore but they're so memorable, and I've heard them so many times, that now I can just play Shaggs songs in my brain. I'm pretty sure the song was "Who Are Parents?"

If I put the Shaggs on, was there some Daniel Johnston, too? Maybe "Speeding Motorcycle"?

Love,

Stacey

P.S. I checked iTunes and what do you know, I remember the Vaselines. The song was either "You Think You're a Man," "Molly's Lips," or "Jesus Wants Me for a Sunbeam."

Some other thoughts:

Meat Puppets: Plateau

Matthew Sweet: Girlfriend

PJ Harvey: Sheela-na-gig

Sonic Youth: Silver Rocket

Mazzy Star: Fade into You

The Lemonheads: Hate Your Friends (or something else by them)

Galaxie 500: Pictures

Redd Kross: Love Is You

T. Rex: A Beard of Stars

It makes me feel like a dork to find all carefully culled nineties musical coolness in a list called "'90s Indie Rock" as part of the iTunes essential collection.

Dear Stacey,

From where are you remembering this stuff? Are you just cribbing from the iTunes compilation? I don't think there was any Matthew Sweet or any Meat Puppets on the tape, nor any Sonic Youth, but I will confess that probably every person who made a tape for me in the early nineties put "Fade Into You" on it. So many, in fact, that I now detest that song. Too much junkie business. Also, I don't remember any of those songs shown above in your most recent note, but I think you are right about Daniel Johnston and "Speeding Motorcycle," which is one of those rare songs where both the original and the cover (Yo La Tengo) are equally good. And I think it was "Jesus Wants Me for a Sunbeam" by the Vaselines, because I think I knew "Molly's Lips" from *Incesticide*, the Nirvana B-side album, right? Wasn't that on there?

And my recollection of the title, now that you mention it, was that it was called "Ribbed . . . For Her Pleasure" Not "Sanitized." I have never been able to see a condom box without thinking of your cassette.

I guess we are probably coming to the end of what I can remember, even though this list of songs would probably barely fit one half of a ninety-minute cassette. Maybe it was a sixty-minute one? And I suppose since we're nearing the end of the cassette discussion, it's fair to say that it was very nice to remember all of this, and that I still love you and think of you as one of my best friends. These were the moments of being young when everything in life seemed to be changing, you know, hurtling forward into some unknown realm of adulthood, and maybe that's why these were all such good songs, because they were all peculiar and memorable at such an important moment. For that reason, and many others, you were an imperative friend then, as you are now.

Love,

r.

Dear Rick,

Aw, you're an imperative friend, too, you know that. Now, I agree we've reached the end of remembering, especially since I've finally realized that much of what I'm recalling is ANOTHER TAPE I made for ANOTHER BOY, Shit! Sorry! I think I am mostly remembering "Sanitized . . . For Your Protection" while you are remembering "Ribbed . . . For Her Pleasure." The nineties were not only a time of hurtling change but also of mild sluttiness. Also, since I only had one record collection, there was bound to be some overlap. Oops. Still, this was fun.

xxo,

Stacey

A dramatic recreation, in order of recollection:

Young Marble Giants: Credit In the Straight World

Stereolab: Lock-Groove Lullaby

The Blake Babies: Cesspool

The Velvet Underground: What Goes On

Mary Lou Lord: Lights Are Changing

Bikini Kill: Suck My Left One

Girly Sound: Divorce Song

Shonen Knife: Twist Barbie

Bettie Serveert: Palomine

Carey's Problem: I Thought It Would Be Good Today

Seefeel: Moodswing

The Shaggs: Philosophy of the World

The Vaselines: Jesus Wants Me for a Sunbeam

Mazzy Star: Fade Into You

Blake Babies: Out There

PJ Harvey: Sheela-Na-Gig

Redd Kross: Love Is You

Carey's Problem: Led Zeppelin

TAPE OF JACK GOODNESS

BY AMY FLEMING

We were seventeen years old and it was 1991. Jack and I were in the same Theater Studies class and, twice weekly, we'd attend lessons in a dance studio on the top floor of a Victorian school building off the smoggy Holloway Road in North London.

We didn't get to know each other very well during the first year of the course. I was busy battling through my acid-fueled first real love affair, and Jack also had a girlfriend. We moved in different circles, too, although, from a distance, I always thought he was interesting and talented.

I, on the other hand, was too painfully self-conscious to have even a shred of acting talent, and Jack got to witness me make a spectacular ass of myself on many occasions; my labored sobbing through a Chekhov monologue mortifyingly springs to mind. We even performed together in a group piece, dressed in metallic boiler suits, pretending we were a production line for socially conditioning human beings—cogs in *the machine*, making more cogs. Could it have been any more trite? I doubt it. Jack was really good at robotic movement though.

By the time the second year came around I was single and, over the next few months, I started noticing more and more things I liked about Jack. It wasn't long before I was harboring a full-blown crush. He was relatively small-boned for a man, but strong from football and yoga (other teenage boys didn't do yoga and I found it hot and adorable that he did). He had full lips, smiled often and seemed different from most other kids, as though he was on his own, distinct, infectious journey.

I started paying him attention, trying to make him laugh, and testing the water. My crush got so out of control that whenever I was near him I felt idiotically light and intoxicated. One time, I nearly levitated from sheer excitement when he stole a potato chip out of my hand. I told my best friend about it later and we analyzed it over and over, trying to work out whether his cheeky theft had been a sign that he fancied me.

Jack's parents were going on holiday so he decided to throw a house party. When I showed up at his home, I was nervous but full of hope. I remember liking it that he had his drum kit set up in the front room. I lingered too long over pictures in the downstairs loo of his pretty family on exotic holidays, and felt like a stalker. Then, out of the blue, he gave me this cassette. He hadn't written on it, or decorated the box (I gave it the title and label some time later). He just handed it to me, all casual. Was it a gesture of friendship, or more? Did he make everyone mixtapes or was I special? Had he even split up with that girlfriend I'd heard about some time ago? Later that night, we somehow ended up alone, talking and stroking his cat, and yes, it turned out, he was single after all. His ex had recently got together with one of their female friends and was now a lesbian. When he finally made a move on me, I couldn't believe my luck.

A few months later, when we'd grown comfy with each other, I asked Jack if his inclusion on the cassette of "When Will You Be Mine," by the Average White Band, had been intended as a musical clue to his feelings for me. Of course it bloody-well had, he said. We were an item for three years and remain friends today, although we hardly ever see each other. Last I heard, he was playing flute and percussion with a Brazilian funk outfit.

TAPE OF JACK GOODNESS

A
DATE
N.R. O YES O NO.

James Brown: Cold Sweat
Fred Wesley and The Horny Horns: Four Play
Stevie Wonder: Higher Ground
Sly and The Family Stone: If You Want Me to Stay
The J.B.'s: Pass the Peas
James Brown: Get on the Good Foot
Stevie Wonder: Maybe Your Baby
Roy Ayers: Everybody Loves the Sunshine

B
DATE
N.R. O YES O NO.

Sly and The Family Stone: Remember Who You Are
Stevie Wonder: Living for the City
James Brown: Get Up Offa that Thing
The Average White Band: When Will You Be Mine
Kool & the Gang: Who's Gonna Take the Weight
Sly and The Family Stone: In Time
Stevie Wonder: Superstition
Pegboy: Field of Darkness

CHRISTMASS TAPE 1982

BY GRETCHEN PHILLIPS

I graduated from high school in 1981 and promptly moved to Austin with my then-girlfriend. I worked at a bakery and one day the lesbian cake decorator said, "Gretchen, I hired a new girl for you." And indeed she had. Teresa and I hit it off right away and suddenly, bye-bye live-in girlfriend, hello heady punk rock lifestyle. It was one drunken adventure after another. We had no furniture and only minimum wage jobs, but we had a cheap apartment and a stereo and could always come up with the cover price for shows somehow.

This nervous, chain-smoking fashion plate taught me a lot. She felt that I really needed help and so she set out to educate me about popular music. She had no time for my old singer songwriter loves of the '70s. Folk music, phaw! Instead she made me sit down and listen, *really* listen to Blondie. I'd previously dismissed them as a vacuous pop band but she would put on an album and talk me through the finer points of their impeccable riffs, playful lyrics, and awesome musicianship. It took a couple of sessions, but I clearly remem-

ber that "aha" moment when I got what she was after. It was a revelation. Wow, the stuff you hear on the radio can have some real validity and not just be a guilty pleasure. I'd been too hung up on notions of sincerity for far too long and had made distinctions between good and bad. "It all has merit," Teresa said. There is no low art and high art. There's just art. There's no such thing as guilty pleasures, they're just pleasures. That lesson changed my life.

Our first, and only, Christmas day together found us with a bunch of pot and the need to make a 120-minute mixtape together. We used the outrageously expensive fifty-dollar TEAC cassette deck that my EST seminar had convinced me that I could actually afford. (And God knows, I did get my money's worth of service from that workhorse.) Teresa set about instructing me on the basics of mixing. She would hit pause after a song in order to avoid the clicking sound of the stop button on the tape. And then she would hit record/pause and cue the next song up and take it off pause just when the song was beginning in order to create a seamless stream of music. The virtue of this way of listening had never occurred to me before. God, she was such a genius.

We mostly raided my record collection, with a few songs from hers. The miracle of the thing was how she combined such disparate offerings from Joy Division to Sonny and Cher in such a satisfying way. In the past, I would never have mixed up the food on my plate like that, certainly not. I would make a punk tape, or a folk tape, but not such a crazy combo tape. But on this fateful day Teresa showed me how to weave themes throughout a mix by combining various styles dealing with certain topics. Since it was Christmas, we needed some Christ, which led us to *Jesus Christ Superstar* and the Psychedelic Furs. Our choices for songs about queers were severely limited back in those days, so we made do with homophobic offerings from Dr. Demento and a stereotyping Elton John. Surely there's a need to critique holiday consumptive habits, how about *Capital* by Gang of Four! And then, of course, since we were smart, self-aware lesbians, we included one cynical song about love after another. But there was one genuinely romantic moment, however, when she put on the

Runaways, and as Joan Jett plaintively pleaded at the end of the song, *Don't go away!* Teresa said, "That's how I feel about you." I remember being so touched.

There were many, many things wrong with our relationship. But our shared love of music and her articulate and pedantic appreciation of it really was the sweet glue that kept us together through all of our lesbian drama. We finally self-destructed in a truly spectacular way, but I never held a grudge or didn't love her with all of my heart. She was too important.

Through the years I've gotten to swap with some of the exquisite makers of the mixtape (Olympia musician Lois Maffeo and WFMU's Irwin Chusid, for example). And if the tapes I offered them in exchange were any good, and contained any internal humor and flow and surprises, I owe that skill to the teachings of Teresa. It all began one Christmas with a 120-minute TDK that, truth be told, has held up amazingly well.

CHRIST MASS TAPE 1982

A DATE
N.R. ○ YES ○ NO.

Sonny and Cher: A Cowboy's Work Is Never Done
Herb Alpert and The Tijuana Brass: The Lonely Bull
Jefferson Airplane: White Rabbit
Gang of Four: Capital
Nina Hagen: Herman's Door
Lydia Lunch: A Cruise to the Moon
Vaselina: Eres Todo Mi Amor
Siouxsie and the Banshees: Cocoon
Dionne Warwick: Anyone Who Had a Heart
Sex Pistols: Submisson
Joy Division: Candidate
The Runaways: Don't Go Away
Siouxsie and the Banshees: Love in a Void
Elton John: All the Girls Love Alice
MDC: Dick for Brains
Dionne Warwick: I Smiled Yesterday
Sam and Dave: Soothe Me
Prince: Dirty Mind
Echo & The Bunnymen: The Puppet
The Roches: The Married Men
Dead Kennedys: Viva Las Vegas

B DATE
N.R. ○ YES ○ NO.

The Roches: We
Crass: Bat a Motel
Billie Holiday: God Bless the Child
***Jesus Christ Superstar*:** Trial Before Pilate
The Psychedelic Furs: Imitation of Christ
10cc: I'm Not in Love
Bruce Woolley and the Camera Club: Johnny
Cheryl Lynn: Got to Be Real
5000 Volts: I'm on Fire
BT Express: Peace Pipe
***Jesus Christ Superstar*:** Heaven on Their Minds
David Geddes: Run Joey Run
Vikki Carr: It Must Be Him
Janis Ian: She's Made of Porcelain
Big Brother and the Holding Company: Summertime
Cheech and Chong: Basketball Jones featuring Tyrone Shoelaces
Ben Gay & The Silly Savages: Ballad of Ben Gay
***Hair*:** Air
The Slits: Love Und Romance

Boo
Fucking
Hoo!
Book
2

Boo Fucking Hoo! Book 2

BOO FUCKING HOO! : BOOK 2

BY MARY HUHN

A. and I first connected through music—Lydia Lunch, the Smiths, the Butthole Surfers—when we worked, circa 1986, as editorial assistants at a trade magazine. Our furious friendship, also rooted in sports (he introduced me to the secret languages of baseball and basketball), writing and exploring New York, evolved into a stormy relationship.

BOO FUCKING HOO! BOOK 2 was made around 1988 when our relationship wasn't going well. When our connection was good, it was Thurston and Kim good; when it was bad, it was Madonna and Sean horrid. A Saturday night of drinking and dancing at the Empire State Soul Club would be overshadowed by a Sunday-afternoon argument over one of our behaviors. We loved each other, but passion—as well as tension, possessiveness and jealousy—was in all-consuming overdrive.

Perhaps he wanted more than I was capable of giving. He pushed. I pulled. Or vice versa. In retrospect, I was probably doing most of the pushing, but A. of greater faith and optimism wouldn't be pushed away. Instead A., who was tremendously introspective, communicated in the one way he knew how—and could be certain I'd listen to—with this tape full of songs iced with a double meaning of love and self-pity, wrapped in a knowing wink.

One mutual friend, however, saw "I'm Your Puppet" on the tape and was appalled that anyone would wear his heart on his sleeve to that degree. I didn't see it like that. I focused more on the love—and the music. Yes, the songs were stuffed with messages of every imaginable heartache, but some were achingly beautiful or just playful. It made it easy to ignore the sender's true message—or at least not talk about it.

The cassette also introduced me to all sorts of country, blues, and indie rock, back in the day without the Internet—only record stores, jukeboxes, indie radio stations, and mixed tapes—to discover songs. I was impatient when it came to new sounds, but A. mixed familiar and unfamiliar songs, so I would stay engaged.

What's astounding is the number of songs I had never heard, which could now be considered standards in my life. Meaning notwithstanding, I had never heard of Bobby and James Purify or their song "I'm Your Puppet." I wasn't a country music fan until A. introduced me to Bob Wills, Rosanne Cash, Chris Isaak, and Lyle Lovett (on another tape, "Don't You Know a More Cheerful Story?", A. put "Nobody Knows Me like My Babe," which embodies the simple intimacy of any relationship). When alt-country rose in the '90s, I fully embraced the genre and appreciated A.'s song selections even more.

I wasn't put off by the deeply personal meaning of A.'s choices, some full of doomed optimism, others rife with stabbing awareness (I think of myself as the town cryer in Costello's song after constant make-up martinis at our local bars, but—upon further consideration—perhaps he was, too).

The feelings behind the songs, all representing a slice of reality or a dream, enhanced them. Charlie Rich's "That's How Much I Love You" was simply a crazy romantic song—a world in which we wished we lived. "Lady Friend" can still make me teary-eyed, particularly as the girl collects her trinkets from his house and moves on. That's the story of any couple who breaks up, as we eventually did.

But, as the song assured me, *And he will learn to live without her and survive.* That line still rips me up. In the end, we both survived, separately.

To be certain that his choice of "Marry Me," didn't sound as meaningful as it actually was, A. wrote "lie lie" in parentheses next to it. Marriage, which we never addressed except in abstract ways, wasn't an issue, but commitment was. At times, his. At more times, mine.

Other songs, such as "I Love My Leather Jacket" and "Indian Summer," have lingered with me, standing on their own musically and poetically, but I still feel the love in the songs and the sentiment

BOO

BRAIN CLOUDY BLUES - BOB WILLS & THE TEXAS PLAYBOYS
THAT'S HOW MUCH I LOVE YOU - CHARLIE RICH
ARE WE DREAMING THE SAME DREAM? - GARY STEWART
I'M YOUR PUPPET - BOBBY & JAMES PURIFY
I DON'T DO WINDOWS - O.V. WRIGHT
STUPIDITY - SOLOMON BURKE
TOWN CRYER - ELVIS COSTELLO
I'M YOUR MAN - LEONARD COHEN
STRANGE WEATHER - MARIANNE FAITHFUL
GOD WILL / IF I WERE THE MAN YOU WANTED - LYLE LOVETT
THIS LOVE WILL LAST - CHRIS ISAAK
I DON'T KNOW WHY (ETC.) - ROSANNE
YOU'LL LOSE A GOOD THING - BARBARA LYNN
NO ONE EVER TELLS YOU - THE CRYSTALS

HOO

MARRY ME (LIE LIE) - THESE IMMORTAL SOULS
INDIAN SUMMER - BEAT HAPPENING
I LOVE HER ALL THE TIME - SONIC YOUTH
REPULSION - ~~NEIL YOUNG~~ (DINOSAUR)
ASTRAL PLANE - MODERN LOVERS
(I LOVE MY) LEATHER JACKET - THE CHILLS
STORM IN MY HOUSE - MINUTEMEN
SLEEP - BIG BLACK
LADY FRIEND - THE BYRDS
THE LADY & THE LIZARD - VERLAINES
CRASH - PRIMITIVES
(I'M NOT HERE) 1967 / GHOSTS OF AMERICAN ASTRONAUTS - MEKONS
TIME TO CHILL - DJ JAZZY JEFF & THE FRESH PRINCE.

of the sender from twenty years ago. And the fact was: I did love my leather jacket, as well as Indian summers, cemeteries, and baked Alaska. A. knew more about me than I would have ever admitted—or which I chose to ignore.

A.'s message was clear. I wasn't appalled by the tape—or the person who bravely sent such personal messages, albeit cloaked in song. I was honored.

What's amazing about this tape is that it's called "Book 2" because I lost the original. A. remade it for me. He didn't get pissed 'cause I lost it. He, being the kind of patient guy he is, painstakingly remade it, probably shaking his head while digging through his albums. He ended BOO FUCKING HOO lightheartedly with "Time to Chill" by that "new" rap duo—DJ Jazzy Jeff and the Fresh Prince.

It was a significant song because it represents the amount of time we spent going to rap shows, taping Mr. Magic's radio broadcasts and dissecting songs to identify the samples. L. L. Cool J.'s "I Need Love" helped, but A. had coaxed me into my rap obsession as well.

After two decades, the tracks take me straight to those days, but not just to the turbulent times. They help me appreciate our struggle to make it as best we could, as well as the days and nights when we could "relax, lay back, unwind, 'cause now is time to chill," as the Fresh Prince rapped.

Less than two years into our relationship, after we finally realized that the DJ powers of Marly Marl, tickets to Elvis Costello, or a cassette didn't possess the power to keep us connected, we broke up. We did that as we had gone out, fighting and making up, over and over, for months. It wasn't lighthearted at all.

Listening to this tape again, twenty years later, I felt more boo fucking hoo than ever. Reminiscing over lost love, without laying blame anymore, and an old cassette will do that to you.

BOO FUCKING HOO!

A DATE
N.R. ○ YES ○ NO.

BOO SIDE

Bob Wills and His Texas Playboys: Brain Cloudy Blues
Charlie Rich: That's How Much I Love You
Gary Stewart: Are We Dreamin' the Same Dream?
Bobby and James Purify: I'm Your Puppet
O. V. Wright: I Don't Do Windows
Solomon Burke: Stupidity
Elvis Costello: Town Cryer
Leonard Cohen: I'm Your Man
Marianne Faithfull: Strange Weather
Lyle Lovett: God Will
Lyle Lovett: If I Were The Man You Wanted
Chris Isaak: This Love Will Last
Rosanne Cash: I Don't Know Why You Don't Want Me
Barbara Lynn: You'll Lose A Good Thing
The Crystals: No One Ever Tells You

B DATE
N.R. ○ YES ○ NO.

HOO SIDE

These Immortal Souls: Marry Me
Beat Happening: Indian Summer
Sonic Youth: I Love Her All the Time
Dinosaur Jr.: Repulsion
Modern Lovers: Astral Plane
The Chills: I Love My Leather Jacket
Minutemen: Storm In My House
Big Black: Sleep!
The Byrds: Lady Friend
Verlaines: The Lady and the Lizard
The Primitives: Crash
The Mekons: (I'm Not Here) 1967
The Mekons: Ghosts of American Astronauts
DJ Jazzy Jeff and The Fresh Prince: Time To Chill

KEN'S CORNER

BY DAVID GREENBERGER

In 1979, I started a literary project called *The Duplex Planet*. At the time it was a self-produced periodical devoted to my conversations with the residents of the Duplex Nursing Home in Boston. I was the activities director there for three years and I met Ken Eglin my first day on the job. He had no family, but made friends easily. During the 1940s he'd hung out in Boston jazz clubs tap-dancing for pocket money and meeting performers like Lester Young and Billie Holiday. It became clear that music was a vital part of his life. I'd bring in my Walkman and play songs for him, getting him to comment on what he'd heard. I turned his spontaneous riffing critiques into a music review column called "Ken's Corner." It was a regular *Duplex Planet* feature and syndicated to a few music publications around the country. Readers and fans of Ken's column began sending me cassettes filled with songs. They wanted to spark my conversations about the music with Ken. These compilations were carefully selected and sequenced, each sent by a different person. In the fall of 1983, Ken's condition began to deteriorate and he was transferred from the nursing home to a nearby VA hospital. On January 26, 1984, a call came in the middle of the night. Ken had died. It was a sad privilege to be the one person close enough to Ken to be the recipient of that final call. I called a funeral home in the neighborhood. Ken would be given a veteran's burial in the national cemetery near Cape Cod. *The Boston Globe* ran a large obituary, headlined "Kenneth Eglin, rock music critic, began as tap dancer in '30s." Because of the newspaper's coverage and through phone calls and word of mouth, dozens of people, most of whom had never met Ken, came by for the wake. Funeral homes are generally somber gathering places but it was Ken's personality and his vibrant response to music that drew us together. I played a tape of some of the songs he loved (including Thelonious Monk, Jonathan Richman, NRBQ, Mal Waldron). One last cassette had arrived that Ken never got to hear. I tucked it into his jacket pocket. I didn't want to listen to it without him.

Songs by Hollow Men (and Women)

By Jessica Agneessens

In the spring of 1996, I walked through the perpetually damp campus of the University of Oregon in search of a kindred spirit. I was disenchanted with the disproportionate number of patchouli-basted students grooving out to their bootlegs of the Grateful Dead. I hadn't made friends save for my roommates, whom I'd known prior to my move to the Pacific Northwest. By the second semester, I noticed a quiet, chestnut-eyed pixie in most of my classes. A feat not easily accomplished with a class inventory that included geology, French, creative writing, and Japanese film. We often caught each other staring. I would learn later that the catalyst for her curiosity was the fact that I was rolling into class in last night's clothing and makeup (my boyfriend played in a jazz band that often gigged out). I hadn't considered my appearance would be notable given the number of half-shirts on campus.

Three weeks into our semester of esoteric classes together, the Chestnut Pixie and I guiltily looked away from a mutual sideways glance. Up to now we'd made it clear that we intended to know one another. We'd blushed, we'd tried to impress each other with our French pronunciations, identification of "drumlin swarms," and knowledge of Japanese cinema that employed benshi narrators or the Japanese Elvis trope . . . but we had yet to properly meet. I was killing time during an excruciating four-hour break between classes—excruciating because, when not out with my boyfriend, I worked nights conducting phone surveys with Malaysian computer companies. There were few places to nap on the soggy grounds of the school. My favorite spot on days like this was the campus art museum. It was quiet and (in the absence of sleep) there was, at least, the potential of a walking nap.

During my somnambulatory tour through the museum, I marveled at the stagnant quality of the campus art collection—I needed a new place to kill time. Suddenly, a milky arm shot through the crook in mine. It wasn't forceful, but it was confident. It was the Pixie. She hooked my arm and guided us out of the museum. She tried to smile and make it seem natural, but she was awkward. The Pixie had a profound sadness to her as if her eyes had been designed to weep—I noted that it took extraordinary effort for her mouth to turn itself up at the corners. Either she was the victim of an existential crisis or an academic who'd wrongly identified happiness as a direct outgrowth of ignorance. She led me through alleys and down unfamiliar streets until we arrived at her apartment. When we got there she said she was sick, "hypoglycemia probably." She ran in for something to eat and returned having commenced eating a flour tortilla that she dragged through a tub of hummus. I stood watching as she sat on her porch resentful of her blood's sugar deficiency. At one point she pulled it from her mouth and a line of saliva held fast. She offered me none. We entered her apartment and I learned that she also had a vinyl collection with many of the rare jazz titles I had in mine. We had, what appeared to be, a lot in common.

She showed me her bedroom in which there hung a translucent plastic dress. This dress suggested the possibility that she was more adventurous than she appeared. I was intrigued. She mentioned that she had a boyfriend, so did I, but we continued to flirt. She did not smell like patchouli.

In the months that followed, every man in my life would fall head over heels for my new friend—she was beautiful and we were all still young enough to believe that there was nothing more alluring than a sad woman.

Our friendship continued on that thin line between envy and desire—the occasional fruit of the female bond. We spent every day together; we sat together in class, we attended my boyfriend's shows, we skipped class and hiked or soaked at the McCredie hot spring. I had found my kindred spirit. A few months before summer break in the first year of our friendship, I informed the Pixie that my boyfriend had been accepted to medical school near my family in Wisconsin and that my grandfather was dying. She saw neither as plausible justifications for a move and promptly quit speaking to me.

It wasn't until the night of my going-away party that she finally appeared. I was found forcing some

Jess-

I wish I could be there for your birthday, but, alas, I must satisfy the asshole gods at U of O and take WR 121 + 122 this summer. Yes, it does SUCK! But hopefully I will see you in August, either here or there... Right now all I have to give you is this tape, which I tried to make as UN-depressing as possible! I love you + your collage is awesome

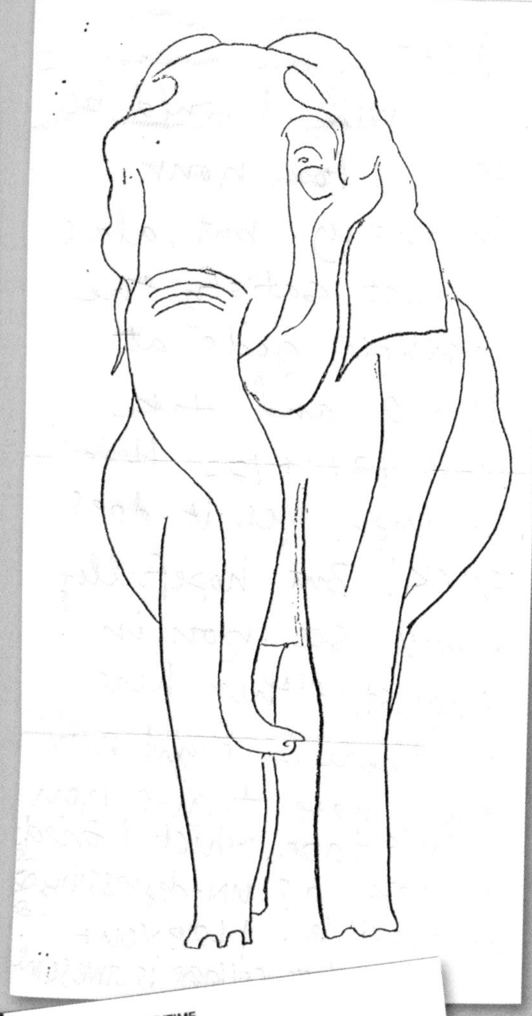

B DATE/TIME NOISE REDUCTION

TDK

Songs by hollow men (+ women)

NO CLUES!

forgotten item in the overloaded car when she arrived with her boyfriend (whom I'd never met), a hot dish, and a cassette tape. It was awkward. The party wouldn't start for an hour. The tape was an early birthday gift—I'd be in my new city by the time I actually turned twenty-one—she intended on me listening to it on the drive. It was terrible to say good-bye. She told me that it would be some time before she made it out to see me, if ever. She left my party before anyone else arrived.

The liner notes stated that it would be a while before she could visit. She blamed her class schedule but the sharp edge of that repeated declaration suggested how abandoned she felt by my departure.

I played the tape repeatedly on the drive to the Midwest and for a long time after. The mix wasn't much different from what my peers across the country were listening to, but it was a far cry from that which my peers in Eugene had been listening to. For this, I was . . . well . . . grateful. It was a montage of popular culture and included artists like Sonic Youth, The Rolling Stones, Modest Mouse, Cat Power. . . . The Pixie had done me a great service, she'd prepared me for life outside of Eugene. It became the soundtrack to my awkward adjustment to a new town and eventually to my grandfather's death.

By midsummer she rescinded and came to visit.

SONGS BY HOLLOW MEN (+ WOMEN)

A

Sonic Youth: Crème Brûlée
Fiona Apple: Paper Bag
Modest Mouse: 3rd Planet
Sebadoh: Narrow Stories
Sebadoh: Punch in the Nose
Yo La Tengo: Cast a Shadow
Cat Power: Back of Your Head
Belle and Sebastian: Get Me Away from Here, I'm Dying
The Rolling Stones: Beast of Burden
Sonic Youth: Sunday
Stereolab: Come and Play in the Milky Night
Sebadoh: Skull
The Spinanes: Suckers Trial
Pavement: Grounded
The Sea And Cake: The Biz

B

Sonic Youth: Androgynous Mind
Lou Barlow: Cause for Celebration
Quasi: Our Happiness Is Guaranteed
Cat Power: The Coat Is Always On
Iron and Wine: March 25th 1998
Modest Mouse: Styrofoam Boots/It's All Nice on Ice, Alright
The Halo Benders: On a Tip
Yo La Tengo: Center of Gravity
Built to Spill: Car
The Rolling Stones: She's a Rainbow
David Bowie: Ziggy Stardust
Jets to Brazil: Conrad
Sentridoh and Lou Barlow: I Will Be Lonely All My Life

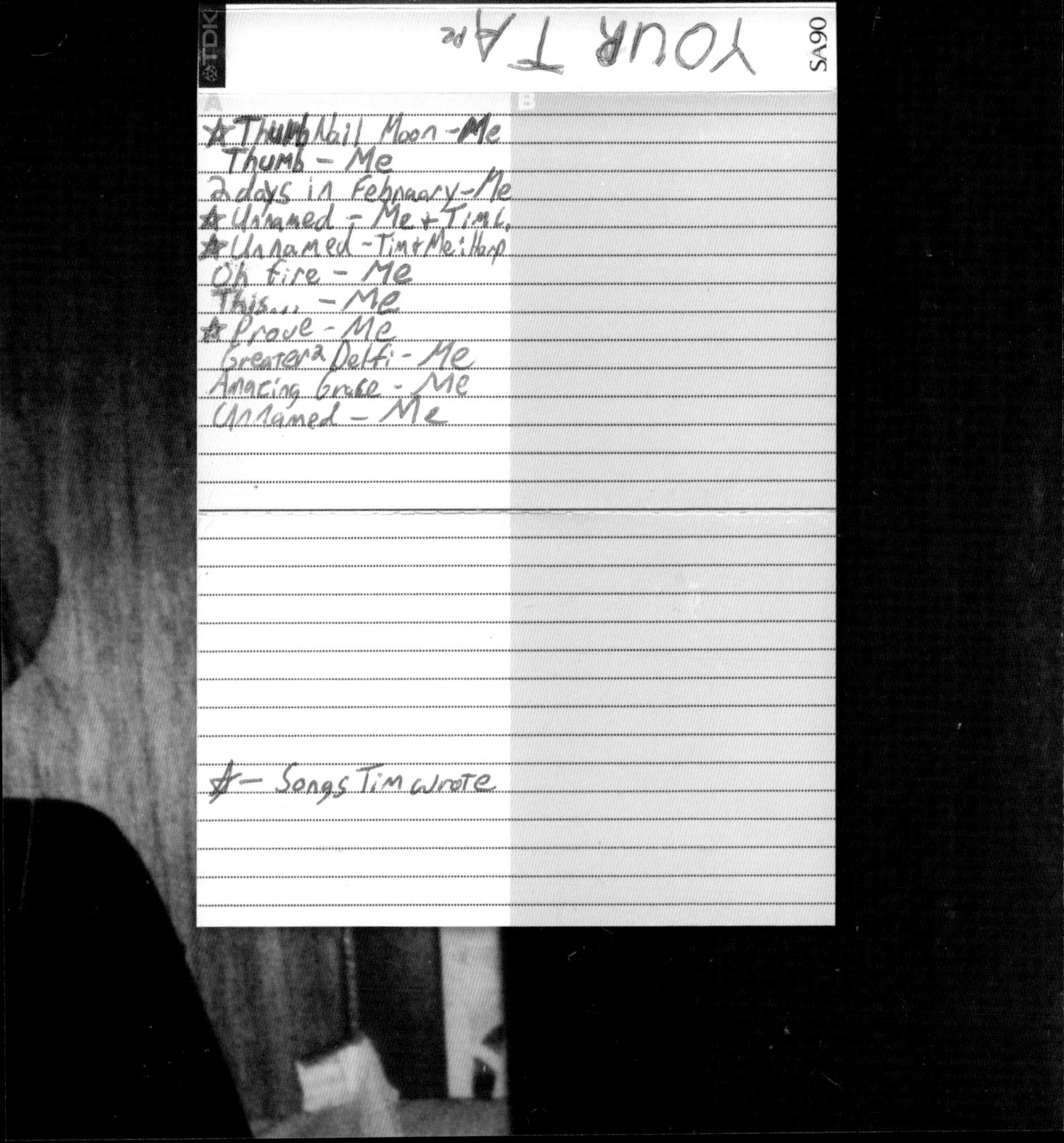

TDK

YOUR TAPE

SA90

A

☆ ~~Thumb~~ Nail Moon - Me

Thumb - Me

2 days in February - Me

☆ Unnamed - Me + Tim C.

☆ Unnamed - Tim + Me: Harp

Oh fire - Me

This... - Me

☆ Prove - Me

Greater a Delfi - Me

Amazing Grace - Me

Unnamed - Me

B

☆ - Songs Tim wrote

ME-4-YOU

BY DIANE BULLOCK

If I could relive any three-month period of my life, the summer of 1995 would easily top the list. I'd just graduated from Indiana University and was still living in Bloomington. It was my shameless plan to delay real life and adulthood and responsibility for a few months before moving to Chapel Hill where I had a grown-up job waiting for me.

I lived with four other women in an off-campus house—"house" being used in the loosest sense. Really, this place should've been condemned. Where I once walked barefoot from the mildew-ridden shower to my moldier concrete basement bedroom, I wouldn't step foot inside now without a hazmat suit. Sure it was a hovel. But it was our hovel and we loved it.

As far as my hovel mates were concerned, I had just one complaint. They'd succumbed to the pestilence that'd swept so many college campuses in the mid-'90s: Neo-hippie-itis. I could tolerate the stockpile of acid blotters in the freezer and constantly tripping over empty whippet canisters on the floor. But as an entrenched member of the indie rock camp, I drew the line at their Phish parties: the preconcert gatherings that transformed our home into an aquarium of decorative paper fish cutouts and Pepperidge Farm Goldfish crackers. I was starving for some camaraderie that wasn't riding in the H.O.R.D.E. caravan.

And then I met Mark—my breath of nitrous-free air. Mark easily met my music credentials with a resume of CDs including Pavement, Sebadoh, Archers of Loaf, Sonic Youth, Pixies, Dinosaur Jr., and though some indie purists may have sneered, Nirvana.

Unlike the rest of us, Mark wasn't a student. And while Bloomington society neatly compartmentalized all residents into students or "townies," Mark wasn't a townie either. He was a summer transplant from Chicago, just hanging out, playing music with his similarly transplanted bandmates, and working at Kroger.

Our courtship consisted of a couple nights of hanging out, drinking, and listening to music and then mutually deciding he'd spend the night. Knowing I'd be moving away at the end of the summer, I approached the romance with a "We'll always have Bloomington" tack. We'd come to spend most of our sleeping hours in my dingy basement bedroom with nothing but a cheap boombox as our sound system. But as long as we had Nirvana bootlegs as our soundtrack, we'd happily inhale asbestos all night.

Contrast this with my previous deadhead boyfriend who took to mocking me for my Nirvana fanship. The day Kurt Cobain died, he actually waited outside my psychology class to be sure he was the one to give me the news in a "nyah, nyah" sort of way. I got him back at the end of that summer with a taunting phone call when Jerry Garcia bit it.

Despite the noncommittal relationship plan, Mark and I ended up getting serious. After I left Bloomington for Chapel Hill, he poured his heart out on his 4-track, creating the most intense

and personal mixtape anyone has ever made me: ME-4-YOU. In the grand scheme of mixtapes, it's pretty short at eleven songs but since he played guitar and sang on each track and even gave sentimental yet goofy commentary in between, I cut him some slack. Plus, according to Mark's commentary, it sounded like some of the tracks took a grueling number of takes. The starred tracks were originals written by the lead singer of his band. The rest were his own acoustic covers of songs by Dinosaur Jr., Sebadoh, and Goo Goo Dolls, which we both loved.

ME–4–YOU

A
DATE
N.R. ○ YES ○ NO.

Mark Walsh: Thumbnail Moon
Mark Walsh: Thumb
Mark Walsh: 2 Days in February
Mark Walsh and Tim Lotesto: Unnamed
Mark Walsh and Tim Lotesto: Unnamed
Mark Walsh: Oh Fire
Mark Walsh: This . . .
Mark Walsh: Prove
Mark Walsh: Greater Delta
Mark Walsh: Amazing Grace
Mark Walsh: Unnamed

B
DATE
N.R. ○ YES ○ NO.

If there's an opposite condition to compulsive hoarding, I've got it. I'm a purger. I loathe clutter. I move practically every two years so I do my damnedest to rid myself of crap that I'll only have to schlep to the next new tiny apartment. The fact that I've kept this tape over the last fourteen years is a testament to its impact. And it means that much more now that I'm able to give it its proper due. Now it's ME-4-YOU . . . -4-YOU.

KICKING AND SCREAMING INTO THE MAINSTREAM

BY KARA ZUARO

By the time this tape traveled from Nome, Alaska, to my dorm room at Notre Dame in Indiana, Andrew was already my ex . . . but not *exactly* my ex-boyfriend.

For a few semesters, Andrew was often the last person I spoke to at night, before I drifted off to sleep in my all-girls building on our pious, Catholic campus. From the other end of the telephone line, in his boys' dorm just across the quad, he'd always say, "Good night, Kara Zuaro." In my mental picture of him, he is forever bundled in olive-green fleece and his smile glows blurrily, like an overexposed photo. But I can still hear his warm, mellow voice saying my name as clearly as I can recall the chorus of my favorite song (which incidentally, is *not* on this tape).

I met Andrew when I was writing an article about his comedy troupe. They called themselves the Humor Artists (aka) HA—oh, already a bad joke). When my story came out, he took me out for fajitas and margaritas at the local Chili's with the rest of the comedy guys and covered for my portion of the bill. Soon, we were signing up for the same English classes, going to the movies, talking about books over endless pints of Guinness, meeting up for lunch at the dining hall, and going to off-campus parties together. He even came to meet my parents during Christmas break.

Our relationship was perfect, aside from two red flags which I conveniently ignored: (1) He was a huge fan of Sarah McLachlan, and no matter how many indie rock CDs I lent him, I wasn't able to show him the light; (2) We barely touched at all.

This troubled me as much as it intrigued me. I was coming out of a Long Island public school system where the Italian stallions had started wearing gold chains, growing facial hair, and chasing tail in sixth grade. I had no experience with innocent Midwestern boys. So, I heeded the advice of my naïve, optimistic, good Catholic girlfriends when they told me to wait for Andrew. Maybe he was still torn up about his breakup with his high school girlfriend. Maybe he was shy. Maybe I should be *happy* that I found someone sensitive enough to appreciate Sarah McLachlan! Needless to say, those girls aren't my friends anymore, but at the time, they were all I had.

Then one night, Andrew and I were at my favorite bar when the girl whom I referred to as That Tammy Faye Bakker Thing came and sat on Andrew's lap and started kissing his neck. She was a Georgia peach from our Southern Fiction class whose wardrobe was a collection of undersized schoolgirl uniforms. She wore more mascara than anyone I've ever seen, and her drawl was as sultry as a summer night in Savannah. Until that moment, I kind of liked her.

But in a split second, TTFBT's boyfriend threw her off Andrew's lap, grabbed Andrew by the throat, and accused him of sleeping with her. I stunned the guy by screaming some supremely threatening obscenities in his face (thanks, public high school!) and quickly whisked Andrew out of the bar.

Once outside, Andrew apologized. He *did* spend the night with That Tammy Faye Bakker Thing. This put an end to our late-night phone calls.

Andrew graduated a year before me and moved to Alaska to work at a "sorta Christian" radio station, which is where he recorded this tape. I was surprised to receive it, since we didn't keep in touch. As I skimmed the track list, I noticed that his overall taste hadn't improved, but he did include "I Don't Want to Get Over You" by the Magnetic Fields, one of the bands I'd pushed upon him. Now, it's fair to argue that *most* Magnetic Fields songs are about yearning for a lost love, but if you're making a mix for an ex, it would be in better taste to choose one with a more subtle title—such as "Deep Sea Diving Suit," "When You're Old and Lonely," "All the Umbrellas in London," or, better yet, "Flowers She Sent and the Flowers She Said She Sent."

Andrew's bold song choice made me wonder. Was he asking for a second chance? I closed my window to seal out the chilling squeaks of the guy practicing bagpipes behind my dorm (I'm telling you, Notre Dame was a weird place), popped the tape in my stereo, and begrudgingly pressed the Play button.

I expected the opening strains of the Cure's "Mint Car," but instead, some cheesy background music and Andrew's voice, with all its familiar NPR-ish charm, piped into my room: "Hey Kara, this is Andrew." He didn't seem to have much to say as he introduced the first track, but then his voice came on again, leading into a cringe-worthy adult alternative pop song by Sarah Harmer. ("She's no Sarah McLachlan, but she's alright," he said.) The song was about a woman who'd been mistreated by her man. Geez, after all the

Archers of Loaf and Lemonheads records I'd sent his way, Andrew couldn't *possibly* think I'd enjoy this crap. What was the meaning of this? Was I supposed to listen to the lyrics? Was he trying to send me a message?

I sat through Paul Simon's "The Obvious Child." (Really? *That* was the best Paul Simon song he could come up with?) But I just couldn't stand the Barenaked Ladies. I got up to hit the Fast-forward button but froze when I realized what the song was about—a man who wanted to get on a plane and beg forgiveness from a woman he'd done wrong. Wait a minute. Maybe this was a fake out. Andrew *knew* how much I hated this band. Maybe he would mercifully cut the song off early, come back on the mic, and tell me that he'd made a big mistake. Maybe he was testing me to see if I'd listen all the way through. Maybe this tape was his way of telling me he'd loved me all along.

Hey, I'd spent about a year of my life trying to figure out if this guy liked me or not, and even after he got with That Tammy Faye Bakker Thing, I wasn't convinced that he didn't have feelings for me. He sent me this tape during the year that everyone was wearing those WWJD bracelets, and since I was trying to get in the Notre Dame spirit and open my heart to the Lord (without actually going to church or anything), I decided that Jesus would want me to sit tight and listen for clues.

It was ninety minutes of torture. Andrew played the whole Barenaked Ladies song and a few more throwaway alt-rock tracks. When he included solid songwriters—Elvis Costello, Neil Young, and Peter Gabriel—he managed to dig up their most boring tunes. I don't know what Wyclef and the

Roots are doing on this tape, but he even made them sound weak.

At one point, he dubbed in a Casey Kasem dedication about a friendship that was marred by a brief romantic affair. But then he dubbed the words "Country Grammar" over the name of the dedicated song, and Nelly's painful Top-40 hit began to play. I angrily listened to the whole track, just in case Andrew cut it short to say something that I might want to hear. He didn't.

He blabs into the mic throughout, but his only explanation for making the cassette was this: "You know I was just thinking of you the other day and was wondering how you're doing and thinking I might as well make you a tape and put my voice on it with the Perry Mason theme in the background, you know, stuff like that." As the tape ran out, I should've breathed a sigh of relief. I should have shoved it back in its case, opened my window, and used it to bean that obnoxious bagpiper.

Instead, I curled up on my couch and cried.

A TAPE FOR KARA ZUARO

A
DATE
N.R. ○YES ○NO.

The Cure: Mint Car
Sarah Harmer: Around this Corner
Paul Simon: The Obvious Child
Barenaked Ladies: Go Home
Tom Petty and the Heartbreakers: Into the Great Wide Open
Cry Cry Cry: Down by the Water
10,000 Maniacs: More than This
Wyclef Jean featuring The Rock & Melky Sedeck: It Doesn't Matter
Toad the Wet Sprocket: Brother
The Magnetic Fields: I Don't Want to Get Over You
The Beatles: Blackbird
The Roots: Adrenaline!
Elliot Smith: Waltz #2

B
DATE
N.R. ○YES ○NO.

Nelly: Country Grammar
Sinead O'Connor: You Put Your Arms Around Me
Blues Traveler: All in the Groove
Elvis Costello: Long Journey Home
David Firth: Yea God!
Black 47: Oh Maureen
The Pretenders: Chain Gang
Thea Gilmore: The Resurrection Man
Peter Gabriel: That'll Do
Zucchero: No More Regrets
Neil Young: Good to See You

"JOHN" TAPE, CIRCA 1986

BY CLAUDIA GONSON

John was my boyfriend from age fifteen to nineteen or so, i.e., my entire high school career. These of course are the years where music leaves a passionate, indelible mark on the core of your being. It's hard for me to comment on these songs (or some of them, anyway) without wanting to shout, "Oh my God, this is the most amazing song EVER!!"

Which is why I am so grateful to John. I met John in the summer of 1983. A few days later, I introduced him to Stephin, my best friend who later became my lifelong bandmate. They were both older than me, and musically precocious. I was a little doe-eyed kid who had only heard of the Beatles. The day they met, they immediately had an argument over which Lindsey Buckingham solo album was the best. I was scared they hated one another, but it turned out this is how some boys show how much they like one another. The conversation then turned to Yoko Ono, and it went on, for months, years . . . Who got the latest single from Flying Nun, or Rough Trade, or Cherry Red? Who had the cool newest solo project from David Roback of the Rain Parade? (See the "Clay Allison" track. They were then renamed Opal, and eventually morphed into Mazzy Star.) We got fake IDs in Times Square, and went to see our favorite bands live, including the Bangles, Game Theory, the Chills, and The Three O' Clock.

It was clear to me that I needed lessons: "What's the difference between the Rain Parade, The Raincoats, and Rainy Day?" These two men infused me with more information in a month than I could have gotten in years by myself. John would buy the first three Bee Gees' albums and then make me a mixtape of the best songs. All I think I discovered for him during our years together was the Smiths and R.E.M.

Anyway, I am grateful beyond words for John and his mixtapes (and Stephin, too, of course). I am certain I would not be the person I am today had I not had this orthodox musical education. I'd probably be a banker or something.

John also showed me how to listen to production. He sat me down on the bed one day and put on the Archies "Sugar Sugar." "Listen," he said, "to the first verse. What instruments do you hear? Do you hear that tambourine coming in on the second verse? That tambourine on the second verse is the first rule of classic bubblegum production!"

Like many mixtape artists, John worked hard to time out each song so that the tape wouldn't have any remaining space at the end. He also began and ended side A of this particular tape with a song featuring the chimes of Big Ben (the Chills and Cheap Trick).

So many of these songs have stories and memories connected to them, I could write a story for each (in fact, John sent me a marvelous email in which he did just that). And, while I don't want to sound like that person . . . but what the hell, I will—some of these songs are the BEST SONGS ON EARTH. EVER EVER EVER.

JOHN TAPE

A DATE N.R. ○ YES ○ NO.

The Chills: Doldrums
The Byrds: Here Without You
Alice Cooper: Be My Lover
AC/DC: Sink the Pink
The Craig: I Must Be Mad
Human Sexual Response: Marone Moan
The Velvet Underground: Stephanie Says
Flipper: Get Away
The Undertones: Family Entertainment
Algebra Suicide: Somewhat Bleeker Street
Leonard Cohen: Seems So Long Ago, Nancy
Clay Allison: Fell from the Sun
Bobbie Gentry: Mississippi
The Everly Brothers: Love Hurts
Cheap Trick: Clock Strikes Ten

B DATE N.R. ○ YES ○ NO.

Yoko Ono: Walking on Thin Ice
Aerosmith: Uncle Salty
Weekend: Sleepy Theory
Three O'Clock: Hand in Hand
Steppenwolf: Tighten Up Your Wig
Dolly Parton: I Will Always Love You
The Zulus: Back to Sleep
The Meat Puppets: Split Myself in Two
Bee Gees: The Earnest of Being George
Gary Lewis: Me About You
Died Pretty: Laughing Boy
The B-52s: Dirty Back Road
Game Theory: Waltz the Halls
The Archies: Suddenly Susan

TYPE II · BIAS: CrO2 / EQ: 70μs

FR-II 90

A

I'm Sticking With You (Velvet Un-
derground) Don't Sit Under the
Apple Tree × Under a Blanket of
Blue × At Last × Serenade in
Blue × Anvil Chorus × 5 o'clock
Whistle × I Want To Be Happy
(Glenn Miller.) Hobo You
Can't Ride This Train × I Hate To Leave
You Now × (You So and So) You'll Wish You'd
Never Been Born × When You're Smiling -
St. James Infirmary - Dinah × (I'll be
glad when you're dead) You Rascal You -

B

Andy's Chest × She's My Best
Friend × Lisa Says* × I Can't
Stand It. (Velvet Underground)
Sweet Sue, Just You × I Wonder
Who* × Snowball × Swing You
Cats × Honey Don't You Love Me
Anymore × Laughin' Louie ×
He's a Son of the South × Some Swe-
et Day × Basin Street Blues ×
Honey Do. (Louis Armstrong)
County Jail Blues × Tell it
to the Judge Part 2

I'M STICKING WITH YOU

BY DAMON LOCKS

I have always been a guy who passes around music—I was more the giver than the getter of tapes. So I don't have a lot of tapes from ex-girlfriends, but I did get a few. This tape is from my ex, Sue Anne. I was about seventeen when we met.

We were both in a magnet art program in high school, which was a hub of creative youngsters. Sue Anne was a quiet girl, an excellent artist. She regularly wore stretched-out V-necked sweaters and her hair (natural color) was like spiked-out wings on the side and an overgrown devil lock in the front. Very cute.

The early stage of our relationship had its share of tumult. We dated then broke up. Young hearts confuse easily. (These things are still not easy to negotiate.) I dated someone else. I moved away to college. That relationship ended. She dated other people. She came up to visit. We wrote letters sent in packages in unusual shapes and textures, littered with drawings rife with emotional subtext. The drawings were sometimes dark and mournful, sometime agitated and jagged. This was the climate in which I received this tape.

Filled with jazz, big band, and the Velvet Underground, the tape captures nicely the juxtaposition of our music tastes. I was knee-deep in the U.K. late '70s/early '80s punk/post punk scene (The Clash, The

~~[crossed out]~~ When it's Sleeptime
down South – Nobody's SWEETHEART.
(Young louis ARMSTRONG.)

(EXCERPT BECAUSE I
cant tape over and its
3:30 AM Sorry.)
– Judge sentanced Her 30 days
But that wont make Her
cry she'll come out
& gamble & sell moonshine
all Her life.
(By Funny PAPA SMITH.)

* I didnt mean To Tape this
SONG But too lATE cuz OF MY
loser Machine.

Stranglers, The Ruts, etc.) and going to D.C. shows like Minor Threat, Scream, and Void. She was more comfortable with folk music and was interested in early jazz well before I was (I remember seeing Grateful Dead records in her early collection; she will probably be mad I mentioned this).

It also captured the strained but continued magnetic attraction lingering just below the surface. Songs like, "I'm Sticking with You" and "Don't Sit Under the Apple Tree (With Anyone Else But Me)" were received like torturous love poems. "Sweet Sue, Just You" . . . I think the message there was obvious. "Honey Don't You Love Me Anymore?" and "I Want to Be Happy" seemed to echo the messages encoded in our drawings. The magic of Glenn Miller's "Serenade in Blue" still haunts me to this day. The songs were hopeful yet miserable at the same time.

We eventually got back together (and stayed together for seven years), but this tape illustrates, without charcoal or paint, the confusion in our young lives. When listening I can still hear the sad and hopeful messages that made their indelible impact on my psyche.

I'M STICKING WITH YOU

DATE
N.R. ○ YES ○ NO.

Velvet Underground: I'm Sticking with You
Glenn Miller: Don't Sit Under the Apple Tree (With Anyone Else but Me)
Glenn Miller: Under a Blanket of Blue
Glenn Miller: At Last
Glenn Miller: Serenade in Blue
Glenn Miller: Anvil Chorus
Glenn Miller: 5 O'Clock Whistle
Glenn Miller: I Want to Be Happy
Louis Armstrong: Hobo You Can't Ride this Train
Louis Armstrong: I Hate To Leave You Now
Louis Armstrong: You'll Wish You'd Never Been Born
Louis Armstrong: When You're Smiling
Louis Armstrong: St. James Infirmary
Louis Armstrong: Dinah
Louis Armstrong: (I'll Be Glad When You're Dead) You Rascal You
Louis Armstrong: When It's Sleeptime Down South
Louis Armstrong: Nobody's Sweetheart

B
DATE
N.R. ○ YES ○ NO.

Velvet Underground: Andy's Chest
Velvet Underground: She's My Best Friend
Velvet Underground: Lisa Says
Velvet Underground: I Can't Stand It
Louis Armstrong: Sweet Sue, Just You
Louis Armstrong: I Wonder Who
Louis Armstrong: Snowball
Louis Armstrong: Swing You Cats
Louis Armstrong: Honey, Don't You Love Me Anymore?
Louis Armstrong: Laughin' Louie
Louis Armstrong: He's a Son of the South
Louis Armstrong: Some Sweet Day
Louis Armstrong: Basin Street Blues
Louis Armstrong: Honey Do
J. T. "Funny Papa" Smith: County Jail Blues
J. T. "Funny Papa" Smith: Tell It to the Judge Part 2

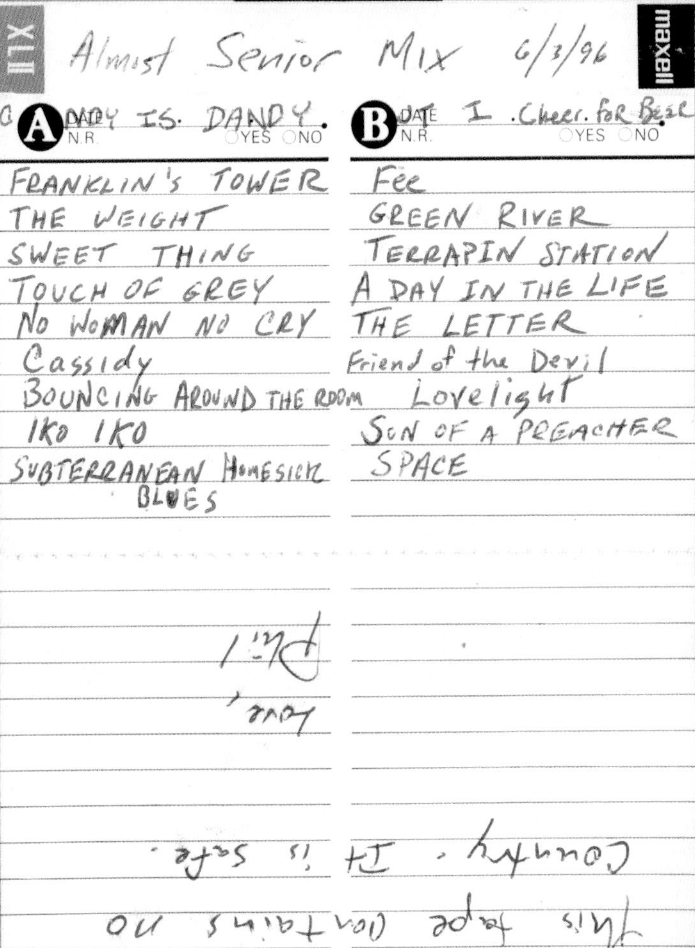
maxell
XLII
POSITION
IEC TYPE II • HIGH (CrO2)
Almost Senior Mix 6/3/96
FRANKLIN'S TOWER
THE WEIGHT
SWEET THING
TOUCH OF GREY
NO WOMAN NO CRY
Cassidy
BOUNCING AROUND THE ROOM
IKO IKO
SUBTERRANEAN HOMESICK BLUES
Fee
GREEN RIVER
TERRAPIN STATION
A DAY IN THE LIFE
THE LETTER
Friend of the Devil
Lovelight
SON OF A PREACHER
SPACE
love,
Phil
This tape contains no Country. It is safe.

Almost Senior Mix

By Jamie Wetherbe

Phil was my high school crush, my prom date, my last innocent relationship. We were barely seventeen, living in the suburbs of the Midwest.

Even at this young age, Phil had a taste for the classics—most of the Almost Senior Mix songs were written well before we were born. We were '90s high school hippies (all tie-dyed and hempy) and the tape is full of Marley, Dylan, Phish, and the Grateful Dead. To be honest, I couldn't stand some of Phil's music: "Space" sounds like something John Cage would have composed while stoned, and a few minutes into the sixteen-minute "Terrapin Station," I was ready to hit Fast-forward. But I pretended to like it all, because I liked him.

Some of his music remains my comfort food. Dusty Springfield's "Son of a Preacher Man" and Van Morrison's "Sweet Thing" will always remind me of the last day of school our junior year, camping together under a Minnesota moon. The mix isn't laden with love songs—most are songs of searching, like "Touch of Grey" by the Grateful Dead or The Band's "The Weight," which are best listened to with your eyes closed. And then there are the strange songs—The Beatles' "A Day in the Life," the Dead's "Cassidy" and Dylan's "Subterranean Homesick Blues"—best listened to with your eyes open.

The top of the tape reads, CANDY IS DANDY and BUT I CHEER FOR BEER. Phil's way of saying side A and side B. That was Phil: A night with him usually ended with empty beer bottles and "Free Bird" on the stereo.

For a year I was at his side. And for years I felt I paled in comparison—I never felt like the blue-eyed crowd-pleaser that he was. He took the advanced classes; he played football; he had all the friends. I felt far too quiet to shine in high school—if Phil and I were to compete in a popularity contest, I was certain he would win. So I took to chasing after his attentions, like he was an absentee father.

The chase got old, and we broke up senior year and the painful high school exchanges followed as we navigated the same group of friends. We went our separate ways after graduation—I headed south to school in Iowa to write, while he headed farther south to Northwestern to become an environmental engineer and save the world with his brains and charm.

After that, our interactions were kept to awkward small talk or silence during holiday breaks.

The last time I saw Phil alive was at a friend's house party, and we did our standard dance: I chased, he sat stoic, and everyone drank beer. Somewhere around 3 A.M., he was passing out on the couch and I was getting ready to leave. I put a blanket on him. "From me to you," I said. And he smiled his Phil smile and there was a comfort between us I hadn't felt in years.

Phil died a few weeks later in a car accident between two off-the-map towns in Australia. It was the summer before his senior year of college.

The last time I saw Phil, he wore a suit and tie inside a coffin—for many of my high school friends, it was our first funeral and we were burying one of our own. Phil was going into the ground.

Phil's been gone almost ten years. Sometimes it seems rude for the world to have gone on that long without him. And still I have his tape. Looking at it again all these years later, I found a drawing of a turtle hidden inside—I guess in reference to the turtles on the Dead's *Terrapin Station* album cover.

Turtle has been a nickname of mine for years; I even have a turtle tattoo across my ribs. And when I saw it, I had to smile a small Phil smile—"My, my, my, my, my Sweet Thing"—perhaps this is our last silent exchange.

ALMOST SENIOR MIX
A
DATE
N.R.
YES NO.
The Grateful Dead: Franklin's Tower
The Band: The Weight
Van Morrison: Sweet Thing
The Grateful Dead: Touch of Grey
Bob Marley: No Woman, No Cry
The Grateful Dead: Cassidy
Phish: Bouncing Around the Room
The Grateful Dead: Iko Iko
Bob Dylan: Subterranean Homesick Blues
B
DATE
N.R.
YES NO.
Phish: Fee
Creedence Clearwater Revival: Green River
The Grateful Dead: Terrapin Station
The Beatles: A Day in the Life
Joe Cocker: The Letter
The Grateful Dead: Friend of the Devil
The Grateful Dead: Turn on Your Love Light
Dusty Springfield: Son of a Preacher Man
The Grateful Dead: Space
maxell
XLII
POSITION
IEC TYPE II • HIGH
XLII
A DATE
N.R.
YES NO
B DATE
N.R.
YES

GHOST TAPE BY CAT MIHOS

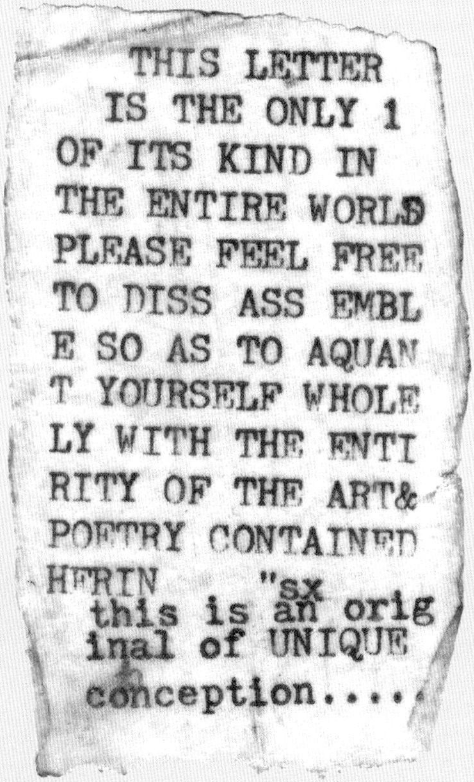

THIS LETTER
IS THE ONLY 1
OF ITS KIND IN
THE ENTIRE WORLD
PLEASE FEEL FREE
TO DISS ASS EMBL
E SO AS TO AQUAN
T YOURSELF WHOLE
LY WITH THE ENTI
RITY OF THE ART&
POETRY CONTAINED
HERIN "sx
this is an orig
inal of UNIQUE
conception....

It started with some letters in the mail from a tall redheaded sailor.

I hand-make a line of one-of-a-kind collage postcards that were sold in a tiny boutique in San Diego. The store owner, a friend of mine, had my photo up on her wall as the artist. The sailor asked her for my mailing address, and he would buy my art cards, sending them back to me along with other interesting postcards he would find on his travels. He also sent me elaborate art-letters, even one made from a pack of rolling papers. The amount of time and effort that went into these creations stirred my romantic moonlit heart.

He began to compile mixtapes for me, telling me there were hidden messages inside the songs. His cassettes put the nail in the coffin. The musical choices were terrific, as I have always been a seeker of new music, but it was more the effort I noticed—the time spent on something

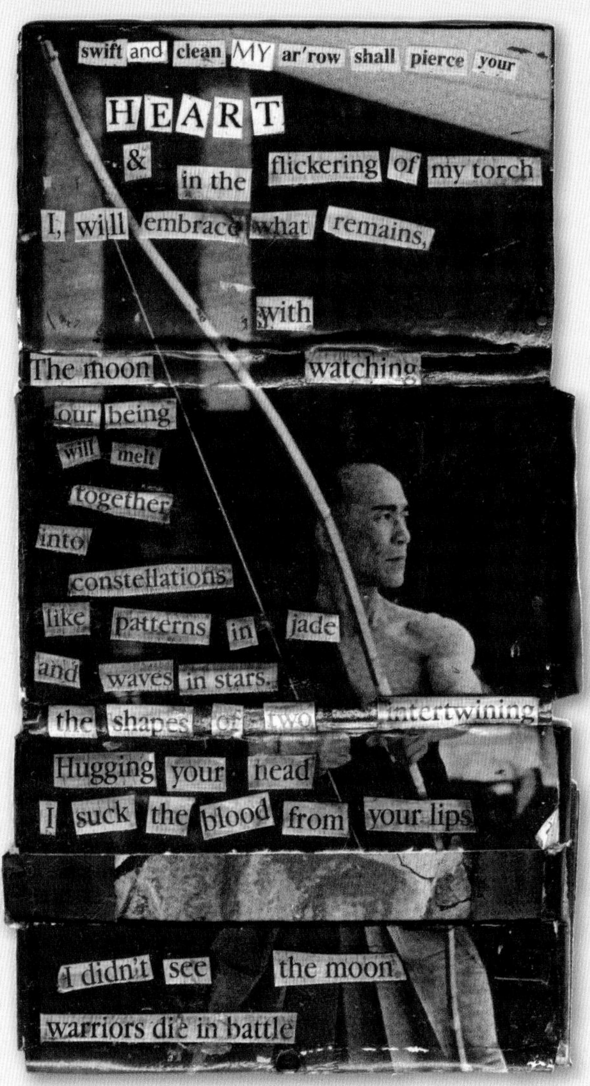
swift and clean MY ar'row shall pierce your
HEART
& in the flickering of my torch
I, will embrace what remains,
with
The moon watching
our being
will melt
together
into
constellations
like patterns in jade
and waves in stars.
the shapes of two intertwining
Hugging your head
I suck the blood from your lips
I didn't see the moon
warriors die in battle

Why does the smell of death trail
I want to fill
I want to be filled
I'll follow the final bird
when my ancestors call me to return

made just for me. He even unscrewed the tiny hardware on the cassette edges to put artwork inside the protective plastic of the case. These tiny details were the dealmaker. The universal code for new love interest was the mixtape, this I knew to be true.

Later, he confessed to putting an actual ritualistic spell upon me, which made sense, in hindsight, in light of the way I acted. We didn't actually meet in person until a year later, when I returned from a four-month backpacking trip through Europe and Africa with my best friend, Anne. (I spent my twenty-fifth birthday on the pyramids of Giza.)

He came to see me in Rehoboth Beach in the off-season and I fell in with him. I leave out the word "love" on purpose; I simply "fell in" with him. I severed ties with my lover in Chicago, in a way I have never been able to comprehend, completely coldly. In a way that I wouldn't act in my normal state of mind . . . I guess that spell proved itself very effective. That three-day visit never ended, not for years. We moved in together. I didn't know much about him, save that he had a gift for art and a mysterious past. He didn't like to talk about himself, preferring instead to tell me stories of the sea, with his tattoos as a reference guide. My close friends did not like him; they observed I wasn't acting like myself and told me so. It was a classic case of him closing me off from the outside world, and me letting him. We lived in the remotest part of Lewes, Delaware, a walk away from the beach, with nothing else around. My cat, Torval, was my only companion in those long lonely winters. I now believe Torv was made up of part psychic blotter paper to protect me, absorbing some of the vampiric aspects of the relationship.

I traveled for my job. We spent time apart, which led to unbalanced shouting matches and a physical tearing apart of our cocoon. I began, rightly, to suspect an affair on his part with the girlfriend of a close friend. We parted ways and later he told me he sat outside a bar in his van, waiting for me and my new man to exit, cradling a gun in his

hand, asking the great spirits for the will-power not to use it. On us, not on himself.

He died some years later, a sad ending to a tortured artist, and at the time I wasn't able to cry for him. I do not hold him in anger, as his death could have been mine; I wrote this as a letting go, an exorcism of sorts. His family, when I did finally meet them, were good and caring people; his death tore a hole in them.

I found this cassette recently, one of many gifts that he poured himself into. The demons chasing him caught up with him.

With this, I'm now able to cry for him. Rest in peace, little ghost.

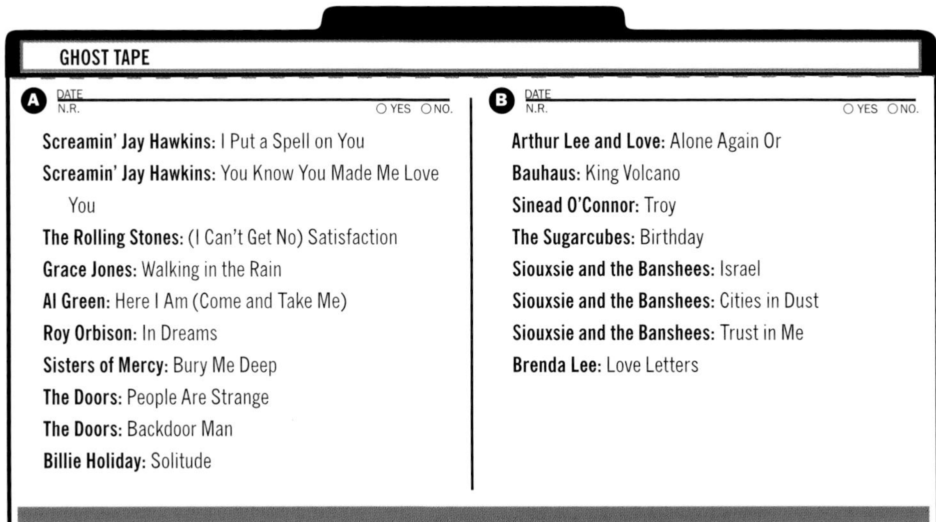

GHOST TAPE

A DATE
N.R. ○ YES ○ NO.

Screamin' Jay Hawkins: I Put a Spell on You
Screamin' Jay Hawkins: You Know You Made Me Love You
The Rolling Stones: (I Can't Get No) Satisfaction
Grace Jones: Walking in the Rain
Al Green: Here I Am (Come and Take Me)
Roy Orbison: In Dreams
Sisters of Mercy: Bury Me Deep
The Doors: People Are Strange
The Doors: Backdoor Man
Billie Holiday: Solitude

B DATE
N.R. ○ YES ○ NO.

Arthur Lee and Love: Alone Again Or
Bauhaus: King Volcano
Sinead O'Connor: Troy
The Sugarcubes: Birthday
Siouxsie and the Banshees: Israel
Siouxsie and the Banshees: Cities in Dust
Siouxsie and the Banshees: Trust in Me
Brenda Lee: Love Letters

DOS AND DON'TS:

Know the Guidelines: Below are a set of dos and don'ts, which are crucial for quality mix-making. Don't be one of those "rules-are-meant-to-be-broken" knuckleheads. Your audience is going to make personal judgments based on your musical creation—and there's a good chance that the mix will live on much longer than your relationship. Take the utmost care while crafting this gem, and use this helpful guide. Your reputation is at stake.

DO:

Do make a tape to woo a possible love. It's like flowers or jewelry, but personal. The gesture will make your intentions known, and it's rarely creepy.

Do use your own music collection. A mix is supposed to be from you—it's impersonal to borrow someone else's collection for this endeavor. Don't be a phony!

Do start exactly five seconds into the tape. There should be no space between the end of the leader tape and the beginning of the magnetic tape. The first song should begin immediately. If you screw this up the first time, rewind and try again.

Do begin side A with (a) a zinger; nothing says I love you like a two-minute corker or (b) a well-chosen piece of dialog. This could be earnest or ironic. These snippets are often chosen from children's records or random thrift store finds.

Do pay attention to audio levels. Keep the levels consistent from song to song so your listener doesn't have to keep reaching for the volume knob.

Do be watchful of the silence between songs. Songs should have two to five seconds between—no more than this unless it's a conceptual tape, or a dumb joke.

Do fill each side with audio all the way to the end. Consider these last few minutes of the tape as carefully as you consider the first minutes. Just make sure you don't cut off the last song.

Do pop the tabs when you're finished. This safety feature ensures the survival of the mix (unless the recipient puts a piece of tape over the openings, rendering your efforts endangered).

Do include original artwork, even if it's just star stickers. The more detailed you make the artwork, the more it shows you care.

DON'T:

Don't use 100-minute tapes. Choose only 60- or 90-minute tapes.

Don't record over a used tape. Songs may bleed through to your new mix. Unless you're going for this effect, you're screwed.

Don't record two songs off a source album in a row. There's been considerable chatter about whether to put multiple songs by the same artist on a tape, but as you can see on many playlists, this guideline is often ignored. Just make sure you never record consecutive songs off an album, as it just seems lazy.

Don't be too consistent. Make sure there's some dynamics on there, unless the tape is "Songs to Sleep To." In this particular instance, no surprises.

Don't make the same tape for multiple lovers or re-gift a mix. If they ever find out, it's over. If they discover it years later, your reputation will be compromised. And they always find out.

Don't use Dolby noise reduction. It never really helped.

Don't forget the track listings! You're either hoarding your knowledge or lazy.

Love And Apologies

By Carrie Friedman

There's a drawer in my home that holds the dissolution of a relationship over the course of twelve years, and almost as many mixtapes. All of them were made by my high school boyfriend years ago. Some are unspooling, some missing altogether, leaving behind only their playlists. I can remember when and why he gave each one to me, over our entire relationship.

We met by a bank of pay phones in high school when I was fourteen and he was fifteen. Just three weeks after we'd officially started going out, he gave me a tape called FOREVER, FOR CARRIE. It was so elaborately decorated with his artwork, as if every stroke of his marker was trying to win my love. In between each song was his cracking voice, serenading me with sweet messages mixed in with suggestions that were really veiled commands: "You'll love this next song," and "If you don't love that last song then I'm sorry, we've got to break up."

And truth be told, aside from "Forever Young" by Alphaville (with lines such as "Let us stay young, let us live forever," that reflected our unabashed innocence at the time), I didn't much care for the music. Of course, I never told him that. My three-week-old love for him had made me deaf to our differences, musical or otherwise.

He gave me WORDS, SONGS, FOREVER a year later. The first blush of infatuation had worn off, and you could tell this both by my hapless care of that cassette and his slightly less invested cover artwork (a simple Polaroid of himself trying to look meaningfully deep). I was almost sixteen and secretly starting to wonder if there might be a better or differently suited boy for me out there in the big world of high school. This tape introduced me to Tom Petty and the song, "Free Fallin'," which remains one of my all-time favorites.

LOVE AND APOLOGIES was the sad, brooding tape (lots of The Cure) he made for me when he kissed another girl on his spring break trip to Spain. He confessed this

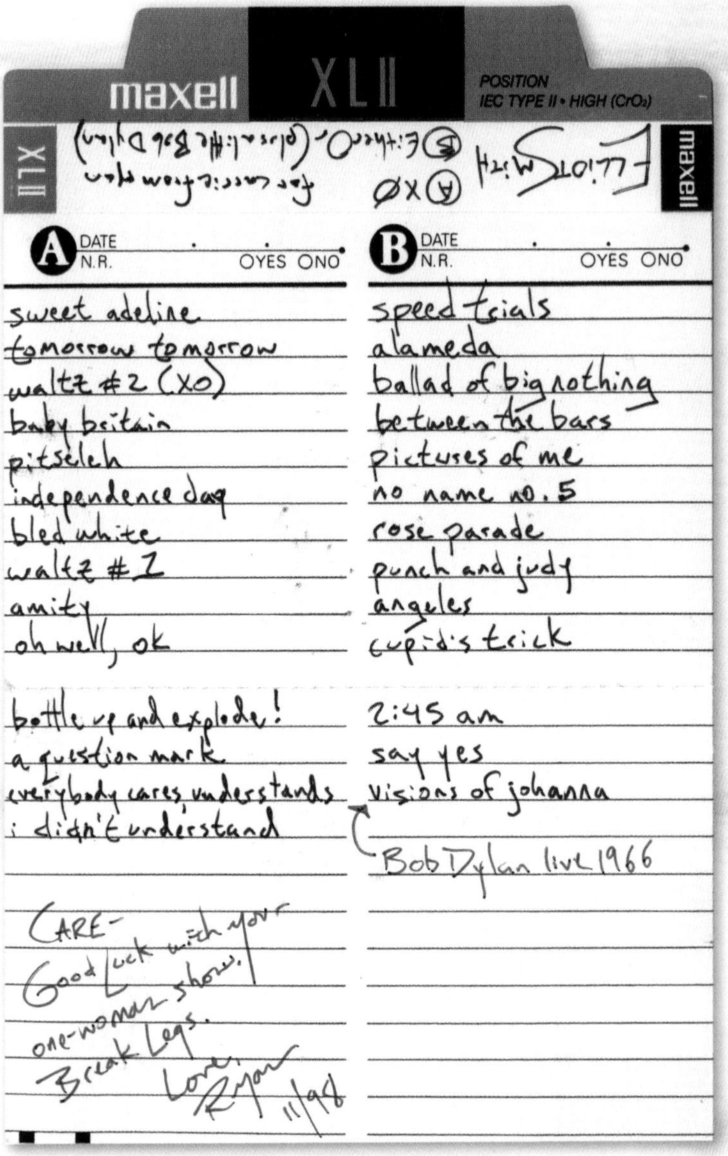

maxell XLII

POSITION
IEC TYPE II • HIGH (CrO_2)

XLII

Elliott Smith
(A) ØXO
(B) Either/Or (plus a little Bob Dylan)
for carrie from ryan

maxell

A DATE . .
N.R. OYES ONO

sweet adeline
tomorrow tomorrow
waltz #2 (XO)
baby britain
pitseleh
independence day
bled white
waltz #1
amity
oh well, ok

bottle up and explode!
a question mark
everybody cares, everybody understands
i didn't understand

CARE-
Good Luck with your
one-woman show.
Break Legs.
Love,
Ryan
11/98

B DATE . .
N.R. OYES ONO

speed trials
alameda
ballad of big nothing
between the bars
pictures of me
no name no. 5
rose parade
punch and judy
angeles
cupid's trick

2:45 am
say yes
visions of johanna

Bob Dylan live 1966

to me in my parents' basement upon his return. He cried so hard he went through an entire package of pink paisley napkins. I remember, even at the time, feeling slightly grateful for his indiscretion, giving me an out and reinforcing my own doubts about our romance.

He gave me SONGS FOR YOU when, after three years of dry-humping, our relationship had dissipated into just friendship, something we'd always been good at. He was off to college and I still had another year of high school. One of the songs was by Simon and Garfunkel, two names we'd mentioned naming our future children, years before. The song was "The Dangling Conversation," and I recall loving it most. I would later realize it mirrored our increasingly mature friendship.

Throughout our college years, his tapes stopped being mixes. Instead, they were cassette re-recordings of CDs he liked. He'd send tapes of Elliott Smith, Ben Folds Five, Bob Dylan, Cake. I'd email him once in a while to tell him about music I had found on my own—singers like Carole King and Fleetwood Mac and Joni Mitchell—all of whom he, of course, had already discovered.

The distance from him had given me some perspective on his mixtapes and, by extension, our relationship: It felt like he was never just sharing his music—he was inflicting his taste on me, trying to shape me, mold me, into the girl he wanted me to be, a female version of himself. We got along beautifully when I was playing the role of student to his teacher. But when I started asserting my own opinions and strong likes and dislikes, our friendship faltered.

A few years after college, there were no more tapes. We had grown up, grown apart. Still, whenever I hear the soaring synthesizer echoes of "Forever Young," I remember falling in lust in front of the pay phones now seventeen years ago, and how we wanted to stay young and live forever.

ELLIOT SMITH

DATE
N.R. ○ YES ○ NO.

Elliott Smith: Sweet Adeline
Elliott Smith: Tomorrow Tomorrow
Elliott Smith: Waltz #2 (xo)
Elliott Smith: Baby Britain
Elliott Smith: Pitseleh
Elliott Smith: Independence Day
Elliott Smith: Bled White
Elliott Smith: Waltz #1
Elliott Smith: Amity
Elliott Smith: Oh Well, OK
Elliott Smith: Bottle Up and Explode!
Elliott Smith: A Question Mark
Elliott Smith: Everybody Cares, Everybody Understands
Elliott Smith: I Didn't Understand

B

DATE
N.R. ○ YES ○ NO.

Elliott Smith: Speed Trials
Elliott Smith: Alameda
Elliott Smith: Ballad of Big Nothing
Elliott Smith: Between the Bars
Elliott Smith: Pictures of Me
Elliott Smith: No Name No. 5
Elliott Smith: Rose Parade
Elliott Smith: Punch and Judy
Elliott Smith: Angeles
Elliott Smith: Cupids Trick
Elliott Smith: 2:45 AM
Elliott Smith: Say Yes
Bob Dylan: Visions of Johanna (live)

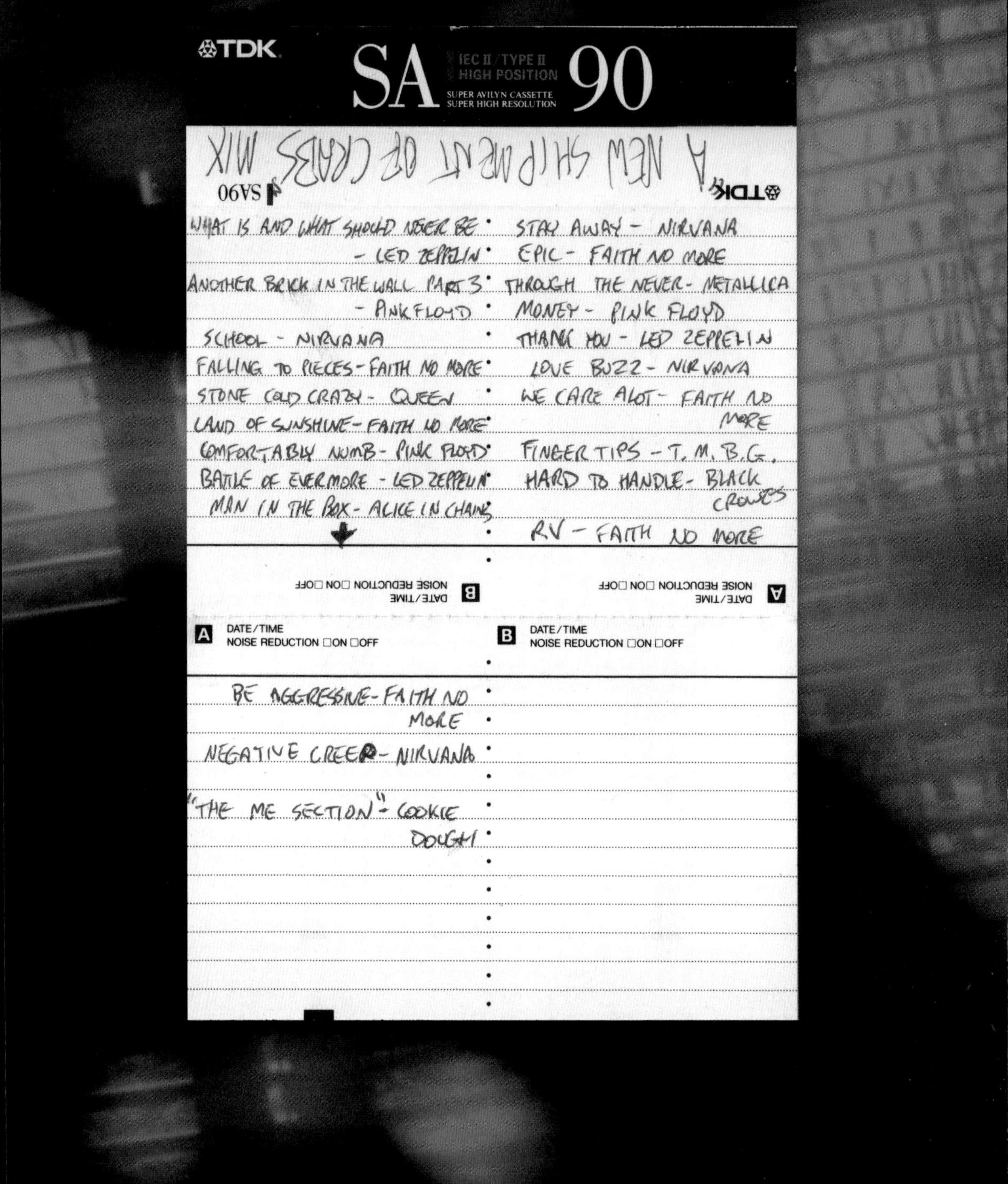

TDK SA 90

IEC II / TYPE II HIGH POSITION

SUPER AVILYN CASSETTE SUPER HIGH RESOLUTION

A NEW SHIPMENT OF CRABS MIX

TDK SA90

WHAT IS AND WHAT SHOULD NEVER BE - LED ZEPPELIN

ANOTHER BRICK IN THE WALL PART 3 - PINK FLOYD

SCHOOL - NIRVANA

FALLING TO PIECES - FAITH NO MORE

STONE COLD CRAZY - QUEEN

LAND OF SUNSHINE - FAITH NO MORE

COMFORTABLY NUMB - PINK FLOYD

BATTLE OF EVERMORE - LED ZEPPELIN

MAN IN THE BOX - ALICE IN CHAINS

STAY AWAY - NIRVANA

EPIC - FAITH NO MORE

THROUGH THE NEVER - METALLICA

MONEY - PINK FLOYD

THANK YOU - LED ZEPPELIN

LOVE BUZZ - NIRVANA

WE CARE ALOT - FAITH NO MORE

FINGER TIPS - T. M. B. G.

HARD TO HANDLE - BLACK CROWES

RV - FAITH NO MORE

B DATE/TIME NOISE REDUCTION □ON □OFF

A DATE/TIME NOISE REDUCTION □ON □OFF

A DATE/TIME NOISE REDUCTION □ON □OFF

B DATE/TIME NOISE REDUCTION □ON □OFF

BE AGGRESSIVE - FAITH NO MORE

NEGATIVE CREEP - NIRVANA

"THE ME SECTION" - COOKIE DOUGH

A NEW SHIPMENT OF CRABS MIX

BY EMILY REMS

As is so often the case with high school relationships, the early stages of my romance with Tom were rocked by indecision. It was 1992, and I was midway through my junior year at Centreville High in Northern Virginia, when I found my on-again, off-again relationship with my guy, Jim, off again. With prom looming large in the spring, I put my heartache aside, and set my sights instead on the shy senior in my Latin class. He was tall with large eyes, and had a mouth so lush and naturally pink it looked like it belonged on a girl. Before this latest breakup, I hadn't ever noticed Tom because he never spoke. But after some ballsy maneuvers that involved me asking our teacher to pair us up for a project, and a few after-school "study" sessions later, he was totally on board to take me to prom. Only as the dance approached, and I made it known that I had a supercool date, the ex took the bait and suddenly we were back together, leaving Tom in the dust.

Of course, once prom was over and college plans kicked into high gear, Jim took off for Ohio with his guitar, his books, and my virginity, and I was suddenly back on the market with a newly awakened appetite for sex and a renewed interest in Tom. He was understandably wary. But I was persistent, and by September he was totally my boyfriend. Unlike Jim, Tom wasn't headed off to college right away, which meant I could enjoy all the perks of having an older boyfriend during my senior year. He'd pick me up after drama club rehearsals in his beige Dodge Dart Swinger, and he even let me call him "Cookie Dough" around my friends. He was easygoing like that. And considerate, too, as evidenced by this mix he made me circa 1993, with a title that references a running gag I had with my best friend about crabs that he co-opted

for my enjoyment. The writing on the track listing for this quintessentially '90s assortment of cock rock and grunge is all very neat and legible. And though the songs aren't particularly romantic, he sweetly filled the space at the end of each side with chatter to keep me company. Mostly it's just him asking if I like the mix and stuff. But at the end of side A, he muses, "Maybe some day, years from now, you'll listen to this and hear my voice, and say 'Oh yeah! I remember him!'"

Which is kinda what happened when my dad unearthed this tape from my parents' basement thirteen years after Tom broke my heart. Our relationship lasted almost three years when all was said and done. After humping constantly throughout my senior year, I went away to college in Boston where I spent every free moment on the phone with him. My second year of college I was studying in Europe, which meant lots of postcard-writing and longing. But by the time I returned to Virginia that summer, things between us had changed. I wasn't sure why, until he called me up while I was moving into my junior-year dorm to tell me it was over. There was someone else. She was sixteen and lived down the street from my parents. I pictured him picking her up from school in his Dodge Dart Swinger and kinda lost my mind for a while. Looking back, I know that given our ages and the distance between us, there was little chance our love would last forever. But at the time I thought I'd never recover.

A NEW SHIPMENT OF CRABS MIX

A DATE
N.R. ○ YES ○ NO.

Led Zeppelin: What Is and What Should Never Be
Pink Floyd: Another Brick in the Wall Part 3
Nirvana: School
Faith No More: Falling to Pieces
Queen: Stone Cold Crazy
Faith No More: Land of Sunshine
Pink Floyd: Comfortably Numb
Led Zeppelin: Battle of Evermore
Alice in Chains: Man in the Box
Faith No More: Be Aggressive
Nirvana: Negative Creep
Cookie Dough: The Me Section

B DATE
N.R. ○ YES ○ NO.

Nirvana: Stay Away
Faith No More: Epic
Metallica: Through the Never
Pink Floyd: Money
Led Zeppelin: Thank You
Nirvana: Love Buzz
Faith No More: We Care a Lot
They Might Be Giants: Finger Tips
Black Crowes: Hard to Handle
Faith No More: RV

WHAT WAS YOUR BRAND?

The audio compact cassette was released and marketed in 1962 by the Philips Company of the Netherlands, primarily for dictation machines. Other companies took note, and the format quickly gained popularity for home taping. Varieties later introduced metal, chrome, and ferromagnetic tape, usually sold in lengths of 30, 45, 60, 90, 100, and 120 minutes. Some of the more popular brands are listed below, Which was your go-to?

3M
AGFA
AKAI
AMPEX
BASF
DENON
FUJI
HITACHI
JVC
MAXELL
MEMOREX
ORWO
PHILIPS
RADIO SHACK
SCOTCH
SONY
TDK
TECHNICS
THAT'S
UNIVERSUM

DAVE AND LISSI'S JUMPIN' JIVE SEXY SOUL CLASSICS MIXTAPE

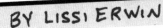

BY LISSI ERWIN

DAVE & LISSI'S JUMPIN' JIVE SEXY SOUL CLASSICS TAPE
A COOL MIX
Have you heard Dave and Lissi's new mix tape?
I sure have, and, boy, can those kids make a jumpin' jive sexy soul mix tape!

Jumpin' Jive Side

kissing my love>bill withers
cockfight>the mighty sparrow
mission impossible theme
donna/hashish>from HAIR
day tripper>sergio mendes&brazil'66
comin' home baby>herbie mann
jumpin' JIVE>cab calloway
shiek of araby>louie & thedukesofdixieland
johnny cake>virgin islands steelband
good ol'beer>the Blazers
whipped cream>tijuana brassband
john's music box>mamasandthepapas
peter gunn>henry mancini
luau>beach boys
annoyingsong>OSCARbrandANDhisHUBCAPS
thunderball>al caiola and HIS orch.
use me>stillbill withers
linus and lucy>vince guarldi
gone home>eddie harris

SEXY SOUL SIDE

minnie the moocher>CAB
jungle fever>the Tornadoes
crazy john>mighty sparrow
doNOTHIN'tilYouHearFromMe>mo(o)seAllison
won't somebody help me>firstclass
Age of aquarius>fifth dimension
o pato>sergio mendes&BRAZIL'66
buzzsaw>turtles
eleanor rigby>standells
the unicorn>IrishRovers
mood indigo>dukeellington
Funky Town>aerobic workout
HOBOFLATS>jimmy smith
wide willy>mission impossible sndtk.
YESwehaveNObananas>mitch miller
margaritaville>jimmybuffet
how sweet itis>j.taylor
mister sandman>chordells

"This is a story of a journey into sound. . . ."

From 1989 to 1993, I was in high school in Westborough, Massachusetts, a small town just outside of Worcester and forty-five minutes from Boston. My boyfriend pretty much throughout high school was a guy named Dave.

Dave (a junior) and I (a sophomore) fell for each other backstage when we were in a play called *Up the Down Staircase*—he was one of the comedic leads, and I just had a bit part where I would walk onstage every once in while to say a funny random thing and then walk off. There was a hilarious smart crew backstage, and we would all sit back there and hang out. I looked forward to this as much or more than the actual play. Dave was especially funny and sarcastic, and we ended up joking around with each other a lot.

Dave and I would drive around all over the Worcester area in his parents' blue Oldsmobile station wagon (wood on the sides) and get into suburban mischief either alone or with a car full of pals, mostly hanging out in coffee shops or

going to punk and hardcore shows at the W.A.G., a warehouse art space in Worcester where there was a scene of punk kids from all over the central Massachusetts area. We met skateboarders from Shrewsbury, and punks from Upton and Mendon, and our world grew bigger than just our small town. Dave and I would also kill time goofing around at Spags (a now-defunct discount empire in Shrewsbury with everything from fish hooks to Dickies to goldfish crackers), hanging late night at all-you-can-drink-coffee Denny's or IHOP, shopping for vintage clothes and Doc Martens at Shaky Jakes, eating late-night cheese fries at Theo's, sipping coffee with the cool kids at the Coffee Kingdom, record shopping at Newbury Comics, or driving into Boston to walk around or go to a show. We also spent a good deal of time at each other's houses hanging out and listening to records.

Dave was also in a band called F.O.E. (Friends of Ed). My friend Kelly and I would hang out at band practice (she was going out with the bass player, Pete). Somehow this was okay because Kelly and I were considered "one of the guys," something we took as a compliment. F.O.E. played at the W.A.G. regularly and became a bit of a Worcester sensation. F.O.E. had a unique graphic presence for the time, because Dave liked to mess around with his father's Corel Draw program, so their flyers were done on the computer as opposed to the typical punk cut-and-paste style. F.O.E. flyers featured clip art of businessmen shaking hands, people at desks, etc. The band even started carrying around the F.O.E. Briefcase, which was a regular leather business attaché with their "official" documents. They would flummox local club owners with their lists of demands.

We traded mixtapes back and forth, though I was probably the beneficiary of most of them. Dave was a great mixtape maker and they would always be kind of funny and a mixture of really cool songs, always a comment on where we were in our relationship and life and the time. One especially boring summer between

sophomore and junior year for me (pre-senior year for him), we made a mixtape *together.* This mixtape would be different! There would be no "cool" songs, and the songs had to all come from our parents' record collections. Neither of us had "normal" parents like our friends, whose parents listened almost entirely to a steady diet of classic rock. Our parents liked jazz and big-band music, comedy records, calypso, Irish drinking records, and AM radio hits. (What sparked this idea was that my cheesy GPX all-in-one "stereo" was dying and only the record player and radio worked, so I had started to explore my parents' record collection.) I had been listening to Sergio Mendes and Brasil '66 on steady repeat and sharing this with Dave. He, too, was finding a wealth of fine recordings such as an entire collection of Mitch Miller and the Gang and some big-band jazz. We spent a couple months going through everything and coming up with what we thought were the true winners. We recorded the tape on Dave's much better component music system. It has a Jumpin' Jive side inspired by Cab Calloway (Dave kept a copy of Cab's *Jive Dictionary* in the F.O.E. briefcase at all times) and a Sexy Soul side probably mostly inspired by Bill Withers or just the concept that this was smooth "sexy" soul. ("Sexy" being a word we found kind of funny at the time since it was so un-punk-rock.) We made two copies, and we each got one so we could listen to it on our own and when we were together.

We loved this mixtape and it went on heavy rotation on drives around town. And a funny thing started to happen—it stopped being ironic music. We actually started to *like* this stuff. I'm pretty sure no one else in high school had a mixtape like this.

Dave and I never fought (which our friends found odd), and stayed together until my first year in college, but things came to an end as the growing pains of our new reality did not bode well for the relationship. We've stayed in touch over the years, though, and even now remember fondly our days of the Jumpin' Jive Sexy Soul Classics Mix Tape. The thing still holds up.

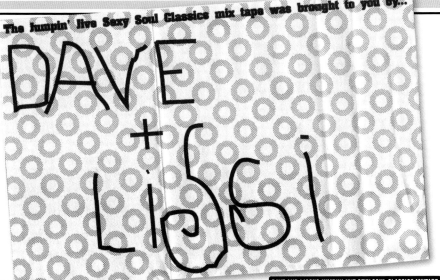

DAVE AND LISSI'S JUMPIN' JIVE SEXY SOUL CLASSICS MIXTAPE

A DATE
N.R. ○ YES ○ NO.

JUMPIN' JIVE SIDE

Bill Withers: Kissing My Love

The Mighty Sparrow: Cockfight

Theme from ***Mission Impossible***

Hair: Donna/Hashish

Sergio Mendes & Brasil '66: Day Tripper

Herbie Mann: Comin' Home Baby

Cab Calloway: Jumpin' Jive

Louie and the Dukes of Dixieland: The Shiek of Araby

Virgin Islands Steel Band: Johnny Cake

The Blazers: Good Ol' Beer

Herb Alpert & the Tijuana Brass: Whipped Cream

The Mamas and the Papas: John's Music Box

Henry Mancini: *Peter Gunn* Theme

The Beach Boys: Luau

Oscar Brand and His Hubcaps: Annoying Song

Al Caiola: Thunderball

Bill Withers: Use Me

Vince Guaraldi: Linus and Lucy

Eddie Harris: Gone Home

B DATE
N.R. ○ YES ○ NO.

SEXY SOUL SIDE

Cab Calloway: Minnie the Moocher

The Tornadoes: Jungle Fever

Mighty Sparrow: Crazy John

Mose Allison: Do Nothin' Till You Hear from Me

The First Class: Won't Somebody Help Me

The Fifth Dimension: Age of Aquarius

Sergio Mendes and Brasil '66: O Pato

The Turtles: Buzzsaw

The Standells: Eleanor Rigby

The Irish Rovers: The Unicorn

Duke Ellington: Mood Indigo

Aerobic workout: Funky Town

Jimmy Smith: Hobo Flats

***Mission Impossible* soundtrack:** Wide Willy

Mitch Miller: Yes, We Have No Bananas

Jimmy Buffett: Margaritaville

James Taylor: How Sweet It Is (To Be Loved by You)

The Chordettes: Mister Sandman

The Jumpin' Jive Sexy Soul Classics mix tape was brought to you by...
DAVE
+
LiSSi

THE LAMEST SUMMER EVER

BY MIKE HANNIGAN

In hindsight, it was achingly simple: We were still years away from life's true worries. And what few concerns we did have—college, summer jobs—were really no bother at all. Boredom was our only true fear.

My friend Melissa was the creator of THE LAMEST SUMMER EVER. Truth be told, I can't remember if she made the tape specifically for me or if I just ended up with it. Melissa and I had been good friends since high school; we only came to date—briefly, disastrously—years later. What I remember most about her was that she was always either giggling or suppressing a giggle beneath her long brown hair; she oozed fun. She was easy to be around in the very best sense of the phrase. Also, we had the shared ignominy of driving K-cars that summer—hers was a craptastic brown wagon while I sported a pale-blue sedan with a stick shift.

The phone calls would go out every afternoon after we got home from our summer jobs. It was usually Heather who would initiate the stagnant ritual.

> *"What are you doing?" she'd ask, knowing the answer.*
>
> *"Nothing."*
>
> *"Want to do something?"*
>
> *"Sure. What?"*
>
> *"I don't know—something."*

There wasn't much to do when you were twenty and stuck in Concord, New Hampshire, for the summer. Like many, my hometown was a good place to grow up, but you really wouldn't want to live there if you had any choice in the matter. What little fun that did exist was a meager mix of cheap beer, cheap pot, and driving about aimlessly in my friend Russ's death-defying Sentra wagon.

She made the tape in 1991, the last summer that most of my friends and I lived at home. We had all dispersed to various colleges and knew from firsthand experience that the world had a lot more to offer than Concord. We'd become accustomed to a certain amount of *entertainment*, a commodity in desperately short supply in our hometown. One could only eat so many D'Angelo's cheesesteaks, getting chased around by the security guards at St. Paul's prep school was a fleeting novelty, and the thrill of seeing how many cigarettes one could smoke at once proved to be ephemeral at best. About the only thing we really had to look forward to were the weekends when my parents would head out of town, which typically resulted in their tastefully appointed, wall-to-wall-white home being turned into a forty-eight-hour frat house.

The music on THE LAMEST SUMMER EVER is classic rock at its finest. It's no surprise that Melissa's tastes ran toward that end of the musical spectrum—the only reliable, somewhat palatable radio station we could pull in was Rock 101, a bastion of '60s-and '70s-era distortion out of Manchester. And beneath Melissa's cute-as-pie preppy exterior lurked a true hippie at heart. It's little surprise that she moved out to San Francisco after college, never to return.

But while she may have chosen *Freedom Rock* songs—and you can practically hear the guy yell, "Turn it up, man!"—at least she chose the *good Freedom Rock* tracks. Sure, there's Little Feat on there, but instead of picking "Dixie Chicken," she went with "Two Trains." Van Morrison made the cut, but rather than "Brown-eyed Girl," it's "Into the Mystic," a song that I still love. Even the occasional clunkers are harmless: Genesis's "Abacab" easily could have been worse—say, "Invisible Touch."

I guess that's the moral of our story—or tape, as the case may be. It coulda been worse. It could have been truly "lame," but it only seemed that way at the time. Our friends all came together in a collective zone defense against boredom. And despite the lame-ass cards we were dealt, we actually wound up having a pretty good ride that summer, even if we failed to appreciate it in the moment.

THE LAMEST SUMMER EVER

A 
DATE
N.R. ○ YES ○ NO.

Fleetwood Mac: Never Going Back Again
Donovan: There Is a Mountain
The Beatles: Here Comes the Sun
Traffic: Who Knows What Tomorrow May Bring
Eric Clapton: Willie and the Hand Jive
Bob Marley and The Wailers: Stir It Up
Simon and Garfunkel: Cecilia
The Doors: Peace Frog
Led Zeppelin: The Battle of Evermore
Cream: Strange Brew
Grateful Dead: Uncle John's Band
Crosby, Stills, Nash & Young: Suite: Judy Blue Eyes

B
DATE
N.R. ○ YES ○ NO.

Michael Hedges: The Funky Avocado
Little Feat: Two Trains
The Rolling Stones: Gimme Shelter
Genesis: Abacab
Blind Faith: Can't Find My Way Home
The Guess Who: No Sugar Tonight
Talking Heads: Take Me to the River
INXS: Mediate
Edie Brickell and New Bohemians: He Said
Van Morrison: Into the Mystic
Tracy Chapman: Freedom Now

TDK
D
NORMAL POSITION
IECI/TYPEI
The LONG OVERDUE TAPE
TDK
IECI/TYPE I
PRECISION
CASSETTE MECHA
Here comes a snowball mix.....
A DATE
N.R.
A DATE/TIME NOISE REDUCTION
B DATE/TIME NOISE REDUCTION
-Kimberly - Patti Smith
-Manic Monday - Walk like an Egyptian - The Bangles
-Groove is in the Heart Dee-Lite
-Cosmic Dancer - T. Rex
- ??? Wyclef Jean
- Don't Be Mean The Raincoats
- Kindhearted Woman Blues
- When you got a good friend Robert Johnson
-Untouchable Face Ani
-Good Things Sleater Kinney
-Introduction The Delta 72
-Camel Walk Southern Culture on the Skids
-Gloria Patti Smith
-Rock Lobster The B-52's
-vs Rahzel The Roots

SNOWBALL'S CHANCE IN HELL

BY VINCENT CHUNG

The piano and violin thing wasn't working out, and adolescent angst was paving the path for punk rock to take over my life. So my parents sent me on a ski trip with the Chinese American Youth Group.

As the bus filled to capacity, friends greeted other friends who greeted everyone but me. The seat adjacent to mine remained empty, and crossing that line from loner to loser kinda stung. Before pulling out, the bus stopped for a straggler. I immediately recognized her from my high school—she was in my biology class and hung out with all the nonconformist kids who smoked on campus. And she was totally hot.

Tera and I shared polite introductions, then sat wordless as the bus pushed out of Raleigh. Being awkward and prematurely misanthropic, I was unwilling to breach the world of initiating contact with the opposite sex. An hour in, she broke the silence by asking if I wanted to listen to music. We split earbud headphones on a Walkman, autoreversing Screeching Weasel's "My Brain Hurts." After the trip, I asked to borrow it so I could make my own copy—and have an excuse to talk to her later.

Over the next four years, we went from cordial greetings to getting scolded for blabbing during class. Tera and I weren't best pals, but sharing a ton of extracurricular activities and classes together can bring two folks pretty close. I was her "reliable" friend, the one whom she could call to get missed homework assignments or when she locked her keys in her car. Or who would let her borrow a sheet of paper because her notebook ran out, which happened every day. Although the crush was long shelved, in retrospect, the doting seemed dorkily pathetic. Color it selfless, but I was just happy to be useful.

Of course I made her a mixtape—sometime around junior year. And of course it took months for her to reciprocate. To me, receiving mixtapes isn't about discovering new music expertly mixed with sweet transitions. They simply have to encapsulate the author's personality, and the cassettes were always ideal in their imperfections. This one was Tera epitomized: a scattered collection of whimsical silliness, reeling from playful diva to fucked-up pop. She even referenced our ski trip in the artwork: her tumbling down a hill while I pointed and laughed. Listening to it, I can only imagine Tera in her messy bedroom, kicking her heels up in dance, and making noises with her mouth that sound straight out of Looney Tunes. These were *her* songs—well, I'm sincerely hoping they're not songs that reminded her of me.

Sometime in college, over winter break, I got a call. Tera was in town and wanted to catch up. We revisited an old stomping ground named the All Children's Playground. Back in the day, we'd come

here in the middle of the night to loiter in the way underaged kids do. As we sat in a dark nook, a light snow started. It became one of those fleeting best-night-ever moments that frequents idealistic young people.

"I realized something over the past couple of years," Tera confessed.

"What's that?"

"You were a good friend to me. Like, really great. You were always there when I was in trouble, and I didn't realize how important you were to me until we went off to college."

I shrugged. "Well, it's not like I disappeared. I'm still in North Carolina. *You're* the one who became a Yankee."

"I know. I just wanted you to know that you're appreciated." She leaned over and kissed me. Not a peck-on-the-cheek-you're-so-sweet kiss, but an openmouthed planter followed by pawing each other like bears mauling prey. I panicked, digging for that crush I had buried under years of platonic memories—not quite processing the surreal moment.

Distance provided a challenge, with sporadic rendezvouses strung out over years. Having our own myopic lives in our respective big cities, I grew emotionally detached. At times, I was a horrible friend to her. Like, really terrible. And my failure to stay in touch trivialized our long history. I forgot. She gave up. In retrospect, it was never about revisiting that high school crush, but venturing into those messy, ambiguous relationships that grown-ups embrace so immaturely.

THE LONG OVERDUE TAPE

A DATE
N.R. ○ YES ○ NO.

Patti Smith: Kimberly
The Bangles: Manic Monday
The Bangles: Walk Like an Egyptian
Deee-Lite: Groove Is in the Heart
T.Rex: Cosmic Dancer
Wyclef Jean: Anything Can Happen
The Raincoats: Don't Be Mean

B DATE
N.R. ○ YES ○ NO.

Robert Johnson: Kindhearted Woman Blues
Robert Johnson: When You Got a Good Friend
Ani Difranco: Untouchable Face
Sleater-Kinney: Good Things
The Delta 72: Introduction
Southern Culture on the Skids: Camel Walk
Patti Smith: Gloria
The B-52s: Rock Lobster
The Roots: ? Vs. Rahzel

RUN-AROUND

BY CHARLIE TODD

In the summer of 1995, I attended a "leadership camp" at Presbyterian College in Clinton, South Carolina. I was sixteen years old. I'm not sure exactly why I was there, but I have a vague memory of being "selected" by my guidance counselor. I do remember thinking it would be a chance to meet some new girls, as I was having very little luck with the girls I already knew. The camp was incredibly corny. We were encouraged to motivate each other by sending compliments via "Happy Grams," little slips of paper that were delivered like Valentines in grade school. We'd receive these notes in our "council meetings" where we sat around and read aloud from a giant three-ring binder filled with Tony Robbins–style essays on leadership.

There were two big social events at the camp: a talent show and a square dance. For the talent show I twirled "devil sticks" on stage while Phish's "Sparkle" backed me up. I was never a hippie, but I was definitely going through a phase. My dorm mate Brian had secured a date to the square dance and talked me into asking out her pretty roommate Holly. The four of us went together and had as much fun as you could at a leadership camp square dance. Thanks to a very literal DJ, Holly and I slow-danced to "The End of the Road" to close out the night and the week. We did not kiss, although I told my friends back home we did.

The next morning at the final council meeting, I got a Happy Gram from Holly.

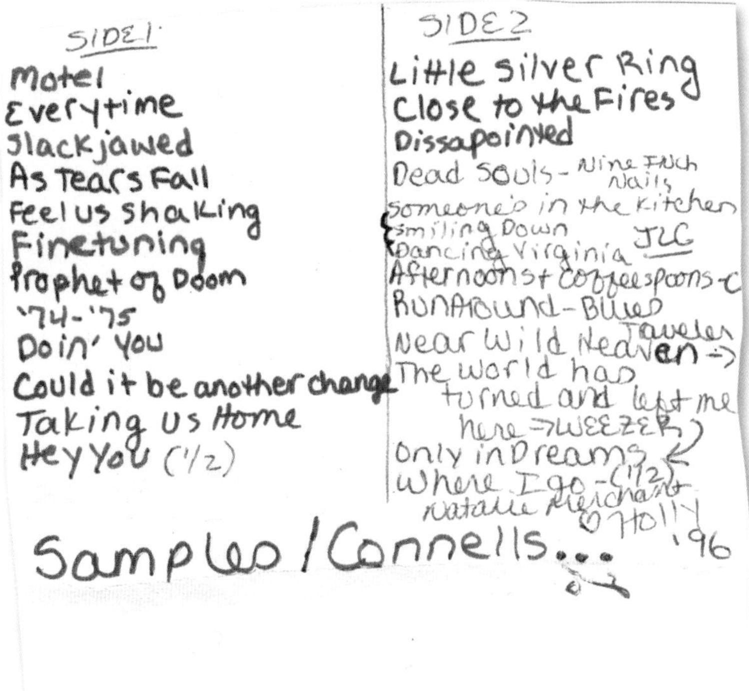

SIDE 1
Motel
Everytime
Slackjawed
As Tears Fall
Feel us shaking
Finetuning
Prophet of Doom
'74-'75
Doin' You
Could it be another change
Taking us Home
Hey You (1/2)
SIDE 2
Little Silver Ring
Close to the Fires
Dissapointed
Dead Souls - Nine Inch Nails
Someone's in the kitchen
Smiling Down
Dancing Virginia
JLC
Afternoons + Coffeespoons - C
Runaround - Blues Traveler
Near Wild Heaven
The world has turned and left me here - WEEZER
Only in Dreams
Where I go - (1/2) Natalie Merchant
Holly '96
Samples / Connells...

"Thanks for being such a great partner last night! I had a lot of fun!!" The final two exclamation marks were made into a smiley face, and the note was signed "❤ Holly." I told her good-bye that afternoon and we promised to keep in touch. This was no easy task with me living in Columbia and her living in Charleston. It being 1995, only nerds like me used the Internet. A phone call would be "long distance" and probably outlawed by parents. So my only way to keep in touch was to write a letter, which I did almost immediately after returning home.

She wrote me back a few days later, called me a "sweetheart," and mentioned that I had "amazing eyes." She even signed the letter "Love, Holly"! I was excited and ran to compose my reply. It was a few months later, around the fourth or fifth letter, when she casually mentioned her new boyfriend, and I realized that my long-distance fantasy girlfriend probably thought of me as a pen pal. Still, might as well keep writing, right? Surely this new boyfriend is just a phase. We discussed music and both lamented Jerry Garcia's death, although "Casey Jones" was the only song I knew. I told her I had never heard her two favorite bands, The Samples and The Connells, and she offered to make me a mix!

When the cassette arrived, I pored over every detail, trying to decipher any hidden messages of love. More than half of it was The Samples and The Connells as promised, but she took the time to sequence it like a mix. This was no high-speed-dub.

Side B came with about a half hour of alt-rock radio bonus tracks and a few cuts from local heroes Jump, Little Children. I liked most of it. The only real stinker was Blues Traveler's "Run-Around." Tragically both sides ended with a song getting cut in half, but at least she took the time to mention it in the liner notes.

I had a math meet in Charleston that winter, and we agreed to get together. "Want to pick me up from my math meet and go out to dinner?" was probably not the best pickup line. By then she had broken up with the new boyfriend, but it was pretty clear she only regarded me as a friend. We had dinner with some of her friends, and then she dropped me off at the hotel where the math team was staying. I had her come inside so my friends could see how pretty she was. Then I walked her to her car and we stood around for a few minutes while I gave her a tour of the night sky. It being winter, Orion was front and center. We did not kiss, but once again I told everyone we did.

That was pretty much the end of our nonrelationship. We stopped writing, although she did send me an anonymous chain letter a month later. I knew from the penmanship and postal code that it came from her. I guess I was one of the ten friends whose postal address she had, and the prospect of "bad luck for life" was too much for her to handle. I broke the chain. I was tired of getting the runaround.

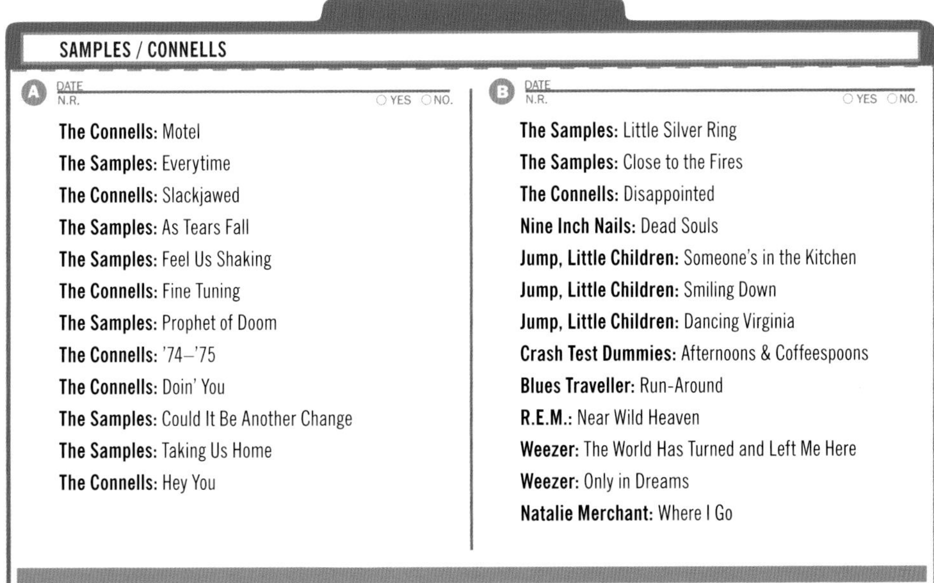
SAMPLES / CONNELLS

A DATE N.R. YES NO.

The Connells: Motel
The Samples: Everytime
The Connells: Slackjawed
The Samples: As Tears Fall
The Samples: Feel Us Shaking
The Connells: Fine Tuning
The Samples: Prophet of Doom
The Connells: '74–'75
The Connells: Doin' You
The Samples: Could It Be Another Change
The Samples: Taking Us Home
The Connells: Hey You

B DATE N.R. YES NO.

The Samples: Little Silver Ring
The Samples: Close to the Fires
The Connells: Disappointed
Nine Inch Nails: Dead Souls
Jump, Little Children: Someone's in the Kitchen
Jump, Little Children: Smiling Down
Jump, Little Children: Dancing Virginia
Crash Test Dummies: Afternoons & Coffeespoons
Blues Traveller: Run-Around
R.E.M.: Near Wild Heaven
Weezer: The World Has Turned and Left Me Here
Weezer: Only in Dreams
Natalie Merchant: Where I Go

TDK
DYNAMIC PERFORMANCE
HIGH OUTPUT
IEC I/TYPE I

TDK REGGAE(+)FI MATURA D

A DATE/TIME NOISE REDUCTION ☐

B DATE/TIME NOISE REDUCTION ☐

AUGUSTUS PABLO - KING TUBBY
MEETS ROCKERS UPTOWN •
I-ROY - DON'T GET WEARY JOE
FRAZIER • JOHNNY CLARKE -
AFRICAN PEOPLE • BUJU
BANTON - COMPLAINT • LKJ -
REGGAE FI RADNI • I-ROY -
SIDEWALK KILLER • J. CLARKE
- EVERY KNEE SHALL BOW •
U-ROY - AFRICAN MESSAGE
• A. PABLO - KEEP ON DUBBING
• I-ROY - SOUND EDUCATION

• BUJU BANTON - MURDERER
• ANTHONY B - NAH GO HIDE

B BUJU BANTON -
CHAMPION • I-ROY - LOOK
A BOOM • BUJU BANTON
- HUSH BABY HUSH •
THE METERS - SOUL
ISLAND • JIMMY McGRIFF
- DIG ON IT • CURTIS
MAYFIELD - BEATIFUL BROS OF
MINE • MILES DAVIS - YESTERNOW

REGGAE (+) FI MAURA

BY MAURA MADDEN

The first time I saw Dave, he was smoking a cigarette on a street corner half a block away from our high school dance. He had been waiting outside while his friends rounded up the girls. He barely looked at me. But I couldn't help myself—I stared at him. He was six feet tall, wearing a dirty flannel shirt with weird military-looking pins on the pocket. His dark wavy hair was hidden under a backward-turned baseball cap, but nothing could hide his huge brown eyes and a face good-looking enough to have graced the cover of any teen magazine. I instantly wanted to be his girlfriend. I was fifteen and had never even kissed a boy, but my mind sped forward into a future as his chosen one, a girl who would suddenly become someone to be wildly jealous of. Out of the pack of girls, however, he chose my best friend, Corey. She smoked cigarettes, too.

But I ended up at the same small college as Dave, one year behind him. I wasn't stalking him, exactly, but I was plenty happy to end up there with him. He and Corey had broken up by the time he got to college, so she was out of the way. I figured I was entitled to go after him—I had liked him before they even started going out. I spent my freshman year following him around, spending late nights in his room just talking, and days desperately pining away for him. The summer between my freshman year and sophomore year, I went to visit him in San Francisco. He was living there for the summer with his current girlfriend. I stayed with them in their basement apartment on the floor, going to see Kubrick movies at the Castro Movie Theater, meeting their friends, the whole time plotting to get him in my clutches. I had no guilt about this, either. I was obsessed with his intelligence, his cynicism, and his good looks that kept getting better.

First semester sophomore year, I doggedly pursued him. When he wanted to start hanging out with new people to get away from the destructive influence of some of his current friends, I was there for him at every turn, ready to lend an ear or a shoulder to cry on. And finally, by December, he had broken up with his girlfriend and was dating me.

We spent every night together, when he was done reading Nietzsche and Kierkegaard and Foucault and I had finished cramming facts about Japanese art and reading critical essays on Edith Wharton. We watched foreign movies we'd rented from the college library while he chain-smoked. We had intense onversations on a nightly basis, about the importance of things that are important in college. We ate ramen noodles with eggs boiled in with the water. We weren't perfect, but we were completely co-dependent. We slept on a bed that covered the whole of his room—two twin dorm mattresses pushed together to make a mattress for two. When I wound up sleeping in the middle, I could feel the crack.

By the time this tape was made, Dave and I had been going out for four years. We had cheated on each other multiple times, thrown things in fits of jealousy, broken up repeatedly, but still moved across country to San Francisco together. We lived on opposite sides of town—he lived in the foggy Sunset and I lived in sunny Potrero Hill. Neither one of us could drive, never having learned in New York City. It took over an hour by bus and train to get from his neighborhood to mine. It was my first year out of college, his second, and we told ourselves we were too young to live together.

At this point, it's hard to know if we were in love anymore, but our lives were totally woven into one. We had been through so much shit, knew every little secret about each other, about our families, it seemed as if we would never pull apart. Dave was spending all of his spare money at Amoeba Records on Haight Street buying CDs and tapes from all the reggae kings. I was more interested in indie rock, not old-school reggae. I listened to this tape when he gave it to me, but not obsessively, the way you listen to a tape from a brand-new love. I just didn't care about Augustus Pablo and The Meters. I wasn't even sure if I cared about us.

I had joined a sketch comedy group with new people, and I felt a change come over me. I was happier. I still cared about Dave deeply, but more and more I was drawn to comedy boys, boys who didn't talk about philosophy or watch foreign movies. Boys who laughed loud and hard and easily, who did bits about language instead of writing essays about it, boys who were strange-looking and warm and listened to indie rock and thought reggae was for hippies. I cheated on him for the last time with one of my friends from my comedy group. We tried to stay together for a few more months, but we couldn't maintain it. The last thread tying us together had frayed.

We would see each other on and off around town after the breakup, and we even hooked up every now and then. We'd have pseudodates at a restaurant in Japantown where they made homemade noodles with egg in the broth, and sometimes I would end up back in his room in the foggy Sunset, wondering if we would always be like this. But Dave moved to Hungary to teach English a year after we had stopped dating. We spent his last night in San Francisco together. I bought him a camera. He left me his CDs to watch over while he was gone.

Ten years have passed since we broke up, but we've managed to keep up a friendship. I am married to Rufus, a handsome funny boy who happens to watch foreign movies and reads philosophy on occasion. We listen to Dave's CDs, which I slowly grew to love, especially the U-Roy and Linton Kwesi Johnson. Rufus has become a fan of Anthony B. He's also a fan of Dave and his lovely Hungarian wife, Anita. They just had their first baby. Someday soon we'll meet their son, and I guess I should give Dave his CDs back. He'll want to introduce the young one to roots, rock, and reggae. We finally unwove ourselves, and still managed to stay connected. Maybe it's our history together, and maybe it's the reggae.

REGGAE +/FI MAURA

A DATE N.R. ○ YES ○ NO.

Augustus Pablo: King Tubby Meets Rockers Uptown
I-Roy: Don't Get Weary, Joe Frazier
Johnny Clarke: African People
Buju Banton: Complaint
Linton Kwesi Johnson: Reggae fi Radni
I-Roy: Sidewalk Killer
Johnny Clarke: Every Knee Shall Bow
U-Roy: African Message
Augustus Pablo: Keep on Dubbing
I-Roy: Sound Education
Buju Banton: Murderer
Anthony B: Nah Go Hide

B DATE N.R. ○ YES ○ NO.

Buju Banton: Champion
I-Roy: Look a Boom
Buju Banton: Hush Baby Hush
The Meters: Soul Island
Jimmy McGriff: Dig on It
Curtis Mayfield: Beautiful Brothers of Mine
Miles Davis: Yesternow

33¢ AT JIVE TIME

BY MAIREAD CASE

At nineteen I had violently violet hair and ate mostly egg whites, grapefruit, and cheese. Wore wrist cuffs and kneesocks. Plastic glitter barrettes. I lived in an apartment up the street from my college, lived with books, insomnia, and three sweet girls who I didn't talk to very much. I was late to every class and stayed up late writing. Two things, mostly. A thesis on *Krapp's Last Tape*—for which I read every word Beckett wrote, analyzed his handwriting, then dreamed he woke up next to me—and lots of music criticism.

At the time, I thought I had Vision. I blew whistles on iffy feminism, "selling out," and recycled choruses, then ran toward anything loud enough, weird enough, to hijack my buzz a while. Bonus points if it sounded like Sleater-Kinney. If purity's the severest kink, then man, I was Queen Venus of All Furs. At least I knew what I didn't like. And I suppose some of the writing was good. But carting around all that anger gets toxic.

One October, I flew home to Seattle for my birthday and took a Rock Crit class at Hugo House. It was taught by the editors of the alt-pop-cult magazine *Bandoppler*, Chris Estey and Jason Dodd, chuckling and stoned and waxing gold about *Grand Royal*, *Creem*, Céline, and chocolate eyeballs. Afterward, outside, I gave them each a clove (ah, twenty: birthday money from parents equals glass in lungs) and three hours later I was on staff for them. The sixth issue featured David Lasky's drawing of Chuck D. in the Oval Office, blue-green and brown, and in retrospect few feminisms are truer.

For the next two years and all practical purposes, *Bandoppler (Dopplebanger, Hangingboppler)* was my boyfriend. I blew off trig to interview Lydia Lunch in my bedroom, and on Sundays, woke up early so I could sit at the grocery store and edit and watch churchkids eat doughnuts. I did not drink. I did not have sex.

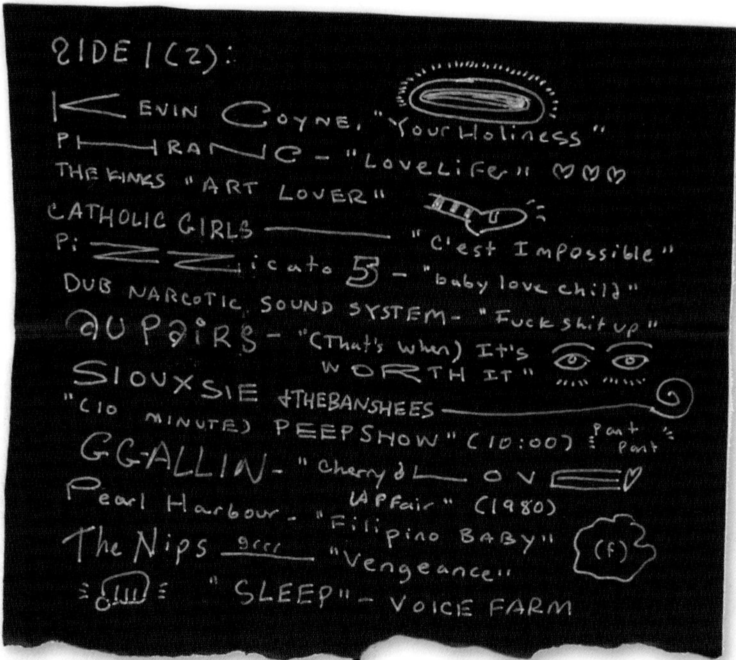

SIDE 1 (2):
KEVIN COYNE, "Your Holiness"
PHRANC - "LoveLife"
THE KINKS "ART LOVER"
CATHOLIC GIRLS — "C'est Impossible"
Pizzicato 5 - "baby love child"
DUB NARCOTIC SOUND SYSTEM - "Fuck shit up"
AU PAIRS - "(That's when) It's WORTH IT"
SIOUXSIE & THE BANSHEES
"(10 MINUTE) PEEPSHOW" (10:00) pant pant
GG ALLIN - "Cherry & LOVE Affair" (1980)
Pearl Harbour - "Filipino BABY"
The Nips grrr "Vengeance"
"SLEEP" - VOICE FARM

I wrote labyrinthine, no-caps, 3 A.M. emails to Chris about religion and lust and infection, and he always listened. He told stories back. He sent quotes from the Hernandez Brothers and Bill-Dale Marcinko and Kristine McKenna. And because Chris never laughed at or hit on me, I'm pretty sure those emails saved my life a couple times. A couple nights. What I really wanted was to be taken seriously. To play.

Eventually Chris, Chris who I now call Capote and he calls me Harper (or Stagger, depending on rum and mood), Chris sent this mix, 33¢ AT JIVE TIME. Two sides, "One-Two" and "Two-One." Track list in silver gel pen on black construction paper, liner notes techno-scrolly and personal, too.

The tape hooked me like a fish. There's a ten-minute remix of "Peep Show," which is nine too long and seventeen too short. There's a song about sex and Jesus, to be cranked cathartically, electric-fencedly, nude as the news from my bike basket. Bass lines are teased out and mysteries are left in and this was the first time I realized sticking around means more than saying no. That sometimes you love someone and also you want to bite off his ear. That soundtracks are soundtracks, not mirrors.

For a while, I was this cassette. I carried it around like a sandwich board or a name tag. A lucky charm. But then all the magazines folded, I graduated and left, and some other stuff happened, and I moved to Chicago. And I realized that everything didn't fit into a song. This happens to everyone, somehow.

And in Chicago, one dear night in the morning, seeing rainbows, P and J and M and I, we biked up a hill and we were listening to the tape and I pressed the wrong button. The red one. Record. I erased Alice Cooper and was surprised to realize that it was okay. It didn't ruin anything. It was even kind of funny. Guess I'm less defiant now. But I still write—and I'll always love Siouxsie.

SIDE 2 (1):

The Stranglers: "WALTZIN BLACK"
PSYCHIC TV - "Godstar"
Life in General - "One WAY"
LEWIS FUREY - "Poetic young man"
LINDSEY BUCKINGHAM "MARY Lee Jones"
THE Selecter —— "Celebrate THE Bullet"
PHIL OCHS — "The Crucifixion"
THE FEEDERZ - "Jesus Entering"
WALL OF VOODOO —— "BACK IN FLESH"
Alice Cooper - "CLONES"
JAPAN - "CANTONESE Boy"
PHRANC - "CAPED CRUSADER"

33 ¢ AT JIVE TIME

DATE
N.R. ○ YES ○ NO.

Kevin Coyne: Your Holiness
Phranc: Lifelover
The Kinks: Art Lover
The Catholic Girls: C'est Impossible
Pizzicato Five: Baby Love Child
Dub Narcotic Sound System: Fuck Shit Up
Au Pairs: That's When It's Worth It
Siouxsie and the Banshees: Peepshow
GG Allin: Cheri Love Affair
Pearl Harbor and The Explosions: Filipino Baby
The Nips: Vengeance
Voice Farm: Sleep

B

DATE
N.R. ○ YES ○ NO.

The Stranglers: Waltzin' Black
Psychic TV: Godstar
Life In General: One Way
Lewis Furey: Poetic Young Man
Lindsay Buckingham: Mary Lee Jones
The Selecter: Celebrate the Bullet
Phil Ochs: The Crucifixion
The Feederz: Jesus Entering
Wall of Voodoo: Back in Flesh
Alice Cooper: Clones
Japan: Cantonese Boy
Phranc: Caped Crusader

THE HAND-ME-DOWN

BY ANNE JENSEN

The hand-me-down was a phenomenon that I was introduced to at birth. Born the youngest of four children into a middle-class family, I was afraid that I would never be able to escape it. Everything I owned was previously used by my sister or brothers. Baby clothes, toys, books. I played softball and used my brother Scott's old mitt; when I was big enough for my own room, I got my sister's old room. For every school dance I was allowed to raid my sister's closet for a dress to wear. As a child, I hated being the "hand-me-down" girl, knowing that when I became an adult, I would have the power to have my own things. Brand-new, never-been-used things.

By the time I was twenty-three, I moved out to Los Angeles, got my own apartment, paid for my own schooling, and found a job, a car, and a new set of L.A. friends, all on my own, in a faraway city that my siblings had never touched before. I also started dating Adam. Adam had been emotionally scarred by his ex-girlfriend, Melissa, and was happy to find someone new.

Adam was my first long-term boyfriend and I loved him a lot, but he never did things the way a boyfriend should do things. Take Christmas, for example. Adam loved Christmas. He spent tons of time discussing what he should buy his friends and family, and he ended up getting them all very elaborate, thoughtful, and expensive gifts. I could only imagine what he'd get me, the love of his life. We exchanged our gifts a couple of days before Christmas. I won't go into much detail about the gifts I gave him, just to say they were of the same caliber of the gifts he gave his friends. Very nice, very thoughtful, very out-of-my-price range. He loved them all. My turn. Adam pushed in my direction what looked to be a shirt box wrapped up, looked at me like he had been defeated, and shrugged. Before I fully opened the gift, he stopped me and said, "If you don't like it, you can take it back." What I opened was a sweater that, most likely, came out of his grandmother's closet. I was shocked and wanted to cry, but thanked him anyway because I knew our love was stronger and deeper than any bad Christmas present. I wore the sweater to dinner that night.

Fast-forward another year. Adam and I were still going strong, minus some minor relationship problems. One night while we were hanging out, he popped in a tape and said it was a mix of his favorite songs and that he thought of me while listening to it. He wanted me to have it. We listened to the mixtape together, and I loved it! I had never heard The Magnetic Fields, Dinosaur Jr., or The Pogues before and never had the proper introduction to Tom Waits. Every song on the tape was beautiful, and I thought it was so thoughtful of him to make a mixtape for me, even though we were well into CD technology, and the only tape player I owned was in my run-down 1991 Mazda. I didn't care, it was the thought that counted. When it was finished, I grabbed the tape from the tape player to claim it as my own only to find on the front of it, another girl's writing. *To Adam, love Melissa*. Melissa. His ex. The one right before me. "You can have it if you want," Adam said with a shrug. He shrugged a lot. I took it. Mostly because the music was fantastic, but also because I loved the idea of having this mixtape. This hand-me-down mixtape. Because, in some strange way, he made it for me.

Adam and I broke up and I started dating Dave. One night while hanging out with Dave, he turned on his CD player, and it played music that had a lot of the same music as on my hand-me-down mixtape. I loved the CD and asked him to make me a copy. Dave said he wouldn't, because his ex-girlfriend made the CD for him. "I'll make you a different mix CD, one that's about us, not about my past relationships. Anyway, the CD kinda reminds me of her. Melissa was pretty crazy." Melissa?!?? After a couple of prying questions, I found out it was the *same* Melissa. The CD had been on rotation in his CD player and he forgot it was even in there. I was mad. Who the heck is Melissa, with her hand-me-down music, and her hand-me-down boyfriends. I hated her for making me feel like a child again.

Dave eventually made me a great mix CD, one that I listened to often, one that was my own. Shortly after Dave and I broke up, my car was broken into and it was stolen.

I'm in my thirties now, and have come to embrace the reality of the still present hand-me-downs in my life. The hand-me-downs have gotten better, too. The car I currently drive was given to me by my sister. It was my car of choice, but was discarded by her for the newer model. My apartment is decorated with my mom's old couch, my brother's old dining-room table, and I eat off my grandmother's old china. These hand-me-downs have saved me so much money that I now understand and appreciate this mess my parents got me into.

THE HAND-ME DOWN

A DATE N.R. ○YES ○NO.

They Might Be Giants: Destination Moon
Tom Waits: Take It with Me
The Muffs: Another Ugly Face
Sheryl Crow: Run Baby Run
Social Distortion: Ring of Fire
Tori Amos: Concertina
Dinosaur Jr.: The Wagon
The Pixies: Where Is My Mind?

B DATE N.R. ○YES ○NO.

The Magnetic Fields: Born on a Train
Tom Waits: Goin' Out West
Screeching Weasel: Hey Suburbia
The Pogues: Fairytale of New York
The Chemical Brothers: Asleep from Day
Beck: Dead Melodies
They Might Be Giants: Hey Mr. DJ, I Thought You Said We Had a Deal
Nirvana: Rape Me
Johnny Cash: Guess Things Happen that Way

Jamie didn't write down the titles of the songs. He didn't even bother to label the cassette. I have to be careful lest it get separated from its hand-scratched case. I've identified many of the songs I didn't know by typing the lyrics into a search engine. It's the same way with Jamie. There's no looking him up on Facebook, not much to be gleaned by Google-stalking that old flame. I've already dug up what I can, an obituary from his hometown paper, another from the online edition of his dad's dojo's newsletter, a MySpace page someone else administers in his honor. I wonder if that person knows I'm more than just some random friend request, that Jamie is Wylie, the groovy young lover who shows up in a few of my books. I wonder what Jamie knew, too, if curiosity ever compelled him to look for me, the way I now look for him.

From what I've been able to piece together, the music he was into at the end was dark to the point of nihilism. He had a lot of friends, though, mostly people from the bar where he'd worked for a number of years. I wonder what these guys would've made of the tape he gave me back in 1991, those romantic, nonverbal interludes from the movie *Betty Blue*, Lenny Kravitz's voluptuous bawl. I doubt Big White, the enormous and scary-looking dude who marked the one-year anniversary of Jamie's suicide with a Happy Death Day message, would put up with Lenny wandering slowly through "Fields of Joy."

Maybe Jamie wouldn't have either anymore, but he remained a lover, as evidenced by a note his fiancée shared with his MySpace friends, in which he spoke of their pending dream move to Vermont, just the two of them and their cat, maybe some sheep.

It's funny to think of him embracing Nature-with-a-capital-N, when the Jamie I knew craved clove cigarettes and afternoons spent sprawled on his messy mattress, listening to Depeche Mode and watching the stereo lights blink. That's how I remember the bulk of our ten months together. That and his fondness for taking baths with each other.

Stranger still to think of him being thirty-eight, short-haired, on the verge of marrying a young woman not that much older than I was when he was nineteen and we were the item, with a whole new set of friends, far removed from the one in whose midst we existed. Online evidence that life goes on, even when it doesn't. The Jamie who lives in my memory, the Wylie who shows up from time to time in my books, is the boy who made this tape. He made it for himself. I'm merely the one who ended up with it.

SOMEBODY

A DATE
N.R. ○ YES ○ NO.

Lenny Krayitz: Let Love Rule
Eric Serra: C'est Le Vent, Betty
Jane's Addiction: Summertime Rolls
Depeche Mode: Somebody
Velvet Underground: New Age
This Mortal Coil: Ivy and Neet
This Mortal Coil: Tarantula
Lenny Kravitz: Rosemary
***Betty Blue* soundtrack:** Zorg et Betty

B DATE
N.R. ○ YES ○ NO.

Jane's Addiction: Then She Did . . .
Lenny Kravitz: Fields of Joy
Chris Isaak: Wicked Game
Lenny Kravitz; Does Anybody Out There Even Care
Gabriel Yared: Cargo Voyage
Lenny Kravitz: Fields of Joy (reprise)
Lenny Kravitz: Blues for Sister Someone
Angelo Badalamenti: Dark Spanish Symphony
Rubber City: Dark Spanish Symphony
Gabriel Yared: Le Petit Nicolas
Paris Opéra-Comique Orchestra: Dôme Épais

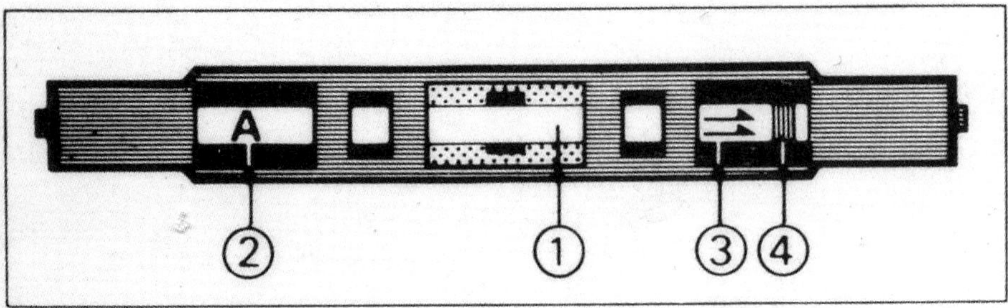

WOW AND FLUTTER

BY THOMAS PERRY

I'm getting older now, and I've made tapes for over half my life. From the neon 90-minuters of my early teens that I taped for car journeys just so I didn't have to listen to Joan Baez or Johnny Mathis (featuring '80s rock taped from the radio and excruciating U.K. rap), to the hand-crafted meister-works of my later years. There have been missteps, audible pops, terrifying wow and flutter, tape chews and snaps, dubious cellotape fixes. But gradually I got really good at making them. And they were a certain thing, part of the process of meeting someone I liked, boy or girl. Eventually I'd make a tape, and that was it. Friendship cemented, love declared, or somewhere in between. One notable example was a sixty-minute tape consisting of twenty-four Lemonheads songs called LEMONY GOODNESS. It finished right on the button for both sides, too. No snazzy cover, but it was probably the best tape I've ever made.

Only ever got one mixtape from a girl I was seeing, though. We met at the Freshers fair at Uni, and gradually, things just fell into place. Sadly I was the other man in a love triangle, and I couldn't make her leave her fiancé. Never asked her to, although it was something I desperately wanted. It just didn't seem right to me, breaking up someone else's long-term relationship. And all I could do was think about her, and think what we were doing was wrong. It was a hard situation. Probably bored half my friends to death talking about it.

Anyway . . . she gave me a sixty-minute tape back in return for one I'd made her, which was a nice surprise. It wasn't the best tape I'd ever heard, but it did have a couple of good things on it. I can't find the outer sleeve, so can't give you the whole track list. You get the highlights.

The Animalhouse doing "Small" (great single, underrated band), an indie pop band called McCabe doing a song called "Nothing" (which lyrically encapsulated her take on our relationship, I suppose). Indian Ropeman doing "Dog in the Piano" (I picked up that dodgy single years later out of nostalgia). It wasn't perfect, but as a tape it worked. There were thirty seconds of an unlisted pop track from the '90s at the end of each side, intended to cut out and allow me a sigh of relief, I suppose. One of them was "Psyche!" by terrifying *Byker Grove* pop duo PJ and Duncan. Evil.

The relationship ended badly (how did you not see that coming?), but we eventually got to the point where we didn't hate each other. Spotted her at a gig the other night, and got that cold chill I used to get when she contacted me out of the blue after a year of silence. She didn't recognize me. I look a bit different now, heavier, glasses, etc. She was with her husband, I think; didn't want to just ghost in, freak her out, and leave. So I didn't, and there you have it.

I've still got the tape in a box somewhere, and although I'll never listen to it again it reminds me of a time when I was really crazy about someone. I'd been that way before, and have since, but that tape serves as a memento of a great time in my life. It's not as if I'd grab it first if there were a house fire, or build it a shrine. But it lives in my house like she lives in my memories. And it'll travel with me when I move.

WOW AND FLUTTER

A DATE
N.R. ○ YES ○ NO.

The Animalhouse: Small
Birth: Gotten Bold
David Bowie: Seven
Placebo: Pure Morning
Elastica: Your Arse, My Place
Papa Roach: Last Resort
My Vitriol: Always Your Way
PJ and Duncan: Psyche!

B DATE
N.R. ○ YES ○ NO.

Indian Ropeman: Dog in the Piano
Laptop: Everyone's Happy You Failed
McCabe: Nothing
Ash: A Life Less Ordinary
Tom Jones and the Cardigans: Burning Down the House
The Wannadies: I Love Myself
Pulp: Mile End
Christina Aguilera: Genie in a Bottle

THE INFAMOUS TAPE

BY JENNY READER

It was the turn of a the century, and the U.K. was still in the passionate embrace of the Spice Girls and having an affair with Europop, filled with paranoia about the Millennium Bug, and partying like it was 1999, because, well, it was. Bucking my usual need for romance above everything else, I had for once put my head before my heart, and had settled in a "sensible" relationship, living in a house I had prematurely bought with my then long-term boyfriend. I was full of the excitement about my first real paychecks in London, and he was jaded by the whole experience, scorned by an ex with whom he had lived before she took more than her share of the pie. Not to be fooled again, he entered our relationship with financial caution and, seven years my senior, I trusted him to make the right decisions by us. It already had all the makings of a bad soap opera, but blinded by a deep-rooted craving for "normality" to combat my penchant for the dramatic, I threw myself in.

I had been convinced to move to the outer echelons of Greater London, trading my dreams of an apartment in the city for a two-bed in an industrial estate in suburban Essex, a renowned not-me part of the country. My best friends lived in South London, and were a family of friends with their own language that hung out together ad hoc—just dropped by each other's houses at random. I sought solace with the South Londoners when 'burbs living got too much; frozen pizza in front of *The Simpsons* now sounds a bit like heaven, but with me itching to just get out in the world, it felt like jail. Life in the South was hardly glamorous, but there was something so endearingly gritty and real, it's no wonder The Streets gained a lot of their inspiration from the area they lived in years later. My friends had grown up there, and for better or worse, this was their life.

It was around this time that I met Will, who was core to this group, happily playing the role of the quintessential "arty" one of the bunch. A student at Central St. Martin's College of Art and Design (as featured in the Pulp song "Common People"), Will worked as a decorator in his spare time to earn money to fund his art projects. He took photos that juxtaposed the bleakness of London against things of beauty—the gray graffitied awnings of South London dwellings against bright blue skies—earning him a spot in sporadic

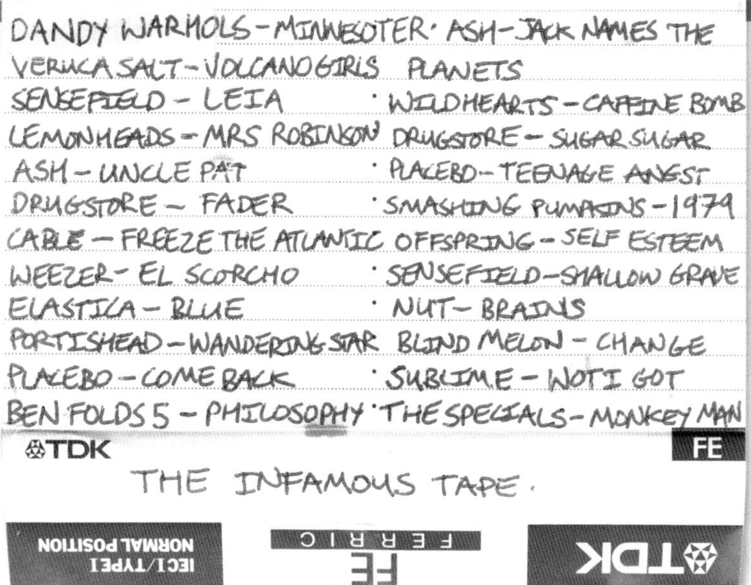

A DATE / TIME
NOISE REDUCTION ON OFF
DATE / TIME
NOISE REDUCTION ON OFF B
DANDY WARHOLS - MINNESOTER · ASH - JACK NAMES THE
VERUCA SALT - VOLCANO GIRLS PLANETS
SENSEFIELD - LEIA · WILDHEARTS - CAFFINE BOMB
LEMONHEADS - MRS ROBINSON DRUGSTORE - SUGAR SUGAR
ASH - UNCLE PAT · PLACEBO - TEENAGE ANGST
DRUGSTORE - FADER · SMASHING PUMPKINS - 1979
CABLE - FREEZE THE ATLANTIC OFFSPRING - SELF ESTEEM
WEEZER - EL SCORCHO · SENSEFIELD - SHALLOW GRAVE
ELASTICA - BLUE · NUT - BRAINS
PORTISHEAD - WANDERING STAR BLIND MELON - CHANGE
PLACEBO - COME BACK · SUBLIME - WOT I GOT
BEN FOLDS 5 - PHILOSOPHY · THE SPECIALS - MONKEY MAN
TDK
FE
THE INFAMOUS TAPE.
NORMAL POSITION
IECI/TYPE I
FERRIC
FE
TDK

exhibits in big airy buildings. His simple vision was to show that the positive side of the seemingly negative things is never too far way, and that the two sit side by side all the way through life. I was a sucker for him from the start, and what might have been seen as him being "aloof" to others just made me want to understand what made this strange and amazing boy tick.

Although I have a feeling that the first time we really got to know each other was at one of my house parties where I believe he fed pizza to my fish ("Come on, everyone likes pizza"), I've glossed over memory with a more exciting first encounter, at a birthday gathering in London's West End around Christmas. Fed up of cohabiting in a dead relationship, I was full of pent-up schemes and subconsciously planning my escape. The group had planned to go to New York City for New Year's and by the end of that evening there were enough stars in my eyes and booze in my belly to convince Will we should go, too. Bonded by our love of pre-'95 music and anything guitar-based with meaning, we headed overseas on a whim to see in the New Year in inebriated, uninhibited style. We danced around each other in a romantic haze, trading the South London palate of gray for the bright lights of Broadway, and taking long subway rides to an abandoned Coney Island, wondering at the Wonder Wheel in hibernation. I remember him lying in the middle of Fifth Avenue to get a picture of the Flatiron Building and while everyone thought he was mental, I thought it was just amazing someone shared the same creative vision as me. In hindsight it's probably not wise to surrender yourself to Manhattan rush-hour traffic for the sake of a picture, but at the time I thought his dedication to capturing the good in the bad was pretty poetic. I still do.

The Infamous Tape was born out of this spontaneous trip, becoming the soundtrack to the bubble we built inside the Big Apple—the edgy, casually cool riffs of Elastica, Weezer, and Veruca Salt giving way to the effortless slacker vibe of the B-side that would provide background noise on shared headphones in the months and years to follow—as we ambled around Soho record shopping on hungover Sunday afternoons. At a time when cohabitation = coma for me, Will reminded me of the youth I still had, the opportunities in front of me, and the meaningful relationships that I now knew could exist that didn't involve talk of IKEA or what drink coasters our neighbors had. I felt *alive*. When we returned to the real world our relationship evolved into a special friendship. And though we tried to make it work romantically, we were just destined for different places, both placing each other on a pedestal; both so consumed by our lives-to-be that—although for a while there the punk shows, cheap drinks and crap dance clubs where we checked off playlists like Keno made sense—we never could quite make it work as a couple.

But isn't that the best ex you could wish for? Not pining for what you didn't have, but happy about what you did, accepting your place in each other's lives, and ultimately, hearts. The INFAMOUS TAPE is the most perfect summation of my life postmillennium—firmly stuck in the early '90s yet accepting that life was about to move on past Girl Power and disposable Ibitha anthems. It is as gritty and real as the people that surrounded me, and for a collection of songs intended to impress someone, its place in my "memories" box as one of the only things I took with me when I moved overseas I think says what I don't need to.

There was an INFAMOUS TAPE 2, which came years after the original, although the music barely altered. I last saw Will in Clapham Common before I left the U.K. all loved up and still dissecting music and all its minutia with the same fervor we did when we first met. Times change, people change, but the tunes that become entwined in the fabric of your life? That's as gritty and real, and as unchangeable, as it gets.

THE INFAMOUS TAPE

A DATE N.R. ○ YES ○ NO.

The Dandy Warhols: Minnesoter
Veruca Salt: Volcano Girls
Sense Field: Leia
The Lemonheads: Mrs. Robinson
Ash: Uncle Pat
Drugstore: Fader
Cable: Freeze the Atlantic
Weezer: El Scorcho
Elastica: Blue
Portishead: Wandering Star
Placebo: Taste in Men
Ben Folds Five: Philosophy
The Ramones: Substitute

B DATE N.R. ○ YES ○ NO.

Ash: Jack Names the Planets
The Wildhearts: Caffeine Bomb
Drugstore: Sugar Sugar
Placebo: Teenage Angst
The Smashing Pumpkins: 1979
The Offspring: Self Esteem
Sense Field: Shallow Grave
Nut: Brains
Blind Melon: Change
Sublime: What I Got
The Specials: Monkey Man
The Muffs: Kids in America
Sugar: Panama City Motel
Tracy Chapman: Fast Car

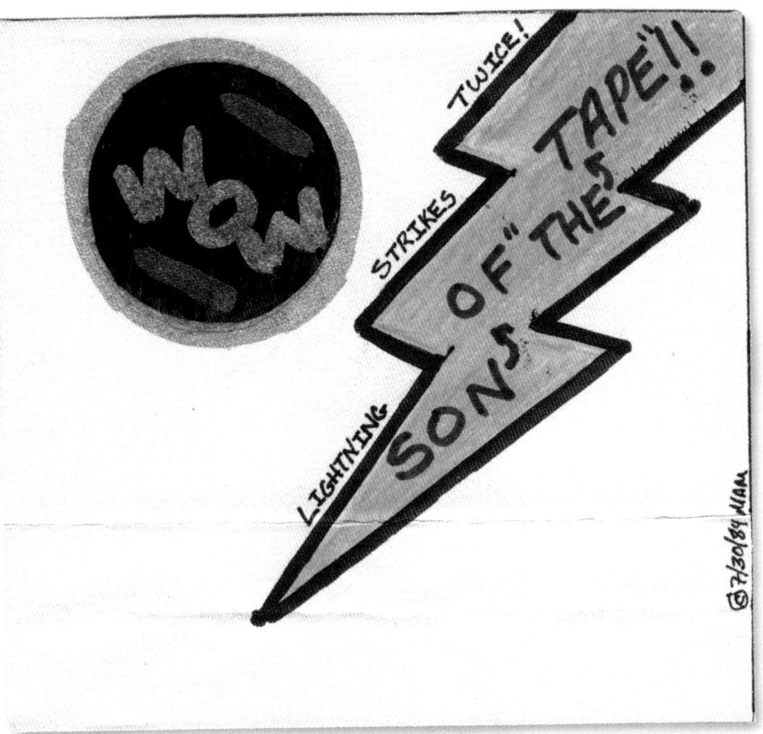

SON OF "THE TAPE"

BY NINA KATCHADOURIAN

I went out with Matt when I was a junior and he was a senior in high school. It was an imbalanced relationship from the start. I had been freshly deceived and injured by my first boyfriend—a bad and confusing first encounter with love—and so when broad-shouldered, laconic, deeply philosophical theater buff Matt came along, I was ripe to be adored and admired. Being with him was comfortable and no work, emotionally. The relationship was a horrible deal for him, and it still ranks very high on my Greatest Hits of Shame when it comes to people I have treated badly in my life.

He told me I looked like Natasha Kinski (ridiculous, but high praise in the early '80s because she had just done that naked pose for Richard Avedon with the python). He gave me Dr. Seuss books with long inscriptions, and he stole a street sign for me that said NINA PLACE. He couldn't make off with the sign alone so he had to rip out of the ground the metal signpost, cement ground plug and all. When I got to his house to see the surprise he was trying to wrest the sign free from the heavy weight of its groundings. We listened to music together in his car and we went to see Simple Minds. Simon and

IF this tape gets to you before a big letter does, don't listen to the tape until the letter comes. This way, you can open the letter after you have listened to the tape. It was cheaper to mail them seperately.

Love,
Matt "The Cheap One"

Garfunkel's "Bridge Over Troubled Water" was declared Our Song.

Summer came and I was leaving to spend it with a French family so I could learn to speak the language. Matt was planning to mourn the entire time I was gone; I was preparing to have an amazing time, and looked forward to writing letters. My adventure began the second I got on the plane and saw an incredibly cute guy walking down the aisle toward the only empty seat available: the one next to me. David was tall and tan, a college freshman in Florida, a semi-pro bike racer. He got us headphones so we could watch the movie together. I made it pretty clear I wanted to make out with him and so we did, for most of the transatlantic flight, under a staticky wool blanket. I kissed him good-bye at baggage claim and never saw him again, and that was fine. The rest of the summer was spent with the charming Veronique, sixteen years old, French, feisty, and incredibly cute, and a boy magnet. We flirted with windsurfing instructors, went to clubs that served us vodka Fantas without carding us, hiked in the mountains, confided in each other, and cracked each other up. The day I got back to the States, Matt and several of my other friends were waiting for me at my house. I broke up with him the first second we were alone together. He crouched in my driveway, looking stunned, and saying, "I knew this would happen." I felt bad. I was also irritated.

All summer long, Matt's letters had arrived regularly, always long and handwritten with frequent switching of felt-tip pen colors. He pined for me, he used the word "love," he signed his name on a diagonal with an underline. He sent me

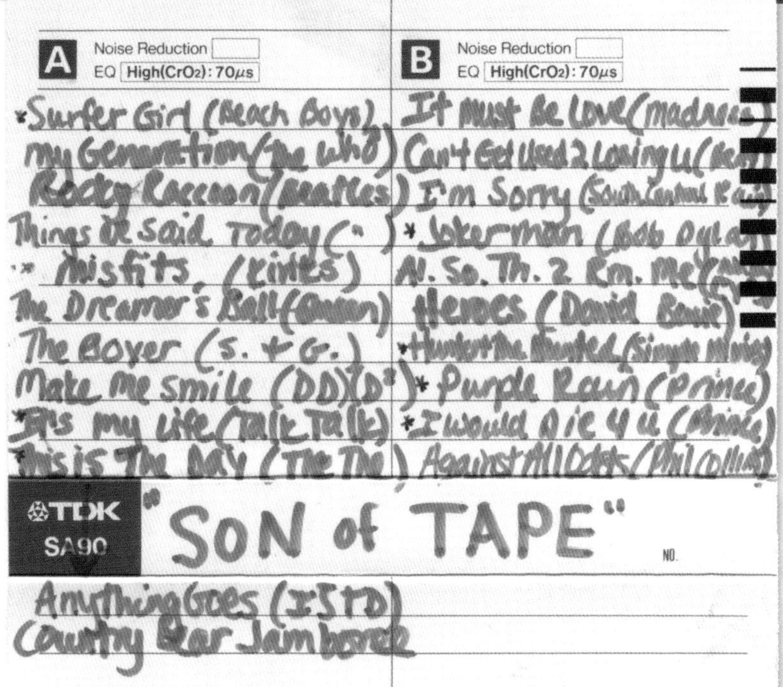

tapes. There were two that came as a pair, sent in installments: first THE TAPE and then SON OF "THE TAPE," emblazoned with an emblem that said "Lightning strikes twice!" The playlist is written in my handwriting, with asterisks that indicate the songs I liked. Inside the tape case is still a handwritten instructional note from Matt, explaining he had mailed the tape and the accompanying letter separately (cheaper) but to wait for the letter before listening to the tape. I am sure I didn't. It was a good mix. The obviously suggestive song titles ("It Must Be Love," "Can't Get Used to Losing You,' and "I Would Die 4 U") were annoying. But there were unexpected and strange songs too, like R.E.M.'s "So. Central Rain" and "Misfits" (The Kinks). I listened to "Joker Man" (Bob Dylan) so often that I knew exactly how long the rewind took to the start of the song, and I learned all the words. I loved "It's My Life" by Talk Talk and cranked it on my Walkman. I realized he put it on the tape for the first line, "Funny how I found myself in love with you," but I chose to hear the song purely as an anthem of independence, the soundtrack that rationalized whatever freedoms I chose to indulge that summer.

A decade later I encountered one of the wisest things I've ever heard spoken in a relationship discussion: "I just need you to be clear in your intentions toward me." These words came from another boyfriend, someone I really loved, at a point in time when we had to make a choice about our very complicated romantic future. It summarizes exactly the way in which I failed Matt so colossally. I never did him the favor of telling him I wasn't serious and I didn't really love him the same way, and I was dishonest about it because I wanted him to keep doing all those things that made me feel good. I liked the pining and the devotion and the love and the attention. I was selfish and stupid in the face of this sweet and well-meaning person. Later, I learned how the lavish expenditure of love on a selfish and untruthful recipient completely robs you of all joy when the truth eventually makes itself clear. SON OF THE TAPE is the only cassette I still have that's worth writing about, since it is an excuse to make a public apology.

Dear Matt,

I am very sorry.

Sincerely,

Nina

SON OF "THE TAPE"

DATE

N.R. ○ YES ○ NO.

The Beach Boys: Surfer Girl

The Who: My Generation

The Beatles: Rocky Raccoon

The Beatles: Things We Said Today

The Kinks: Misfits

Queen: The Dreamers Ball

Simon and Garfunkel: The Boxer

Duran Duran: Make Me Smile (Come Up and See Me)

Talk Talk: It's My Life

The The: This Is the Day

***Indiana Jones and the Temple of Doom* soundtrack:** Anything Goes

Country Bear Jamboree

DATE

N.R. ○ YES ○ NO.

Madness: It Must Be Love

English Beat: Can't Get Used to Losing You

R.E.M.: South Central Rain (I'm Sorry)

Bob Dylan: Jokerman

Naked Eyes: Always Something There to Remind Me

David Bowie: Heroes

Simple Minds: Hunter and the Hunted

Prince: Purple Rain

Prince: I Would Die 4 U

Phil Collins: Against All Odds

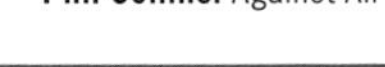

When Things Were Good

By Fiona Maazel

Something Sweet From NYC, JL
A N.R. ON OFF (B)
B N.R. ON OFF (B)
I DON'T KNOW WHAT TO WRITE
Going To California
I Could Have Lied
Solace of You
Classic Girl
Knockin' On Heaven's Door
Wave of Mutilation
Jump In the River
All I Ever Wanted
Angel
Wish U Were
Little Martha
Starfish + Coffee
2 Princes
Broken Hearts
Bold As Love
7 turns
PATIENCE
So Far Away
The End
FUJI PHOTO FILM CO., LTD., TOKYO 106.
MADE IN JAPAN / FABRIQUE AU JAPON / FABRICADO EN JAPÓN

My first high school boyfriend, we called him little John. There were two's between us—inches and years—he was older, I was taller, it equaled out in the end. Before me, he'd been with a girl whose left breast could hold eight of mine. She was sexy and zaftig; I was a virgin. Ha, a virgin—I'm pretty sure I'd kissed only one boy by then, whose lips, incidentally, I can still feel today. I was fifteen, but already, I'd had my heart snapped twice. So for this older guy (he played lacrosse, wore combat boots and a bomber jacket, was—in sum—anarchic, alienated, and thus: hot), there'd be no snapping. If I even got within striking distance, I was going to be whatever he wanted. I started to wear flats. I started watching *The Wonder Years* for news of how to give a *hand job* and when this information was unavailing, I sought example in the burlesque impresario Robin Byrd—friends and I would actually sing the show's theme song, "Baby Let Me Bang Your Box," out loud—only to find there was no *interacting* on the show. No states of arousal to study, no techniques to adopt. John and I started going out and I was terrified.

Fast-forward a year. I'd had a boyfriend for a whole year! I bumbled along, embarrassed myself, but it didn't matter: this guy loved me. Given the heartwreck that has become my experience of romance since then, I've learned to put a premium on the people who, quite simply, love you.

In May of that year, my parents announced we were moving to Los Angeles. I'd had a party in our apartment a couple months before, which sent one kid to the hospital with kidney failure, so there was no trusting me to stay behind and finish out high school in New York. Me and John were doomed. I didn't take it well, he took it worse. I tend to shut down when hurt seems lethal—think of the emergency

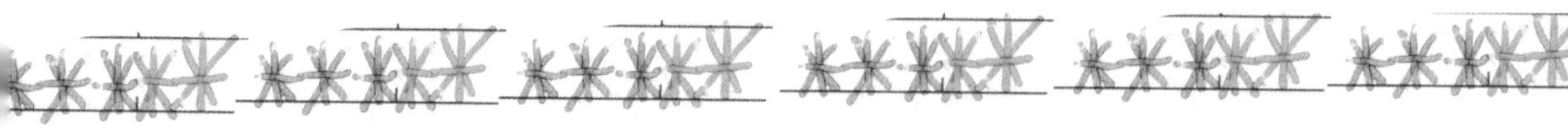

switch on a reactor—but his method was to feel the hurt and record it. I was going to California. The first guy who ever loved me was not. He made me a mixtape. It was full of mainstream music that meant something to us, maybe because though he was troubled and struggling and I was—quite obviously—a little weird, our relationship was conventional as could be.

I listened to the tape all the time. I'd sit in French class at my new high school and stare at the girl who played Winnie on *The Wonder Years*—she really was in my French class—and think about talking to her after, but just putting on my headphones, instead.

SOMETHING SWEET FROM NYC, JH

A DATE N.R. ○ YES ○ NO.

Led Zeppelin: Going to California
Red Hot Chili Peppers: I Could Have Lied
Living Colour: Solace of You
Jane's Addiction: Classic Girl
Guns N' Roses: Knocking on Heaven's Door
The Pixies: Wave of Mutilation
Sinéad O'Connor: Jump in the River
Lenny Kravitz: All I Ever Wanted
Jimi Hendrix: Angel
Pink Floyd: Wish You Were Here
The Allman Brothers Band: Little Martha

B DATE N.R. ○ YES ○ NO.

Prince: Starfish & Coffee
Spin Doctors: Two Princes
Living Colour: Broken Hearts
Jimi Hendrix: Bold as Love
The Allman Brothers Band: Seven Turns
Guns N' Roses: Patience
Dire Straits: So Far Away
The Doors: The End

40 OZ. TO FREEDOM MIX

BY SARA STRAHAN

After growing up in the suburbs of Chicago and attending a high school that was like a bad John Hughes movie, going to UC Santa Cruz seemed like an incredible accomplishment. I went from high school hallways filled with meatheads and young Republicans to a "clothing optional" campus in a grove of redwood trees looking out over some of the best surfing beaches in the world. I was going to a university that didn't have grades, and whose earliest students had chosen the banana slug as a mascot not only because they are hermaphrodites with huge penises, but also despite being able to impregnate themselves, they still have sex with each other for days on end. I was definitely not in Chicago anymore.

Music was another part of my cultural landscape that had totally changed. Those California kids who were now my peers were just so . . . advanced. I had listened to "X" in high school; they had been at the Whisky A Go Go show where they recorded their live album. I knew some people in a band; they had grown up with Offspring and The Minutemen. I went to this really crazy hardcore show one time with my friend; they had been going to shows at Gillman Street since they were thirteen, It all made for an amazing music scene in Santa Cruz and far from being intimidated I was thrilled to jump in—which is how I first met Eric.

It was 1989 and my second year at college, and I was going to yet another house party with a band. The party was at Eric's house and the draw was a death metal band that Eric was fronting. The cops broke up the party and the band never really got going, but Eric and I hit it off and became fast friends. He was six-feet-one-inches with red hair, freckles, and beautiful bone structure courtesy of his Filipino mom. He had grown up with the punks in San Jose and had crazy stories about all the violent shit that he had been involved in. But beneath his leather jacket, his Misfits

T-shirt and the spiked bracelets, Eric was a real sweetheart. He was extremely loyal and protective of his friends, especially the ladies, and with me he had good reason to worry. I was feisty, and would refuse escorts home after a night of partying and then occasionally wander down to the beach alone in my bikini to go for a dip in the middle of the night. Eric had chased me down there more than a couple times and finally put an end to it by dragging our friend Dave over one night to tell me the story of how he and three friends used to go swimming at night, and how one night only two of them had come back.

Eric and I both stayed in Santa Cruz the year after we graduated. We lived together in a house crammed full of our closest friends and worked together at a hand-made glass company with an angry hippie named Redwood packing up large quantities of eighty-five-dollar dinner plates for fancy stores around the world. It was a stupid job, but solid work for a beach town and we made the best of it. By the time the next summer came around, people were starting to go in different directions. I was getting ready to move to Japan to work and travel around Asia for a year, and Eric spent most of the summer sailing in a race to Hawaii and back on a thirty-two-foot boat with his dad. By the time he got back to Santa Cruz, I was leaving in less than a month. I spent a lot of my time with Eric in those final days—going to the beach or on bike rides during the days and drinking whiskey and playing poker and craps at night. In hindsight, I can see that something else was developing between us and that Eric liked me more than a friend. Whether it was naïveté, denial, or both, I didn't see it at the time, and along with the rest of my friends in Santa Cruz, I said good-bye to him and left.

I went to Japan to meet up with a bunch of Santa Cruz gals and to work as "hostesses" in bars for Japanese businessmen. After three months we had to leave the country to renew our tourist visas so a few of us had decided to go to Thailand for a few weeks around New Year's. Sometime that fall, Eric and our friend John had decided to go on a trip to Southeast Asia so we all picked a date and a restaurant on a remote beach that we had found in a travel guide to meet at. By the time Eric and John arrived, the girls and I had already settled into life on our tropical island—bamboo huts, tropical fruit smoothies, and all-night drug-ravaged raves at clubs in the middle of the jungle brought to you by the international rave circuit that had converged on the island. Days were spent recovering on the beach by swimming and smoking the ounce of weed that we had bought for about three dollars. It was paradise for a twenty-three-year-old, but when Eric and John announced that they were leaving for India, I was feeling restless and so the three of us traveled together for the next seven weeks.

We were the quintessential budget travelers and shared everything from the one Walkman we had between us to our single room with one double bed that we got at each guesthouse. Days and weeks just passed with varying degrees of activity. We'd leave a town when one or all of us got restless enough to leave and we'd hop a train to the next random place. We had spent so much time together that we started to finish each other's sentences, and the same stupid in-jokes never failed to crack us up. We all had a complete mental inventory of every tape we had between us and could probably sing all the songs on them from memory. We were all really close, but things were definitely shifting with Eric. I'd fall asleep on his chest during bus and train rides; over the course of our trip our sleeping order in the double bed had gone from random to Eric

FUJI DR-I Extraslim IEC I / TYPE I NORMAL

40 OZ to Freedom Mix
No. DR-I

A N.R. ☐ON ☐OFF ( )	B N.R. ☐ON ☐OFF ( )
Jen Side	Grandma Side
DRI	Cypress Hill - Insane in the Brain
Alice Donut - Untidy Suicide	Run DMC / Public Enemy -
Sublime / Beastie Boys	Victim's Family -
Bad Religion - Fuck Armageddon	Sick & Wrong - Wesson Oil
Butthole Surfers - Goofy's Concern	C.O.C. - Painted Smiling Face
Duran Duran - Save A Prayer	Rage Against the Machine
Men At Work - Helpless Automation	- Bullet in Your Head
the Gits - Another Shot of Whiskey	Juliana Hatfield - My Sister
Green Jello - House Me Teenage	Neneh Cherry - Move with Me
Rave	Alice Donut - Come Up w/
Kid Frost - the Volo	Your Hands Out / over

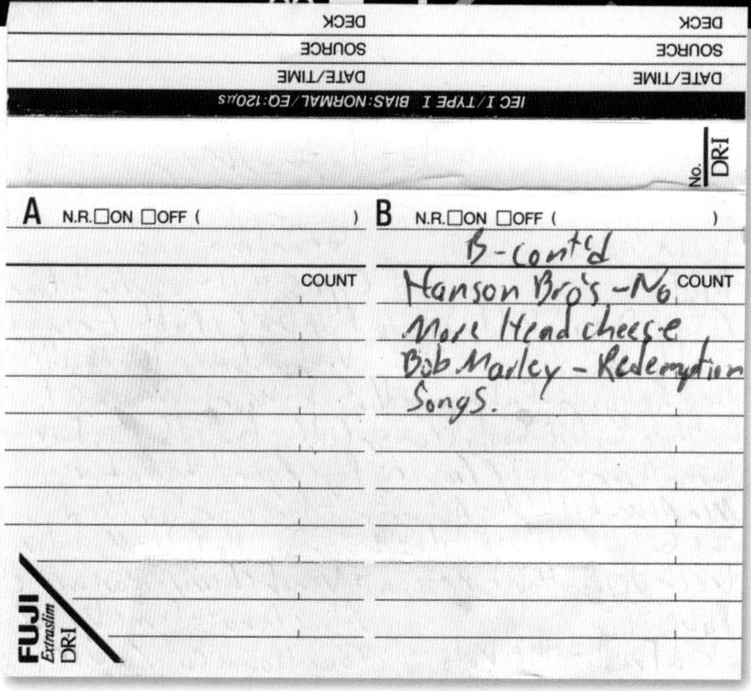

and I always sleeping next to each other. It progressed like a PG-13 movie from lying next to each other, to spooning, to a full-on snuggle plus a few stolen quiet kisses when John was snoring and definitely asleep.

Five weeks had passed in India and I announced that I was going to Thailand for one last week before I had to go back to Japan. The boys decided to go with me and we went to a tiny unpopulated island near Cambodia. Monsoon season was starting to come in and we spent our days writing, reading, and playing cards while watching out over the stormy sea from the porch of our bamboo hut. While it was definitely time for me to head back to Japan, I was sad about leaving the boys, especially Eric. We both knew that things had changed and we were both avoiding having that conversation. Because we were so nervous to talk about it, we decided to write each other letters about what we thought we should do about "us" and then exchanged the letters and read and discussed them. The letters were funny and adorable, but after lots of giggles and a heartfelt discussion we decided that we shouldn't pursue a relationship. The main reasons were that we didn't want to fuck up a good friendship and that Eric had gone out with a mutual friend for years in college who we knew would be upset and hurt if we started dating. We agreed that it had been a special and interesting time in our friendship and left it at that.

I waved good-bye at the ferry, confused about how sad Eric seemed at my leaving. I made my way back to Japan while Eric got so sick that he and John had to leave the island and fly back to the States much sooner than they had originally planned. Eric and I kept in touch through letters and the black-market phone cards that I bought and then one day a package arrived. Inside was a homemade batch of chocolate-chip cookies and a mixtape on which Eric's chicken scrawl read, 40 OZ. TO FREEDOM MIX. I loved that tape from the minute I got it and listened to it constantly while wandering past pachinko parlors and ramen stands or riding on the crammed trains of Osaka. Some of the songs I knew and they took me right back to the moment of driving around in Santa Cruz in Eric's Dodge Dart, hanging out with our friends or some show that we had gone to together. But even if I didn't know the song, I knew why Eric had put it on that tape—what line meant the most to him or cracked him up or reminded him of his San Jose days—and that was enough to make me like it, too. The tape as a whole somehow reflected all the intimacies that Eric and I had shared during our five-year friendship—in nothing less than a punk rock kind of way.

One day I was walking around Osaka with an Australian girl I was friendly with. We were talking about boys and love and relationships. She asked me to describe the qualities I was looking for in a guy and I rattled off a list of things. She pressed me to give examples and so I did, suddenly realizing that every example ended with "like my friend Eric." I went back to my apartment that night and wrote the boldest letter that I have probably ever written. I told Eric that I had decided to move to San Francisco after my stay in Japan and that when I got there I wanted us to be together.

A couple months later Eric drove up from Santa Cruz to pick me up from the airport in San Francisco and shortly after my return, he moved there to be with me for the next three and a half years. Although our relationship had more than its share of ups and downs, he was my best friend and the first person that I trusted enough to truly fall in love with. To this day, no courtship has ever compared to ours and no love of mine has ever rivaled Eric's sweetness.

40 OZ. TO FREEDOM MIX

A DATE
N.R. ○ YES ○ NO.

D.R.I.: Suit and Tie Guy
Alice Donut: Untidy Suicide
Sublime: 40 Oz. to Freedom
Beastie Boys: Boomin' Granny
Bad Religion: We're Only Gonna Die
Butthole Surfers: Goofy's Concern
Duran Duran: Save a Prayer
Men at Work: Helpless Automation
The Gits: Another Shot of Whiskey
Green Jelly: House Me Teenage Rave
Kid Frost: The Volo

B DATE
N.R. ○ YES ○ NO.

Cypress Hill: Insane in the Membrane
Run-D.M.C.: Can I Get It, Yo
Public Enemy: You're Gonna Get Yours
Victims Family: In a Nutshell
Sick & Wrong: Wesson Oil
Corrosion of Conformity: Painted Smiling Face
Rage Against the Machine: Bullet in Your Head
The Juliana Hatfield Three: My Sister
Neneh Cherry: Move with Me
Alice Donut: Come Up with Your Hands Out
Hanson Brothers: No More Headcheese
Bob Marley: Redemption Song

Scissors and Snare Drums

By Michael Hearst

In the summer of 1996, the year after I graduated from VCU, I worked as a screen printer for an art-supply store in Richmond, Virginia. I slaved away by myself in an old wooden attic, which was perhaps one of the most miserable environments that I've ever experienced. Aside from the toxic chemicals wafting through the air in abundance, the temperatures in the attic on any given afternoon were unbearable. This was partially due to the greenhouse effect of trapped summer heat, but largely caused by the plastisol-curing oven that leaked temperatures of up to one thousand degrees. My only relief came from large jugs of water, which I refilled in the bathroom sink just about every hour.

The one good memory from that job was a girl named Nina who worked downstairs in the store. She was semi-Goth, with black stockings, black skirts, and black nails. Her un-Gothness came in the form of indie rock T-shirts and bleach-blond hair with a single red dreadlock that hung to the side. Nina and I quickly developed a flirtatious friendship. We often spent lunchtime together, heading to the Village Café for burgers and coffee.

One afternoon, while perhaps delirious from the summer heat, I misprinted a NASCAR T-shirt. Instead of throwing it away, I hand-painted her name on the side of the crooked race car, and brought it to her as a gift. It must have been a week or two later that she presented me with a mixtape. Aside from the uninspired selection of songs broadcast over the Richmond radio airwaves, this cassette quickly became the soundtrack to my summer. I specifically remember making fun of her for putting "Back In Black" on the tape.

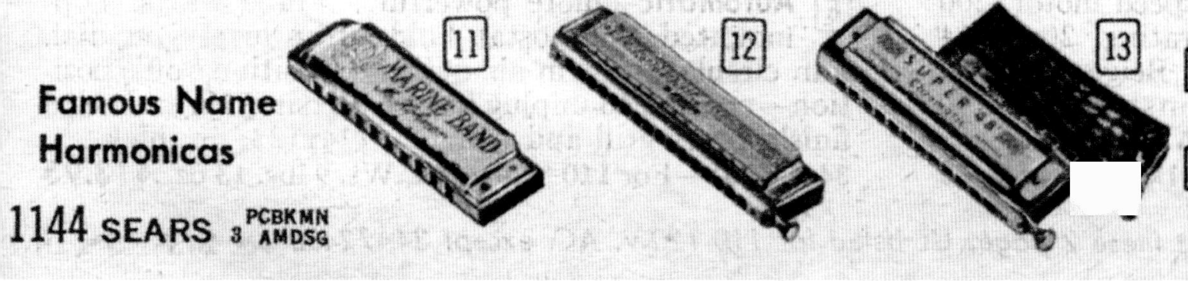

She firmly argued, "Come on, it's one of the most perfect rock songs ever created!"

Funny thing is, I now kind of agree with her. I also remember being disappointed that she put Chrome Daddy Disco on the mix. CDD were a local rockabilly band whose singer I didn't particularly get along with at the time. Alas.

As much as Nina and I seemed to hit it off, nothing ever really came of our relationship. Once or twice she hinted at a boyfriend she had back at college in Northern Virginia. For some reason I never pried into the subject. I think I was just too shy. Regardless, summer ended, and Nina went back to school. I quit the job soon after, overjoyed to land a much better gig as a harmonica technician at Hohner, Inc. I never heard from Nina again.

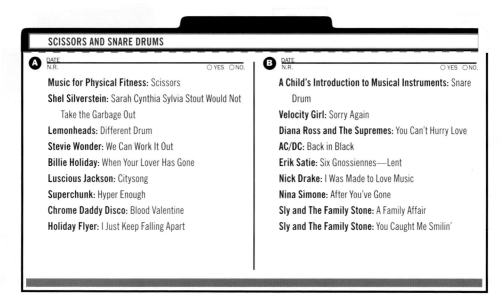

SCISSORS AND SNARE DRUMS

A DATE N.R. ○ YES ○ NO.

Music for Physical Fitness: Scissors
Shel Silverstein: Sarah Cynthia Sylvia Stout Would Not Take the Garbage Out
Lemonheads: Different Drum
Stevie Wonder: We Can Work It Out
Billie Holiday: When Your Lover Has Gone
Luscious Jackson: Citysong
Superchunk: Hyper Enough
Chrome Daddy Disco: Blood Valentine
Holiday Flyer: I Just Keep Falling Apart

B DATE N.R. ○ YES ○ NO.

A Child's Introduction to Musical Instruments: Snare Drum
Velocity Girl: Sorry Again
Diana Ross and The Supremes: You Can't Hurry Love
AC/DC: Back in Black
Erik Satie: Six Gnossiennes—Lent
Nick Drake: I Was Made to Love Music
Nina Simone: After You've Gone
Sly and The Family Stone: A Family Affair
Sly and The Family Stone: You Caught Me Smilin'

BARELY A MIXTAPE

BY KATIE KRENTZ

It was the summer of '99, and I had just finished my freshman year of college at Indiana University. There, I gained the freshman fifteen, some amazing friends, and a whole lot of perspective. This came to a screeching halt once finals were over, and my childhood friend Luke and I were forced to move back home. There we both were, teenagers with a fabulous identity at college, but back home we were our parents' kids where last names matter. But I was a changed woman! I had layers now, dammit! I spent a ton of time with Luke that summer because we were both experiencing college withdrawal, and because we were both really bored.

I'd known Luke since preschool back when he had a bowl cut, and when I, well, had the same bowl cut. We grew up together in the same small town, witnessing each other's awkwardness. He had a constant Kool-Aid–stained mouth and chubby cheeks, and I was rocking a mullet and headgear. We had a history, so it made it easy to pick up where we left off.

Our summer days consisted of his mowing lawns and painting fire hydrants, and my scooping ice cream and making coffee drinks for the locals. At night, he'd pick me up in his Jeep Grand Cherokee, and off we'd go down the country roads past the prison farm and on the highway up to New Buffalo, Michigan, a quaint beach town on Lake Michigan. We'd scarf down burgers and baskets of crinkle-cut fries from Redamak's and then head to the beach, where we'd sit and watch the sunset. No hugging, no kissing, just sitting in silence watching the sky turn from pinks and oranges to grays and blues. It was magnificent. I sensed that there was nothing less we'd rather do than screw. Add a huge heap of crippling Catholic guilt, and you have a safe summer relationship where no one gets hurt (or pregnant!).

I don't really remember the night Luke gave me the mixtape. I think it was at the end of our summer together. The year he made this tape was the birth of the Winamp and Napster. The mixtape had already been replaced with the much easier mix CD, so I was a bit confused when he gave me a tape when both of us only had CD players in our cars. Plus, he had made the tape from a new thing called a Playlist from his computer. It was sweet of him to give me the tape despite my inability to actually play the tape.

The contents of the tape run as deep as a conversation on a Friday night at a frat

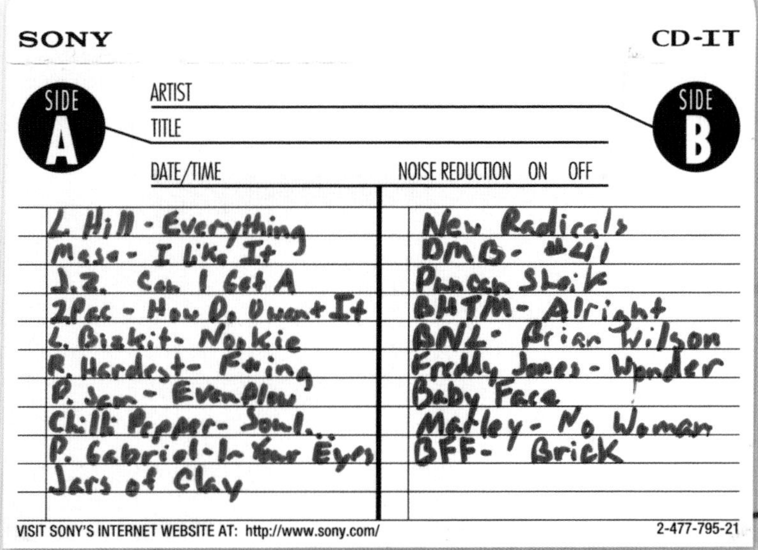
SONY CD-IT

SIDE A

ARTIST

TITLE

DATE/TIME NOISE REDUCTION ON OFF

SIDE B

Side A	Side B
L. Hill - Everything	New Radicals
Mase - I Like It	DMB - #41
J.Z. Can I Get A	Pancam Shaik
2Pac - How Do U want It	BHTM - Alright
L. Bizkit - Nookie	BNL - Brian Wilson
R. Hardest - F*ing	Freddy Jones - Wonder
P. Jam - Evenflow	Baby Face
Chili Pepper - Soul...	Marley - No Woman
P. Gabriel - In Your Eyes	BFF - Brick
Jars of Clay	

VISIT SONY'S INTERNET WEBSITE AT: http://www.sony.com/ 2-477-795-21

house (which he belonged to). What was this tape? Looking back on it now, was this cassette him making a move? With titles like "How Do You Want It" and "Nookie"—maybe. The tape had most of the songs we played on the nights where we had nowhere to be, because our town celebrated those *in* high school, not those who were now a year out of high school. Now we're a part of the ones who do the slow fade from the town. At least we knew we had each other.

This tape is full of mainstream songs that don't dare go below the surface. Kind of like us at the time. There's just too much complexity there, so let's keep things playful and fun like the tape. He was barely my boyfriend, and this was barely a mixtape. Gone were the days of syncing your tapes on a dual-deck boombox to make a carefully thought-out tape that took hours to make. This was a drag-and-drop situation with an export from a computer to a cassette that masked itself as a mixtape. Just like the drag-and-drop summer from college back to our hometown with him that masked itself as a relationship.

Back at school, I had my first taste of diversity, and Luke had just had his first taste of conformity, and we were both hooked. Somehow though, we were both able to meet halfway for the summers during college and enjoy the crappy music he liked on full blast down the lonely Indiana roads. Soon we'd find ourselves traveling down two very different paths, he pursuing a job in finance in-state, and I pursuing a career in entertainment in Los Angeles.

The songs on this tape don't remind me much of Luke. And I'm pretty sure these songs don't remind him of me, either. These songs reminded us of our respective friends we so desperately missed, because at that age finding people who get you is everything. We were each other's filler till August rolled around, and until then we could replay the year from the comfort of Luke's stereo.

GOOD STUFF / VOL I

DATE
N.R. ○ YES ○ NO.

Lauryn Hill: Everything Is Everything
Mase: I Like It
Jay Z: Can I Get . . .
2Pac: How Do You Want It
Limp Bizkit: Nookie
Rich Hardesty: I Never Wanna See You Again
Pearl Jam: Evenflow
Red Hot Chili Peppers: Soul to Squeeze
Peter Gabriel: In Your Eyes
Jars of Clay: Flood

B

DATE
N.R. ○ YES ○ NO.

Brand New Radicals: Get What You Give
Dave Mathews Band: #41
Duncan Sheik: Barely Breathing
Big Head Todd and the Monsters: Alright
Barenaked Ladies: Brian Wilson
Freddy Jones Band: Wonder
Babyface: I'll Make Love to You
Bob Marley: No Woman, No Cry
Ben Folds Five: Brick

WHO'S CALLING, PLEASE?

BY DAVE FISCHOFF

Sometime late in the summer of 1998, I got an email from a girl named Emma. I'd just released my first record, and Emma wanted to know if she could interview me for her "Web gazette" (this is before "blog" had entered the vocabulary). This was completely exciting to me—not only was it my first interview with someone outside my friend-with-a-zine sphere, but it was with someone on the other side of the planet! Emma was from Sydney, Australia. Of course I said yes, and the interview took place over the course of several emails. Even from those first exchanges I could tell that she was smart and charming, and I wanted to know more about her. We kept writing each other well after the interview was over, and the emails began to get more personal. She was a painter and a designer, and she wanted to move to New York one day. She liked cats and chamomile tea, and she played toy piano in a band. We traded photos. She was definitely a cutie. I really, really wanted to meet this girl.

Of course, Australia isn't easy or cheap to get to, but around this time my stepgrandmother passed away and left me a little bit of money. Not enough to live off or anything, but definitely enough to make a trip Down Under. Emma's birthday was coming up in a few months and I got an amazing vision in my head: What if I surprised her by showing up on her birthday unannounced? If I could get in touch with her roommate, Julie, she could set up a birthday party for Emma and I could show up dressed in a gorilla costume. What? Yeah, I don't know why, but for some reason I pictured myself showing up at Emma's backyard birthday barbie dressed in a gorilla outfit, prancing and dancing around for a bit, and then removing the gorilla mask to reveal my true identity. Perfect.

Anyway, I knew Emma and Julie were renting out an apartment that was in Emma's mother's name, and I knew the street she lived on from her mentioning it in an email. I got online and found a phone book for Sydney, Australia, with a listing for her mother on the correct street. Excellent. Now all I had to do was call up the apartment and ask for Julie (in an Australian accent, of course). If Julie answered, I'd just explain who I was and we'd start concocting our plan, but if it was Emma, I'd pretend I was Julie's friend or something and say I'd try calling back later. I spent about ten minutes pacing in my bedroom, rehearsing my best Australian accent (" 'Ello, is Julie there, playse?") and then dialed. *Ring ring.* A female voice answered, and I asked if Julie was there. No, she wasn't. Nerves started to creep in, and my accent started to slip. The voice

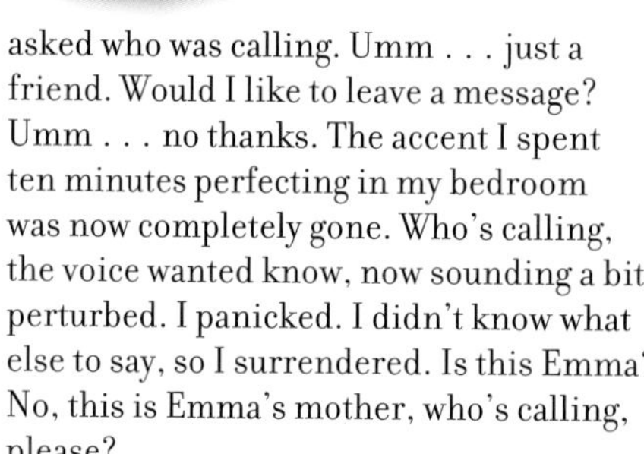

asked who was calling. Umm . . . just a friend. Would I like to leave a message? Umm . . . no thanks. The accent I spent ten minutes perfecting in my bedroom was now completely gone. Who's calling, the voice wanted know, now sounding a bit perturbed. I panicked. I didn't know what else to say, so I surrendered. Is this Emma? No, this is Emma's mother, who's calling, please?

And there it went. Fake accents, gorilla costumes, all of my best-laid plans straight down the tubes. As it turns out, Emma's mom was staying in the apartment as well (a situation that's more common for Australian twenty-somethings than in the United States). I came clean, told her I was Emma's friend Dave from the United States. Emma was sleeping, but her mom would let her know I called. Emma did call me back the next day and I explained the whole situation. I ended up flying to Sydney and yes, the romance bloomed, and we did our best to sustain a long-very long-distance relationship. This mix was from the period when we were still trying to figure out a way to make it work, still hoping that she'd be able to move to the States one day, though that part of the plan never quite worked out. Looking back over the tracklisting, it doesn't strike me as a particularly thematic mix, but more of a snapshot of the kind of music we were both really into at the time. Some of the songs feel completely locked to that period (indie rock like Sebadoh and Pond), and others, like the Spiritualized and Smokey Robinson tunes, will probably sound as great as ever thirty years from now. And those two Palace songs, with Will Oldham's creaky wooden voice, still remind me of a night in Sydney when we were laying in her bed that was draped over with a giant mosquito net. The windows were open, Palace was on the stereo, and we felt secure.

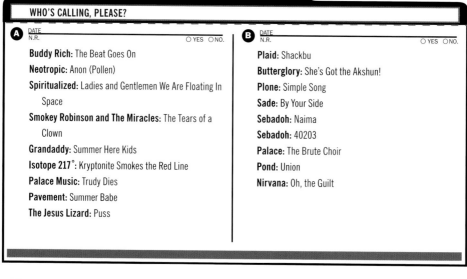

WHO'S CALLING, PLEASE?

A DATE
N.R. ○ YES ○ NO.

Buddy Rich: The Beat Goes On
Neotropic: Anon (Pollen)
Spiritualized: Ladies and Gentlemen We Are Floating In Space
Smokey Robinson and The Miracles: The Tears of a Clown
Grandaddy: Summer Here Kids
Isotope 217°: Kryptonite Smokes the Red Line
Palace Music: Trudy Dies
Pavement: Summer Babe
The Jesus Lizard: Puss

B DATE
N.R. ○ YES ○ NO.

Plaid: Shackbu
Butterglory: She's Got the Akshun!
Plone: Simple Song
Sade: By Your Side
Sebadoh: Naima
Sebadoh: 40203
Palace: The Brute Choir
Pond: Union
Nirvana: Oh, the Guilt

// one: the beat goes on: buddy rich
// two: anon (pollen): neotropic
// three: ladies and gentlemen we are floating in space: spiritualized
// four: tears of a clown: smokey robinson and the miracles
// five: summer here kids: grandaddy
// six: kryptonite smokes the red light: isotope 217°
// seven: trudy dies: palace music
// eight: summer babe: pavement
// nine: puss: the jesus lizard
// ten: shackbu: plaid
// eleven: she's got the akshun!: butterglory
// twelve: simple song: plone
// thirteen: by your side: sade
// fourteen: naima: sebadoh
// fifteen: 40203: sebadoh
// sixteen: brute choir- palace
// seventeen: union: pond
// eighteen: oh, the guilt: nirvana

TDK
IEC II/TYPE II
POSITION CHROME
CDing2 90
A
ONE DAY
N.R. YES NO

TDK
IEC II/TYPE II
POSITION CHROME
CDing2 90
B
WE'RE GOING TO FIND THE SUN
N.R. YES NO

ONE DAY... WE'RE GOING TO FIND THE SUN

BY CECILIA FAGE

I first got to know T in a dingy East End pub—on a drunken summer Sunday afternoon he sat with a pint of Guinness, his bemused blues eyes watching me sing Shania Twain on karaoke. As the evening went on, we laughed at a mutual friend dancing bare-chested in a fringed leather jacket. An afro wig which was passed from head to head. The old ladies who'd been propping up the bar butchered "The Shoop Shoop Song" with a group of us on backing vocals. I sat next to him, and looked at his pale arms next to mine. And the next morning at the bus stop, I was still with him.

In three weeks I would be leaving London for a new life as an Agent Provocateur girl in Los Angeles, so we had no idea that this would be anything more than a fling. But within days of my arriving out there, we had both written to each other, sending the first of what would be a long dialogue of mixtapes.

His mission was to get me hooked on garage bands and a jug being played by the 13th Floor Elevators; mine was to convince him of the seriousness of Dolly Parton's talent.

In less than three months he'd left his job in the U.K. and had come out to be with me; we flew to Las Vegas on my day off work, knowing full well what our intention was by going there, but too terrified to mention it out loud. That night we huddled in a UV-lit strip club, possibly the least romantic place on Earth, watching a huge lady in a glowing bikini gyrating in front of us and our luminous frozen margaritas; and I realized this would be my last night single.

So we were married the next day at the Wee Kirk o' Heather Chapel in denim and stripy T-shirts, him cringing at the lecture he was given by the pastor, me refusing to carry a plastic bouquet; then back to L.A. that night on the red-eye (with the requisite loved-up fumbling under the itchy airline blanket).

We looked so much like each other that people would mistake us for brother and sister, or ask if we were just narcissists. We were a couple of pale, black-haired lovers wandering around the desert together . . . we were that couple that people shouted "Get a room!" at . . . we were joined at our skinny hips.

Practicalities were never our strong point; he had no visa and had to leave. The months we were apart were spent writing to each other, with a cassette; the A/B sides named with a story: BEWARE THE DARKNESS / UP SUNSHINE, WANDERLUST SIDE (TO TURN YOU ON) / HOMESICK SIDE (WANTING TO WALK ON WATER).

What had started out as a way of influencing each other's music taste began to take on more significance; the people in the tapes became our eccentric family members to keep us company while we were alone: Leo Kottke and his twelve-string guitar, Al Stewart's geeky geography teacher voice, David Crosby's drug binges, Mike Heron singing a lullaby of folky fa-la-las.

Almost a year to the day after I left, I joined him back home. Strangely though, the music we'd sent to each communicated better than we did. The cassettes petered out . . . until something important needed to be said; on the day our marriage was over.

His last tape for me was ONE DAY / WE'RE GOING TO FIND THE SUN.

My sister helped me load my boxes into my parent's old VW Golf, parked outside our marital home in leafy, suburban North London. I sat behind the wheel unable to start the car or drive, pushed the cassette in the deck and wept.

I guess what Michael Nesmith was singing said it all:

> *And all this talk about leavin' is strictly bad news.*

ONE DAY WE'RE GONNA FIND THE SUN

DATE
N.R. ○YES ○NO.

Leo Kottke: The Tennessee Toad

Jefferson Airplane: Coming Back to Me

McGuinness Flint: Heritage

Michael Nesmith: Some of Shelley's Blues

Blanche: Song of Trust

Brian Jonestown Massacre: Some Things Go Without Saying

Mike Heron: Audrey

All Night Radio: Anchovya Suite Winter Light

Earth Opera: To Care at All

Moby Grape: I Am Not Willing

Manassas: And So Begins the Task

Brian Jonestown Massacre: Let Me Stand Next to Your Flower

B

DATE
N.R. ○YES ○NO.

Poco: Renaissance

The Beta Band: Dry the Rain

Brian Jonestown Massacre: Lost Inside You

Neil Young: Harvest Moon

Simon and Garfunkel: April (Come She Will)

Les Razilles Denudes: Interlude

Brian Jonestown Massacre: Tschusse

The Monkees: Porpoise Song

The Rolling Stones: Harry Flowers

All Night Radio: Sad K

Jethro Tull: Reasons for Waiting

Leo Kottke: The Sailor's Gone on the Prairie

THE TAPE I FINALLY MADE

BY SARAH GRACE McCANDLESS

In Michigan, March notoriously comes in like a lion and goes out like . . . well, a lion, and 1991 was no different. It was yet another unseasonably cold start to Spring, but despite the weather and a pair of very loud orange and purple parachute pants, a tragic teenage love was about to blossom. To be fair, the pants were meant as an early April Fool's joke, worn by senior David Rivard to our incredibly generic Spring Fling school dance. I suppose it was an attempt to liven up what might have otherwise been a rather bland, predictable affair, but it was a gesture that definitely stood out. This was Grosse Pointe, after all, and while plenty of my classmates had trust funds, that didn't mean they had senses of humor to go along with them.

It was my junior year, and my girlfriends and I were trying desperately to look like we didn't care about anything while huddling in one corner of the gym. The same room that had served as my torture chamber by day had somehow transformed into a dark, mysterious den of opportunity by night. This wasn't a date dance, like Homecoming or Sadie Hawkins, where nearly everyone attending was already paired off; no, *this* was a teenage meat market, complete with a disco ball hanging from the rafters above over the waxed foul lines.

I spotted David (or just "D." as he was known) across the room, jumping around in those crazy pants with a few of his other friends. I convinced my group to move closer to his, and soon enough we had all merged into one giant blob, dancing in hysterics to, of all songs, the Divinyls's "I Touch Myself." Oh, sweet masturbation—how you were once so taboo! Oddly enough, this song never ended up on any mix either of us made for each other. I guess it would have been sort of an odd choice as "our

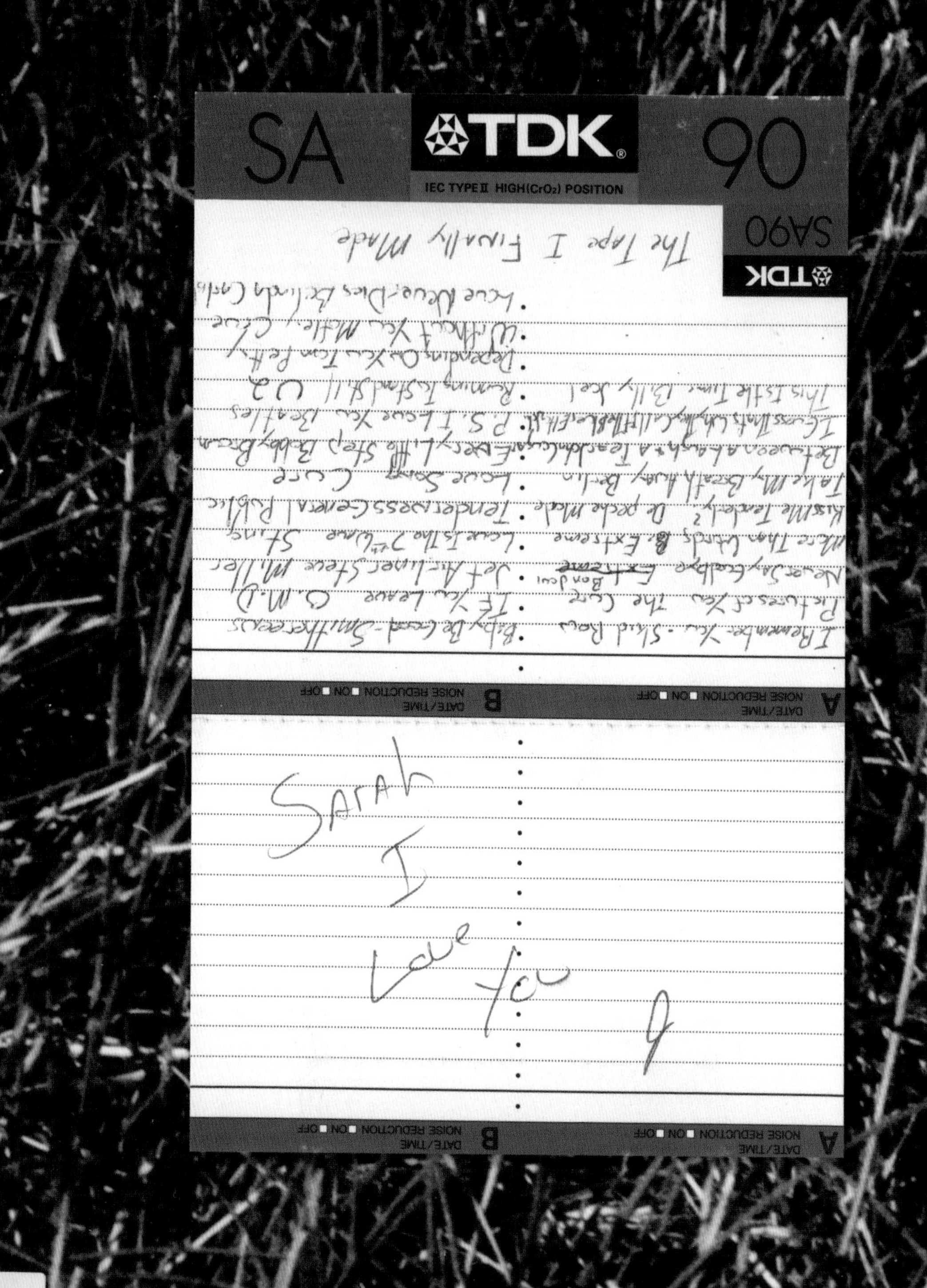
SA
TDK
90
IEC TYPE II HIGH(CrO2) POSITION
SA90
TDK
The Tape I Finally Made
I Remember You - Skid Row
Baby Be Good - Smithereens
Pictures of You The Cure
If You Leave O.M.D.
Never Say Goodbye Bon Jovi
Jet Airliner Steve Miller
More Than Words Extreme
Love Is The 7th Wave Sting
Depeche Mode
Tenderness General Public
Take My Breath Away Berlin
Love Song Cure
Every Little Step Bobby Brown
P.S. I Love You Beatles
This Is the Time Billy Joel
Running to Stand Still U2
Depending On You Tom Petty
Without You Motley Crue
A DATE/TIME NOISE REDUCTION ON OFF
B DATE/TIME NOISE REDUCTION ON OFF
Sarah
I
Love
You
J
A DATE/TIME NOISE REDUCTION ON OFF
B DATE/TIME NOISE REDUCTION ON OFF

song," especially for a guy who was, by all outward appearances, the poster child for All-American Kid—basketball player, preppy, solid grades, nice friends, popular but not pompous, religious parents, a family Labrador, and good-looking to boot.

D. seemed like someone I could bring home, and so I did. Much to the pleasure of my parents, I was never late for my 12:30 A.M. curfew—instead, we would just leave wherever we were thirty to forty-five minutes early so we could park down the street from my house, going from base to base against a soundtrack of '90s hair metal and new wave. He asked me to his senior prom, and I wore a ridiculous, off-shoulder, knee-length white dress, with a piece of lace tied in my hair—looking not unlike a child bride or pageant contestant at best.

Despite my fashion faux pas, we endured, but at his graduation, the reality of his impending departure for college finally started to sink in, as did the fact I would still be here, a good five-and-a-half-hour drive from Miami University in Oxford, Ohio. I started keeping a shoebox of our mementos—notes we had passed, my prom corsage, movie ticket stubs. It wasn't the first shoebox I'd created for a boy, but I was convinced it would be my last, never mind the fact that I was barely seventeen years old.

I spent that summer working the closing shift as a lifeguard at one of the local country clubs, and at dusk, D. would pick me up. We tried our best to stretch out those nights, but instead they seemed to shorten into minutes, and suddenly it was August and time for him to leave for school. I borrowed my best friend Carla's white Chrysler LeBaron, and drove the 3.15 miles from her house to D.'s to say good-bye. He'd been promising me a mix for months, and finally handed it over through our stream of snot-filled tears.

I popped in the tape as I drove away, thinking it might ease the pain, but song after song was about love and loss. He had labeled it, THE TAPE I FINALLY MADE, but he might as well have called it "Slow Songs to Slit Your Wrists To," because I remember thinking, *I'll never be as sad in my life again as I am right now! NEVER!*

(Little did I know the type of *true* heartache that awaited me in the future—like the day they would cancel *Freaks and Geeks*.)

Though I listened to D.'s mix faithfully on a daily basis, we of course managed to fade away completely by the following Spring. Eventually, his shoebox became less of a time capsule and more of a cardboard coffin, so I got rid of most of those contents as well. But I held on to the tape, and I'd like to think he still has those parachute pants tucked away somewhere—because satire *never* goes out of style.

THE TAPE I FINALLY MADE

A DATE N.R. ○ YES ○ NO.

Skid Row: I Remember You
The Cure: Pictures of You
Bon Jovi: Never Say Goodbye
Extreme: More Than Words
Depeche Mode: Somebody
Berlin: Take My Breath Away
John Mellencamp: Between a Laugh and a Tear
Elton John: I Guess That's Why They Call It the Blues
Billy Joel: This Is the Time

B DATE N.R. ○ YES ○ NO.

The Smithereens: Baby Be Good
OMD: If You Leave
Steve Miller Band: Jet Airliner
Sting: Love Is the Seventh Wave
General Public: Tenderness
The Cure: Love Song
Bobby Brown: Every Little Step
The Beatles: P.S. I Love You
U2: Running to Stand Still
Tom Petty: Depending On You
Mötley Crüe: Without You
Belinda Carlisle: Love Never Dies

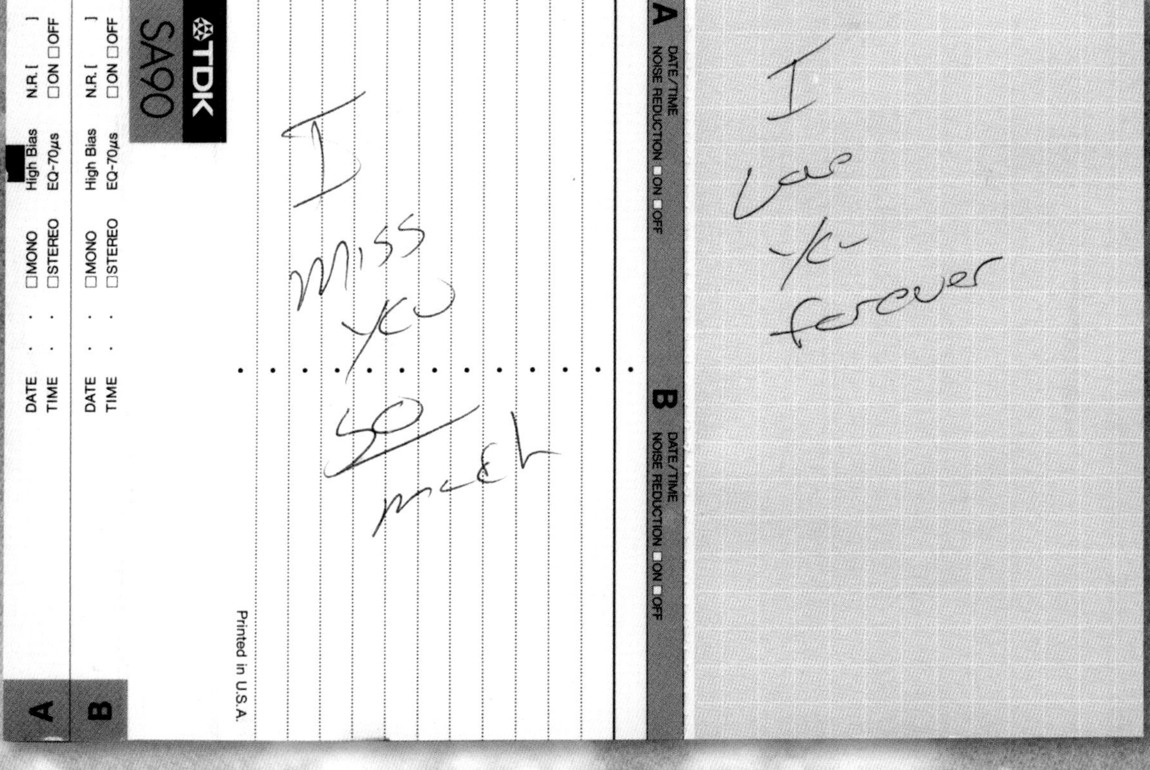

TDK
SA90
DATE
TIME
MONO
STEREO
High Bias
EQ-70μs
N.R. [ ]
ON OFF
A
B
DATE/TIME
NOISE REDUCTION ON OFF
Printed in U.S.A.
I miss you so much
I love you forever

7559-79111-4
killing my lobster gets some action - september 98 sf/
Recordings for THE ENJOYMENT OF MUSIC
Sixth Edition, Shorter
THE
BIG
vol. VII
BIG BANDS
KATE
TDK
D90

PROMISE
PUMPKINS
TDK SA90
Music From The Motion Picture Purple Rain

Cassette Tape and Accessories

LAFAYETTE CASSETTE RECORDING TAPES
CRITERION® DELUXE BLANK TAPE CASSETTES

- Head Cleaning Tape on Each Cassette
- Super-Calendered Tape to Minimize Wear and Improve Frequency Response
- Sensing Foils to Actuate Machines with Reversing Mechanisms
- With Plastic Album Storage Box

Lafayette's best recording tape cassettes manufactured to our specifications, with extra deluxe features. Deep lubricated, super-calendered tape in an improved black plastic cassette, minimizes tape head wear and provides better low and high frequency response. Head cleaning tape at one end removes accumulated material from recorder heads. Sensing foils at each end actuate recorders having automatic reversing capabilities, but may also be used on all cassette recorders. Comes in hard plastic album storage box. Imported. Shpg. wt., 4 oz.

Stock No.	Model No.	Playing Time	NET EACH 1 - 9	NET EACH 10 up
28 K 01298	C-30	30 Minutes	1.23	1.11
28 K 01306	C-60	60 Minutes	1.50	1.35
28 K 01314	C-90	90 Minutes	2.40	2.16
28 K 01322	C-120	120 Minutes	3.18	2.86

LAFAYETTE ECONOMY BLANK TAPE CASSETTES

As Low As 69c

High quality tape assures full fidelity recording. Records and plays 2-tracks at 1⅞ ips. Super strong polyester base. Proper lubrication for longer tape life. Protects heads. Imported. Shpg. wt., 4 oz.

Stock No.	Model No.	Playing Time	NET EACH 1-2	NET EACH 3-9	NET EACH 10 Up
28 K 01280	C-30	30 Minutes	.99	.79	.69
28 K 01223	C-60	60 Minutes	1.19	.99	.89
28 K 01207	C-90	90 Minutes	1.99	1.79	1.59
28 K 01215	C-120	120 Minutes	2.49	2.19	1.99

SOLID STATE CASSETTE AM & FM RADIO TUNERS

AM RADIO TUNER 6.95

FM RADIO TUNER 12.95

- Converts Most Cassette Tape Recorders and Players into a Sensitive Radio

Miniaturized, solid-state radio tuner circuit with self-contained battery (included). Same size as any standard blank or prerecorded cassette. Take it anywhere, play it anywhere. Plays directly through the amplifier and speaker system of your cassette player or recorder. High-impact break resistant case. Size 4x2½x⅜". Imported. Wt. ½ lb.

28 K 43019L AM Radio Tuner ... Net 6.95
FM Radio Tuner ... Net 12.95

TDK C-60SD HI FI CASSETTE

- Low Noise Level.
- Frequency Response 30-20,000 Hz.

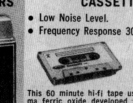

2.99

This 60 minute hi-fi tape uses a new gamma ferric oxide developed for high-density recording. The wide dynamic recording range 32-20,000 Hz. Makes available low noise, distortion-free output for the highest performance that can be expected of a cassette tape. Imported. Shpg. wt., 4 oz.

28 K 01249 .... Net 2.99

LAFAYETTE FOOT SWITCH

3.95

- Ideal for Stenographic Transcribing

Gives your cassette recorder the versatility of a dictating machine. Plays when the foot switch is depressed, stops when released. Simply plugs into "remote" jack. 5 ft. cable with micro-miniature plug. Imported. Shpg. wt., 1 lb.

CASSETTE TAPE CARTRIDGE STORAGE RACK

10.95

- Holds Up To 46 Tapes
- Lazy Susan Type Base

Attractively styled wood and masonite cassette cartridge storage rack with simulated walnut vinyl finish. Has "Lazy Susan" type base for easy access to your cassettes. Size: 7⅞x7⅞x10"H. Shpg. wt., 5 lbs.

28 K 78056W .... Net 10.95

CASSETTE HEAD CLEANER AND TEST TAPE

1.49

3-in-1 Cassette

1) Tests for Proper Head Alignment
2) Tests for Stereo Balance
3) Cleans Tape Head

Keep your cassette player sounding like new with this professionally calibrated test tape. Cleans tape heads to restore full richness of tone. Checks for proper alignment of heads to eliminate crosstalk. Checks for proper balance and equalization of channels. Shpg. wt., 6 oz.

28 K 92024 .... Net 1.49

CASSETTE TEST STROBE

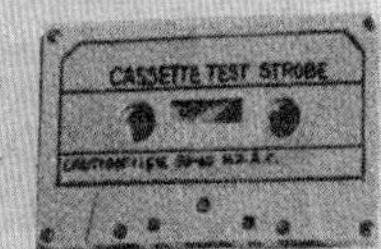

3.69

Checks your cassette recorder/player for proper speed. Too fast causes flutter; too slow creates tape drag or wow. Strobe tape and light built into standard cassette. For 110 VAC 50/60 Hz. Shpg. wt., 5 oz.

28 K 72414 .... Net 3.69

CASSETTE TAPE SPLICER

1.95

Sturdy precision instrument for use in all splicing and editing of cassette tapes. Shpg. wt., 8 oz.

Net 1.95

Scotch

SCREAM'R™

Blank Audio Cassette

45 min
67m

SCREAM'R™

Blank Audio Cassette

Your Music Should Sound This BIG!

Presenting the **SCREAM'R**™ audio cassette–a different tape with a face of its own. Made for the music you like to hear, the way you like to hear it. Offering clear, sharp recordings, and long-lasting quality.

LIMITED WARRANTY
See details on inside.

3M Consumer Video and Audio Products Division
3M
Hutchinson, MN 55350-2927
Made in Korea 34-7027-5088-5

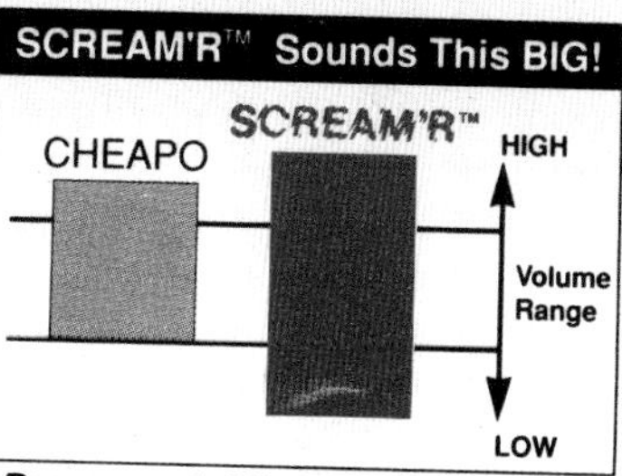

Recommended Usage: EVERYTHING!

Premium Quality

Normal Bias

MANUFACTURER'S COUPON • EXPIRES 12/31/91

SAVE 35¢

on Scotch™ Scream'r Audio Cassettes

Redeem this coupon for 35¢ OFF on your next purchase of 2 or more Scotch SCREAM'R Audio Cassettes.

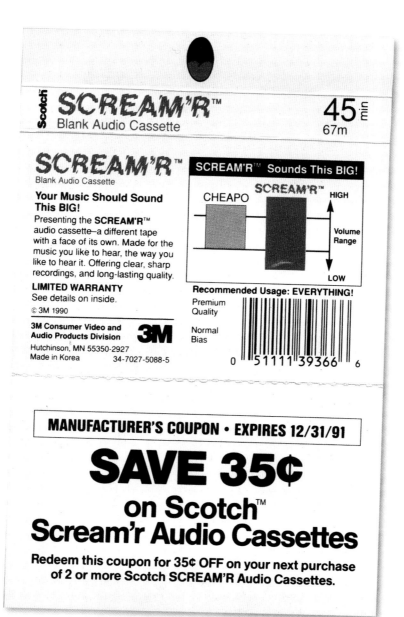

About the Contributors

Jessica Agneessens

Jessica Agneessens is a graduate of the University of Wisconsin-Madison where she majored in English literature with an emphasis on creative writing. She was managing editor at the *Madison Review*, was a recipient of the Cy Howard Memorial Scholarship in Creative Writing, and is an active member of Phi Beta Kappa. Agneessens currently works in operational finance at Whole Foods Market and is based in Austin, Texas. She is founder and director of an annual symposium that pays equal homage to Bluestockings, Gertrude Stein, and Dionysus.

Vinnie Angel

Vinnie Angel is a filmmaker and purveyor of social justice consumer products. He is likely the most renowned tampon-case distributor who ever lived. Visit him at www.vinnieangel.com.

Todd Bachmann

Todd Bachmann is managing producer and director for the nationally distributed public radio program *Sound Opinions* out of Chicago. Prior to the "world's only rock 'n' roll talk show," he was production manager for the public radio show *This American Life*. He currently lives in Evanston, Illinois.

Jennifer Brandel

Jennifer Brandel is not certified in anything and a couple of times, she's almost died. Her hobbies include subscribing to tons of magazines and podcasts and never reading or listening to them, and impersonating famous female vocalists. She's been pen pals with an international drug trafficker in a Bolivian prison, filmed an exercise video of Olympic swimmer Dara Torres, and worked for movie director John Hughes. Recently she's been playing the part of a public radio journalist. Her audio and photographic work has been featured on Chicago Public Radio, NPR's *Day to Day* & *Latino USA*, PRI's *Weekend America*, and *The New York Times* online. She's cofounder of the ladies-only *Dance Dance Party Party* Chicago chapter and coedits *Mule Magazine*.

Diane Bullock

Diane Bullock has been writing comedy for over ten years with credits including *The Onion*, HBO, AOL, VH1, and *Saturday Night Live*'s "Weekend Update." She wrote an original pilot for Comedy Central, an upcoming book for the *Would You Rather?* book series, and is currently working on her first feature film script. She lives with her boyfriend and writing partner in Brooklyn, New York.

Mairead Case

Mairead Case lives and works in Chicago. She has written and edited for publications including *Pitchfork*, *Punk Planet*, *Proximity* Magazine, and the *Stranger*. Mairead's fiction and zines are available at featherproof books, the SQUID Collective, and ZAPP. She curated a radio show about dreams for Neighborhood Public Radio at the 2008 Whitney Biennial.

Matt Casper

Matt Casper is a sentient, bipedal yaz generator and the hell-bound co-author of "Jim & Casper Go to Church." He also rocks: check out www.myspace.com/hellyeahtheband.

Vincent Chung

Vincent Chung is a designer and writer residing in Chicago, Illinois. He has written for *Flavorpill Chicago*, *HeartattaCk*, *The Huffington Post*, *Maximum Rock'n Roll*, *Punk Planet*, and *Ten by Ten*. He also scribes and illustrates things in the snow when he feels the urge.

Leah Dieterich

Leah Dieterich is a writer, filmmaker, and artist living in Los Angeles. She currently works at an agency writing commercials for Jack in the Box and other clients. Her film *Prioritaire* was an official selection at the AFI Dallas Film Fest as well as others. She is working on a screenplay as well a conceptual art project/book of short stories.

Anna Domino

Anna Domino was born in Tokyo and raised in the United States, Italy and Canada. In 1977, she went to New York for a two-week trip and stayed for twenty years. In the early '80s Anna began recording for Belgian label Les Disques du Crepuscule, releasing half a dozen records through them. Back in New York, Anna and husband Michel Delory began a project called Snakefarm, which takes traditional American ballads and rearranges them mercilessly. They have released a selection of these re-works titled *Songs from my Funeral*. Anna and Michel live in Los Angeles where it is always June.

Jancee Dunn

Jancee Dunn grew up in Chatham, New Jersey. She was a writer at *Rolling Stone* from 1989 to 2003, where she wrote twenty cover stories for the magazine. She has written for many different publications, among them *The New York Times*, *Vogue*, *GQ*, and *O: The Oprah Magazine*, where she writes a monthly ethics column entitled "Now What Do I Do?" From 2001 to 2002 she was an entertainment correspondent for *Good Morning America*. Prior to that she was a veejay for MTV2. Her novel *Don't You Forget About Me* is out now from Villard Books. She and her husband live in Brooklyn, New York.

Lissi Erwin

Lissi Erwin is an art director who designs books, CDs, websites, and other ephemera under the moniker of Splendid Corp. She loves old audio equipment and instruments, especially any sort of organ, and plays a Casiotone 701 Keyboard that makes atomic sounds. She loves old things, letterpress and silkscreen printing, rebellion, the color brown, absurdity, and her fiancé Ryan Murphy. Visit her at SplendidCorp.com.

Cecilia Fage

Cecilia Fage is an actor and musician who lives in Bloomsbury, London. She spent her earlier years in a pink dress, working for Agent Provocateur in London and Los Angeles. She loves country music, old musicals, and collecting bows. Lately she's been working with actor/comedian Matt Berry (The IT Crowd, Garth Marenghi's Darkplace, The Mighty Boosh), playing recorder, clarinet, and singing on his album *Witchazel*.

Dave Fischoff

Dave Fischoff puts out records under his own name, composes music for film and television, and remixes other people's songs under the name Spoolwork. He's a Midwesterner now living in Brooklyn, New York.

Amy Fleming

Amy Fleming grew up in London, where she still lives. She works as a writer and editor for the features department of the *Guardian* newspaper. In her spare time she likes to collect graffiti from rock 'n roll venue bathrooms.

Carrie Friedman

Carrie Friedman is a freelance writer living in Los Angeles. Her book *Pregnant Pause: My Journey Through Obnoxious Questions, Baby Lust, Meddling Relatives, and Pre-Partum Depression*, was published in April 2009. Her work has been featured in several magazines, including *Newsweek*. Her website is www.carriefriedmania.com.

Jessica Gentile

Jessica Gentile is a freelance writer who lives just outside New York City, but hopes to live within it. She has written for *CMJ*, *Crawdaddy!*, and *The Paste Magazine*, among other publications. She's currently seeking steadier employment so she'll happily write for you, too. Jessica spends her precious free time photographing strangers with bad hair who block her view at Mountain Goats shows.

Julie Gerstein

Julie Gerstein is a writer and editor living in Brooklyn. She loves her bike, her friends, and snacks. Also traveling. She has written for *Dazed & Confused*, *Anthem*, *Nylon*, and Lemondrop.com. She would like to ghost ride the whip some day.

Claudia Gonson

Claudia Gonson is the pianist/drummer/backing vocalist for The Magnetic Fields. Her day job is as Stephin Merritt's manager, handling all his band projects as well as theater, ads, and film work. Currently Stephin is writing a musical version of the Neil Gaiman story *Coraline* for the stage, and The Magnetic Fields are touring to support their newest CD, *Distortion*. As a drummer, she has also played with the bands Astrud and Honey Bunch. Along with her performances with The Magnetic Fields and Future Bible Heroes, her drumming and backing vocals also appear on the Tender Trap album, *6 Billion People* and Astrud's *Performance*.

David Greenberger

Artist David Greenberger began publishing his conversations with the elderly as *The Duplex Planet* in 1979. It has since been collected into books, adapted into a comic book, been the subject of a couple documentaries, and the source for a series of performances and monologues. He has been a regular commentator for National Public Radio's *All Things Considered*. His paintings and designs have appeared on hundreds of album covers.

Ben Greenman

Ben Greenman is an editor at *The New Yorker* and the author of several acclaimed books of fiction, including *Superbad*, *Correspondences*, and the recent novel *Please Step Back*. He lives in Brooklyn, New York.

Ayun Halliday

Ayun Halliday is the author of four self-mocking memoirs, *No Touch Monkey! And Other Travel Lessons Learned Too Late*, *The Big Rumpus*, *Job Hopper*, and *Dirty Sugar Cookies: Culinary Observations, Questionable Taste*. She has also written one very serious and instructive book for children, *Always Lots of Heinies at the Zoo*. In her spare time, she is the chief primatologist and sole staff member of the quarterly zine, *The East Village Inky*. Ayun lives in Brooklyn with her husband, playwright Greg Kotis and their increasingly well-documented children. Dare to be Heinie and hie yours to www.AyunHalliday.com

Mike Hannigan

Mike Hannigan grew up in Concord, New Hampshire, and now makes his home in Burlington, Vermont, where he is a writer, aspiring ski bum, and consumer of all things pop culture. He is the creative director and owner of Methodikal, Inc., a design, advertising, and creative services shop. You can also see him portraying a surly grandmother in the short film *Roof Sex*, at www.eatpes.com.

Marie Hansen

Marie Hansen is a librarian in New York City. Her shoe size and taste in music have remained the same since eighth grade. When she isn't reading or listening to records, she acts as a supporting member of the Moody Wallen Phantasm Band.

Jen Hazen

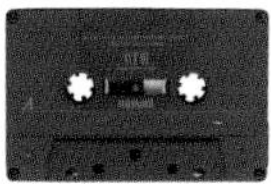

Jen Hazen is a freelance writer/editor who lives in Chicago. She also runs a design business, SuperKonductor.com, and spends way too much time fawning over her miniature dachshund, Talia.

Michael Hearst

Michael Hearst is a musician and a writer. He is a founding member of the band One Ring Zero, which has released at least seven CDs, including the acclaimed lit-rock album *As Smart As We Are*. His most recent work is a solo album titled *Songs for Ice Cream Trucks*. Hearst has toured as the opening act for The Magnetic Fields, performed with The Kronos Quartet, and has also appeared on such shows as NPR's *Fresh Air*, A+E's *Breakfast with the Arts*, and NBC's *The Today Show*. As a writer, Michael's work has been published in such journals as *McSweeney's*, *Parenthetical Note*, and *Post Road*. He also hosts a podcast series with Rick Moody called *18:59*.

Andrew Huff

Andrew Huff is a professional blogger living in Chicago. He is the editor and publisher of *Gapers Block*, a Chicago-centric web publication he cofounded in 2003, and usually has several other projects going on that he somehow manages to keep in the air simultaneously.

Mary Huhn

Mary Huhn grew up listening to AM radio in Devon, Pennsylvania, in the Philadelphia suburbs. Lou Reed's "Walk on the Wild Side" and Vicki Lawrence's "The Night the Lights Went Out in Georgia" were among her first 45s, but she didn't discover the Velvet Underground or Led Zeppelin (and then the Clash and Soft Cell) until attending Penn State. Mary moved to New York in 1985, where she worked at *Adweek* magazine, Rolling Stone Online, and, currently, the *New York Post*. She lives on the Lower East Side overlooking the Williamsburg Bridge.

Anne Jensen

Anne Jensen is the coproducer of the Los Angeles chapter of MORTIFIED. She has been an actor and writer for the past eleven years and cocreated the hit Los Angeles stage show, *The Almost Grown-ups*.

Arthur Jones

Arthur Jones is a designer, illustrator, animator, and writer, living in Brooklyn, New York. He's collaborated with *Cassette From My Ex* editor Jason Bitner on DIRTY FOUND magazine and FoundMagazine.com, and worked with Starlee Kine on the Post-it Note Reading Series. His work can be seen at byarthurjones.com.

Felix Jung

Felix Jung is a blogger and Flash Developer living in Chicago. He received his MFA from the Ohio State University in 2000, and has since developed a deep interest in combining poetry and technology. He currently manages a team of designers at Emmis Interactive, and in his spare time enjoys playing around with Adobe Flash and any API he can get his hands on. He writes about living in Chicago, working in a growing software company, and general web ephemera on his blog (avoision.com)—a site he's been updating daily, since July 2002.

Nina Katchadourian

Nina Katchadourian is a visual artist who works with a wide variety of media including photography, sculpture, video, and sound. She has exhibited domestically and internationally at places such as PS1/MoMA, Museum of Contemporary Art San Diego, and the Palais de Tokyo. In June 2006, the Tang Museum presented a ten year survey of her work with an accompanying monograph entitled "All Forms of Attraction." Katchadourian is represented by Sara Meltzer gallery in New York and Catharine Clark gallery in San Francisco. She leads a sublife as a musician and recently released an album entitled *The Marfa Jingles*. Her work can be seen at www.ninakatchadourian.com.

Starlee Kine

Starlee Kine is a contributor to the public radio program, *This American Life*. She is also the cocreator of the Post- it Note Reading Series in New York. Her writing has appeared in *The New York Times Magazine*, and she is currently working on a book about self-help titled, *It IS Your Fault*.

Katie Krentz

Katie Krentz works at Twentieth Century Fox TV, helping to develop and to produce prime-time animated shows. At night, Katie writes and directs funny things. Her work has been featured on the Second City LA and Improv Olympic West stages. More importantly, she can karaoke *all* of the parts to "Bohemian Rhapsody" and blow your mind. She lives in Santa Monica, California, but her heart is all Midwest.

Sara Lamm

Sara Lamm is a filmmaker and performance artist living in Los Angeles. Her documentary, *Dr. Bronner's Magic Soapbox*, was released theatrically in 2007. For five years, she coproduced and performed in *The Dog & Pony Show*, a regularly occurring variety show in New York City.

Robert Lanham

Robert Lanham's writing has appeared in *The New York Times*, *Maxim*, *Radar*, *Nylon*, *Playboy*, *The Huffington Post* and *Time Out New York*, among others. He is the author of the satirical anthropological studies *The Hipster Handbook*, *Food Court Druids* and *The Sinner's Guide to the Evangelical Right*. Lanham is the founder and editor of the trend-setting publication *FREEwilliamsburg.com*. He lives in Brooklyn, New York.

Joe Levy

Joe Levy is the editor of *Maxim* magazine.

Damon Locks

As lead singer and keyboardist of the Chicago-based band The Eternals and the vocalist in the large scale group, Exploding Star Orchestra, Damon is well known for luring listeners into a brand-new world of music. Before that, he fronted another equally border-blurring band, Trenchmouth. In addition to bringing great music to the people, Damon is a visual artist. He has also designed countless album covers as well as providing art for features in *URB*, *XLR8R*, *Flaunt*, and *Resonance*. You can catch examples of another of his trades, music writing, in magazines like *Stop Smiling* and *Time Out*.

Fiona Maazel

Fiona Maazel's first novel, *Last Last Chance*, was published by Farrar, Straus & Giroux and in 2008. She is a National Book Foundation "5 Under 35" honoree, winner of the Bard Giroux Fiction Prize for 2009, and in 2005, she was awarded a Lannan Literary Fellowship.

Maura Madden

Maura Madden is a writer a performer, a producer, and a crafter working at Comedy Central in New York City. Her first book, *Crafternoon: A Guide to Getting Artsy and Crafty All Year Long* was published by Simon Spotlight Entertainment in 2008. Maura was a member of the San Francisco comedy group Killing My Lobster from 1998 to 2002 and was a cohost of *Two for the Show*, a monthly variety show at Mo Pitkin's House of Satisfaction in New York City from 2005 to '07. She lives in Brooklyn, New York with her husband and her *Two for the Show* cohost, Rufus.

Sarah Grace McCandless

Sarah Grace McCandless is the author of two novels, a regional producer for *Mortified Live*, and a contributor to a variety of publications and websites. She lives with her husband, Ian, and her Corgi, Awesome-O, outside of New York, where she is currently working on a new book and putting the "White Wine and Cupcakes Diet" into daily practice.

Cat Mihos

Cat Mihos is a roadie for a living, touring with bands ranging from Tori Amos to Tool, Britney Spears to Mötley Crüe. When she is off the road, she assists author Neil Gaiman in his various amazing incarnations. She also writes movies in between being a thrift-shop queen, a comic book hoarder, a popcorn expert, and a glass candy bar maker. Find her at www.neverwear.net.

Abby Mims

Abby Mims's stories and essays have been published in several literary magazines and anthologies, including, *The Santa Monica Review*, *Swink*, *Other Voices*, and *Woman's Best Friend: Women Writers on the Dogs in Their Lives*. She has received awards from various writers conferences and was featured in 2006 at the New Short Fiction series, presented by the Beverly Hills Library. She has an MFA in Creative Writing from UC Irvine and currently resides in Portland, Oregon. She is at work on a collection of essays and is collaborating with her sister on a two-woman show about their shared experience of her sister's breast cancer treatment and fairly miraculous remission.

Rich Moody + Stacey Richter

Rick Moody is the author of four novels, three collections of stories, and a memoir, *The Black Veil*. He also plays music sometimes in The Wingdale Community Singers and in Authros. He is at work on a new novel.

Stacey Richter is the author of two short story collections, *My Date with Satan* and *Twin Study*.

Anne Elizabeth Moore

Anne Elizabeth Moore is a writer and an artist. Her most recent book, *Unmarketable: Brandalism, Copyfighting, Mocketing, and the Erosion of Integrity* (The New Press, 2007), received favorable reviews from *Forbes*, the *LA Times*, and the *Guardian*, and was called "an anticorporate manifesto with a difference" by *Mother Jones*, and "sharp and valuable muckraking" by *Time Out New York*. Coeditor and publisher of now-defunct *Punk Planet*, founding editor of the popular Best American Comics series from Houghton Mifflin, outspoken media critic, and exhibiting artist, Moore's work has been the subject of films, college lectures, and police investigations. She teaches at the School of the Art Institute of Chicago.

David Nadelberg

David Nadelberg is the creator of MORTIFIED (getmortified.com), a comedic forum (on the stage, on the page, and on the screen) for adults to share the strange and embarrassing things thing they created as kids. Born in Michigan, Nadelberg now lives in Los Angeles. His latest mixtape is a CD for toddlers that makes his pal Marty's kid incoherent with joy.

Thomas Perry

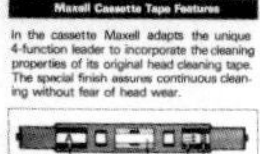

Thomas Perry is a music writer by trade, writing for Beat Happening Online and DrownedinSound.com. He loves Korean films, indie rock, his family, his friends, and his three cats. He lives and works in London. Check him out at tracksfromthestack.blogspot.com

Gretchen Phillips

Gretchen Phillips is an Austin-based musician whose first album, *Meat Joy*, came out in 1984. Since then she has performed with Two Nice Girls, Girls in the Nose, The Gretchen Phillips Ministries, Phillips&Driver, and A Joy Division Cover Band to name a (very) few. She currently performs various solo shows centered around themes such as her latest offering, *Manlove*. She has a new solo record out entitled, *I Was Just Comforting Her*. And she's also studying furniture making and has a side business rendering pet portraits on pieces of wooden scraps, "likeness not guaranteed."

Alan Rapp

Alan Rapp is a writer and visual book editor. After fifteen years in San Francisco, he now lives in Brooklyn, New York.

Jenny Reader

Jenny Reader is a publicist for a leading independent record label. In her many incarnations, she has been a children's magazine editor, a freelance journalist for teen magazines, author, webmaster, assistant TV producer in music television, and recently moved from the United Kingdom to Chicago to indulge her love of Cracker Barrel, crafts, road trips, and to grab her slice of American pie. Currently she's abandoning social network sites to go maverick with her own blog, www.EmbraceYourInnerGeek.net.

Emily Rems

Emily Rems is a feminist writer, editor, rock star, playwright, and occasional plus-size model living in New York's East Village. Best known as Managing Editor of the young women's pop culture magazine *BUST*, Emily is also a movie reviewer for Premiere.com, is the drummer of the all-grrrl punk band Royal Pink, and from 1997 to 2002, saturated downtown New York City with her bizarre original stage productions and adaptations, lampooning cultural icons from Barbie to Olive Oyl to Elvis with a feminist twist.

Julie Shapiro

Julie Shapiro is the artistic director of the Third Coast International Audio Festival, an organization that supports and celebrates producers and other artists creating audio documentary and feature work of all styles for radio and the Internet. Prior to joining the TCIAF staff in 2000, Julie worked at the Center for Documentary Studies at Duke University. These days Julie makes audio art for public presentation and can occasionally be heard on the public radio airwaves. She keeps some thoughts about sound at notetheslantoftheovals.blogspot.com.

Rob Sheffield

Rob Sheffield is the author of the *New York Times* best-seller *Love Is a Mix Tape: Life and Loss, One Song at a Time*. It has been translated into French, Japanese, Swedish, Italian, German, Chinese, Korean, and other languages he cannot read. A longtime writer for *Rolling Stone* he's also written about rock and roll and pop culture for *Spin*, the *Village Voice*, *Blender*, and many other publications, as well as MTV and VH1. He is married and lives in Brooklyn, New York.

Larry Smith

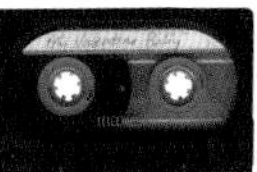

Larry Smith is the cofounder of *SMITH* Magazine (smithmag.net), an online storytelling community obsessed with personal narrative. He's the coeditor of *Not Quite What I Was Planning: Six-Word Memoirs by Writers Famous and Obscure* from *SMITH* Magazine.

Jodyne L. Speyer

Jodyne L. Speyer lives in Los Angeles and is the author of the book *Dump 'em: How to Break Up with Anyone From Your Best Friend to Your Hairdresser* published by HarperCollins. She has made a googolplex of mixed tapes in her day and is proud to be from the Granite State. Live Free or Die!

Sara Strahan

Sara Strahan hails from Chicago and now resides in New York City after recently completing a master's degree in media studies at The New School. These days, she can be found trying to juggle experimental filmmaking, documentary, and other media projects of social value with commercial work for products aimed toward lawn enthusiasts or that celebrities such as Beyonce Knowles may endorse.

Charlie Todd

Charlie Todd is the founder of Improv Everywhere, a prank collective based in New York City. He is also a teacher and performer at the Upright Citizens Brigade Theatre.

Annie Tomlin

Annie Tomlin's writing career began at the tender age of two, when she dictated *Paddington Bear Goes to the Mailbox* to her mother. Since then, her writing has appeared in magazines including *Ms.*, *BUST*, *Bitch*, *Alternative Press*, *Punk Planet*, and *Venus Zine*. She lives in San Francisco, where she occasionally updates her website at http://annie.newdream.net.

Jamie Wetherbe

Jamie Wetherbe is an assistant editor at the *Los Angeles Times* in addition to writing for several LGBT publications, including *IN*, *Frontiers*, and *Curve* magazines. She also teaches journalism and design at community colleges throughout Southern California and traveled the world from Antarctica to Antigua as the assistant editor for *TravelAge West* Magazine. She lives in West Hollywood with her two mutts, Butch and Meow.

Kara Zuaro

After college, Kara Zuaro became a music and food journalist. She met all her favorite bands, collected their favorite recipes, and published them in a cookbook called *I Like Food, Food Tastes Good*. She lives in Brooklyn, New York with her husband, who makes the best mix CDs ever.

Songs for 2nd
NR YES NO
NORMAL BIAS 120μs EQ
NOISE REDUCTION
U.S.A.
TAPE®
GOLD
60

Acknowledgments

I'm deeply indebted to the efforts of six people—Danielle Smith, Michael Hearst, Larry Smith, Katie Krentz, Damon Locks, and Dexter Randazzo—for growing a little website into this anthology. Since day one, they've all worked tirelessly to get the word out about *Cassette from My Ex* and to track down each of the talented writers here in this collection. I'm also thankful for all of the writers' parents who've kept these mixtapes in their basements for the past decade or two. Without your storage, many of these would be lost to time.

There's a few more people who get a big what-what for a variety of reasons, each one of them essential: Alan Rapp, Amy Fleming, Arthur Jones, Benjamen Walker, Christina Lee, Claudia Gonson, Dave Nadelberg, Davy Rothbart, Eric Parrott, Fiona Maazel, Hope Gangloff, Jeff Howe, James Molenda, Jesse Hardman, John Bracken, John Hess, Jolene Siana, Julie Shapiro, Melissa Walker, Katie O'Callaghan, Sarah Grace McCandless, Starlee Kine, and Tod Lippy. Thanks to Rob Sheffield for helping pave the way with *Love is a Mix Tape* and to Thurston Moore for his *Mix Tape: The Art of Cassette Culture*, as well as the kings of "confessional culture": Davy Rothbart and *FOUND*, David Nadelberg and *Mortified*, Frank Warren and *PostSecret*, and Smith Magazine's *Six-Word Memoirs*. Let's keep it going.

Working with editor Kathryn Huck, with the assistance of Alyse Diamond, and everyone at St. Martin's Press, has been a huge pleasure. Thanks for all of your patience and feedback and advocating for the best possible *CFME* book. Big ups to Jud Laghi, super agent at LJK, for shepherding this project into such formidable hands, and for years of proper guidance and Makers Mark. Thanks also to Lissi Erwin, for her putting in tons of skilled effort and love into the design of these pages. We're really lucky to have her.

And thanks go to Joel Meyer at WNYC, Joe DeCeault at WBEZ, Jocelyn Gonzalez at WNYC, Kai Hsing at Current TV, Charles Monroe-Kane at WPR, *Buzzfeed*, *Gawker*, and *Entertainment Weekly* for helping get the spread the word about *Cassette from My Ex* early on, helping to get these mixtapes flowing in.

And, of course, I have to thanks Kate, Heidi, Katharine, Catherine, and Amber, for making me mixtapes back in the day. I've still got them in a suitcase downstairs. Let me know if you want to hear them again—I'll make you a copy on our dual-cassette deck, in real time, none of this 2x business.

And much love to everyone in my amazing and ever-expanding family, especially Danielle.